FAST SIMULATION OF COMPUTER ARCHITECTURES

FAST SIMULATION OF COMPUTER ARCHITECTURES

EDITED BY

Thomas M. Conte
University of South Carolina
Columbia, South Carolina

Charles E. Gimarc
AT&T Global Information Solutions
West Columbia, South Carolina

SPRINGER SCIENCE+BUSINESS MEDIA, LLC

Library of Congress Cataloging-in-Publication Data

Fast simulation of computer architectures / edited by Thomas M. Conte,
 Charles E. Gimarc.
 p.   cm.
 Includes bibliographical references and index.
 ISBN 978-1-4613-6002-5   ISBN 978-1-4615-2361-1 (eBook)
 DOI 10.1007/978-1-4615-2361-1
 1. Computer architecture--Evaluation.   2. Digital computer
simulation.   I. Conte, Thomas M., 1964-   . II. Gimarc, Charles
E., 1953-   .
 QA76.9.A73F28 1995   95-19087
 004.2'4'011--dc20   CIP

Printed on acid-free paper.

CONTENTS

CONTRIBUTORS

Santosh G. Abraham
Hewlett-Packard Laboratories
Palo Alto, California

Bob Boothe
University of Southern Maine
Portland, Maine

Bob Cmelik
Sun Microsystems, Incorporated
Mountain View, California

David Keppel
University of Washington
Seattle, Washington

Bill Mangione-Smith
University of California at Los Angeles
Los Angeles, California

Kishore N. Menezes
University of South Carolina
Columbia, South Carolina

Trevor N. Mudge
University of Michigan
Ann Arbor, Michigan

Jim Pierce
University of Michigan
Ann Arbor, Michigan

Michael Smith
Harvard University
Cambridge, Massachusetts

Rabin A. Sugumar
Cray Research Inc.
Chippewa Falls, Wisconsin

1

INTRODUCTION

This is a book about sophisticated techniques for simulating computer architectures. It is intended for two groups of readers: the practicing computer architect who is looking for good solutions to tough evaluation problems, and the computer architecture student who would like to augment knowledge obtained from more traditional architecture textbooks. It can also be used as a second textbook for first- or second-semester architecture courses. To this end, each chapter includes 10 to 20 exercises useful as class assignments or as study aids.

It has often been said that computer architecture is not a quantitative, systematic design process, rather it is an art form. There is some truth to this observation. Engineering design involves several steps: (1) innovating potential designs, (2) evaluating the performance of the designs, and (3) selecting the best design. The initial innovation (step (1)) involves creativity. The later evaluation and construction steps can largely be expressed as optimization problems, which are often solved systematically (although tremendous creativity is often applied to devising optimization techniques).

Unfortunately, there is no general theory for systematic computer architecture evaluation and selection. This is partly due to the complexity of the problem: successful general-purpose computer systems must have the capacity for a very diverse set of applications. The workloads used in the design process must capture this diversity. (The field of *workload characterization* addresses this problem.) Once a workload has been determined, one must face another, more pressing problem. The number of potential designs is large. Consider a uniprocessor workstation. The design of the memory system must be determined. So must the capacity of the network, the disk, any interconnecting channels, and the processor itself. If the processor is also being designed, the number of variables increases dramatically: the processor pipeline, the branch handling scheme, the role of the compiler, etc. The fact that the workload must be large in order to capture diversity further frustrates the evaluation problem. Fast, efficient, and accurate evaluation techniques are essential for systematic, quantitative computer architecture design.

This book presents several powerful techniques to evaluate the performance of common design tradeoffs. We have attempted to collect what are the most-common and useful of these approaches. We have also included two chapters on how to collect the workload trace itself, since this problem is inextricably intertwined with the evaluation problem.

In Chapter 2, Cmelik and Keppel discuss the basic concepts of instruction-level computer system simulation. This introduction includes a summary and comparison of over 45 modern simulators, virtual machines, and tracing tools. Simulators run target system programs on a host machine. The authors note that simulation is useful for analysis, design, and tuning of HW and SW systems, permitting feedback to improve the design before implementation of ideas. Shade is given as an example of tracing and simulation tools. Shade combines tracing, simulation, and analysis capabilities in a single tool, eliminating the need for multiple tools, and providing high performance. Various levels of functionality are implemented in the variety of tools available. Some features such as tracing signals, self-modifying code, dynamic links, system mode, data references, and tracing speculative execution are typical of most tracing environments. Shade provides some of these features along with the capability for cross-compilation, and several tracing and simulation speed enhancements.

The ability to gather run-time information of executing programs is central to the simulation and analysis of computer architectures and the optimization of applications. In Chapter 3, Pierce, Smith and Mudge present a survey of methods for collecting trace and run-time information. These instrumentation tools typically modify the program under study, either at the compiler level or at the object module level. Once the altered program is run, it generates traces or profile statistics, at some cost in program performance. Examples of source-code, link-time, and executable modification are given. Late-code modification techniques are treated in detail, as they are widely used, and typically the most challenging to implement. Eight of these tools are described and compared. Since instrumentation of multitasking applications and operating system kernels have their own set of unique problems, two of these tools are discussed separately. Instrumentation tools are typically tied to a specific

ISA. This chapter contains examples of tools useful on MIPS, ALPHA, ix86, RS/6000, PA-RISC, 68000, and SPARC architectures.

Cache and memory system analysis can be either analytical or trace driven. The analytical techniques have the advantage of speed - permitting analysis of a large design space. Their disadvantage is relatively poor accuracy. High accuracy is very important in cache performance analysis since the absolute hit rates are typically very close to 100%. Fast simulation techniques are often required.

In Chapter 4, one of the editors (Conte) describes the single-pass, stack-based cache simulation technique. Stack-based simulation is desirable for several reasons. First, since it is a single-pass method, its speed permits performance measurement of a large number of cache and memory system designs in one step. Second, since many caches can be evaluated simultaneously, its speed permits use of traces of long-running benchmarks. Chapter 4 explains a specific stack-based approach, the recurrence/conflict method. Many extensions to stack-based techniques have been proposed. The chapter discusses one in detail: an extension to capture the effects of multiprogramming. Algorithm psuedo code and examples are used to present the technique.

Alternatives to the stack-based simulation algorithms of Chapter 4 are presented in Chapter 5 by Sugumar and Abraham. These non-stack-based single-pass methods rely on m-ary trees. The theory of these techniques are used to develop new simulation algorithms for caches and write buffers.

One of the highest performance simulation methodologies is execution-driven simulation. Of these, the highest-performance execution-driven simulators do only the work that is required to obtain the desired results. Additional uninteresting events are not simulated, but are accounted for in other ways. In Chapter 6, Boothe presents three multiprocessor execution-driven simulators and explains their fundamental design choices. Simulation design decisions include techniques for preprocessing (insertion of probe instructions in the application), and execution of select application instructions on a model of the target system while gathering statistics of that execution. Details are given for one simulator in particular, the author's FAST simulator. FAST runs on a uniprocessor host and simulates shared memory multiprocessors.

Simulation is often performed to capture a few, key performance metrics. These metrics are summary statistics. In Chapter 7, Menezes explores techniques to speed up simulation by using statistical sampling theory to approximate the summary statistics. The general theory of sampling is presented, followed by a literature review of cache and processor statistical sampling methods. Menezes then develops a new method for processor sampling and discusses its applications.

In Chapter 8, Mangione-Smith prevents research in establishing performance upper bounds. Bounds are an attractive alternative to simulation for either tuning existing systems or designing new systems. In the context of the research, these bounds are computed for well-behaving scientific kernels. Examples evaluate performance of a subset of the Livermore Fortran Kernels executing on a wide range of computers (Cray-1, Cray X-MP, Cray-2, Convex C-240, Astronautics ZS-1, RS/6000 and MIPS R2000). A hierarchical methodology of computing these bounds is presented. Each level provides a more detailed analysis, yielding tighter, more accurate bounds. Of course, the tradeoff is in analysis effort versus results accuracy. In its current state, this analysis is useful for comparing expected performance with achievable performance with measured performance of applications on specific system implementations. Such comparison could point to optimization opportunities.

Instructors using this book for can teach largely in the order of occurance of the chapters in the text. However, for specific focus on tracing, Chapters 2 and 3 are recommended, with partial coverage of Chapter 6. A treatment of cache and memory hierarchy simulation should include Chapters 4, 5 and 7. A course that focuses on supercomputer architecture should include special attention to Chapters 6 and 8, in addition to the above chapters.

This book has been constructed with close interaction between the authors and editors. We would like to thank the chapter authors for adjusting their texts when we saw conflicts, and working above and beyond the call of duty to help us deliver a coherent, cohesive volume on fast architectural simulation.

This book would not have been possible without the patient and helpful aid of our editor, Alexander Greene. The preliminary work for this book was motivated by a successful session we organized at the *Hawaii International Conference on System Sciences*. The crowd that attended was lively and provided all with a high-quality discussion. In addition to the chapter authors who attended that session, we would also like to thank: Si-En Chang (Chung Yuan University), Gary Lauterbach (Sun Laboratories), Mario Nemirovsky (University of California, Santa Barbara), Jim Smith (University of Wisconsin), Patricia Teller (New Mexico State University), and Larry Wittie (SUNY-Stony Brook).

–TMC and CEG

2

SHADE: A FAST INSTRUCTION-SET SIMULATOR FOR EXECUTION PROFILING

Bob Cmelik*, David Keppel†

*Sun Microsystems, Incorporated, Mountain View, California
†University of Washington, Seattle, Washington

1 INTRODUCTION

Simulation and tracing tools help in the analysis, design, and tuning of both hardware and software systems. Simulators can execute code for hardware that does not yet exist, can provide access to internal state that may be invisible on real hardware, can give deterministic execution in the face of races, and can produce "stress test" situations that are hard to produce on the real hardware [4]. Tracing tools can provide detailed information about the behavior of a program; that information is used to drive an *analyzer* that analyzes or predicts the behavior of a particular system component. That, in turn, provides feedback that is used to improve the design and implementation of everything from architectures to compilers to applications. Analyzers consume many kinds of trace information; for example, address traces are used for studies of memory hierarchies, opcode and operand usage for superscalar and pipelined processor design, instruction counts for optimization studies, operand values for memoizing studies, and branch behavior for branch prediction.

Simulators and tracing tools appear at first to perform very different tasks. Simulators allow a *host* machine to run programs written for some *target* machine, while tracing tools collect run-time information about a program's execution. In practice, though, simulators and tracing tools do much the same work: both are concerned with machine-level details of a program's run-time behavior. For example, simulators and tracing tools often both capture the application's program counter. Likewise, simulation and tracing are often implemented using similar techniques. For example, simulators and tracing tools often work by analyzing the original program instructions and cross-compiling them to sequences of instructions that simulate or trace the original code.

For the purposes of this chapter, then, we can consider simulation and tracing as two facilities provided by a single tool. Several features can improve the utility of such a tool. First, the tool should be easy to use and avoid dependencies on particular languages and compilers. Ideally it should also avoid potentially cumbersome preprocessing steps. Second, it should operate on a wide variety of applications including those that use signals, exceptions and dynamically-linked libraries. Third, trace generation should be fast, both so that traces can be recreated on demand, instead of being archived on bulk storage, and so that it is possible to study realistic workloads, since partial workloads may not provide representative information [6, 7]. Fourth, a tracing tool should provide arbitrarily detailed trace information so that it is useful for a wide variety of analyzers; in general, this means that it must be extensible [58, 59] so that it can be programmed to collect specialized information. Finally, it should be possible to run and trace applications for machines that do not yet exist.

These features are often at odds with each other. For example, static cross-compilation can produce fast code, but purely static translators cannot simulate and trace all details of dynamically-linked code. Also, improved tracing flexibility generally means reduced performance. An interpreter that saves address trace information may be reasonably fast, but adding control over *whether* it saves an address trace will slow the simulation, if at every instruction the simulator must check whether to save trace information. Providing finer control over where to save trace data slows simulation even more; adding the flexibility to save other kinds of trace information slows simulation yet further.

Because of the conflict between generality and performance, most tools provide only a subset of the features listed above. Shade is a simulation and tracing tool that provides the features together in one tool and uses five general techniques to achieve the needed flexibility and performance. First, Shade dynamically cross-compiles executable code for the target machine into executable code that runs directly on the host machine. Second, the host code is cached for reuse so that the cost of cross-compiling can be amortized. Third, simulation and tracing code are integrated so that the host code saves trace information directly as it runs. Fourth, Shade gives the analyzer detailed control over what is traced: the tracing strategy can be varied dynamically by opcode and address range. Shade then saves just the information requested by the analyzer, so clients that need little trace information pay little overhead. Finally, Shade is *extensible*: it can call special-purpose, analyzer-supplied code to extend Shade's default data-collection capabilities.

Shade uses these techniques together to perform many useful tasks in combination. Shade performs cross-architecture simulation, collects many kinds of trace information, allows fine control over the tracing, is extensible, and simulates and traces the target machine in detail, including tricky things like signals and self-modifying code. Despite its flexibility, Shade has performance competitive with tools that just cross-simulate without tracing, with tools that do only simple tracing, and even with those that omit details to improve simulation and tracing efficiency. Thus, this study of Shade shows how a general-purpose tool can be made efficient enough to effectively replace many other tools. This chapter also presents a framework for describing simulation and tracing tools.

2 RELATED WORK

This section describes related work and summarizes the capabilities and implementation techniques of some other simulators, virtual machines and tracing tools. In most cases we try to evaluate the capabilities of each tool's technology, but as we are evaluating particular tools, we sometimes (necessarily) evaluate limits of a specific implementation.

2.1 Capabilities and Implementation

Table 1 summarizes the capabilities and implementations of a number of tools. The columns show various features of each tool and are grouped in three sections. The first group, *Purpose* and *Input Rep.* describe the purpose of the tool and how a user prepares a program in order to use the tool. The second group *Detail*, *MD*, *MP*, *Sig.*and *SMC OK*, shows the level of detail of the simulation and tracing, and thus the kinds of programs that can be processed by the tool. The third group *Technology*, and *Bugs OK* show the implementation technology used and the tool's robustness in the face of application errors.

Purpose describes how the tool is used: for cross-architecture simulation (*sim*); debugging (*db*); for address tracing or memory hierarchy analysis (*atr*); or for other, more detailed kinds of tracing (*otr*). Tools marked tb_C are *tool-building* tools that provide analyzers with access to arbitrary state of the simulated target machine; the subscript C indicates that they usually use C as the extension language [58, 59].

Table 1 Summary of some related systems. *(Continued next page)*

Name	Purpose	Input Rep.	Detail	MD	MP	Sig.	SMC OK	Technology	Bugs OK
Accelerator [2]	sim	exe	us	Y	N	Y	S	scc+ddi	Y
ATOM [24, 75, 76]	tb$_C$	exe*	us	N	N	Y	S	aug	N
ATUM [1]	sim/atr	exe	us	Y	Y$_=$	Y	Y	emu	Y
Cerberus [10]	otr	hll	u	N	Y	N	Y	scc+gi	Y
Cygnus [30]	sim/db	exe	u	N	N	N	Y	tci	Y
dis+mod+run [27]	sim/atr	asm	u	N	N	N	N	scc	N
Dynascope [70]	db/atr/otr	hll	u	N	N	S	Y	pdi	Y
Dynascope-II [71]	db/atr/otr	exe	u	N	N	S	Y	ddi	Y
Executor [37, 54]	sim	exe	u	N	N	Y	Y	pdi+dcc	Y
FAST [8]	atr	asm	u	N	Y$_1$	N	N	aug	N
FlashPort [28]	sim	exe	u	N	N	Y	S	scc	N
g88 [4]	sim/db	exe	usd	Y	N	Y	Y	tci	Y
GNU Simulators [11, 29]	sim/db	exe	u	N	N	N	Y	ddi+tci	Y
IDtrace[60]	atr	exe	u	N	N	S	N	aug	N
IMS [39]	sim	exe	u	Y	N	Y	Y	emu	Y
Kx10 [31]	sim/db/otr	exe	usd	Y	N	Y	Y	ddi	Y
Mable [19]	sim/db/atr	exe	u	N	Y$_1$	N	Y	ddi	N
mg88 [5]	sim/db/atr/otr/tb$_C$	exe	usd	Y	Y$_1$	Y	Y	tci	Y
Migrant [68]	sim	exe	u	Y	N	Y	Y	scc+emu	Y
Mime [67]	atr/otr	exe	u	N	N	N	N	emu+tci+cr	N
Mimic [55]	sim	exe	u	N	N	N	N	dcc	N
MINT [83]	atr	exe	u	N	Y$_1$	Y	N	pdi+dcc	Y*
Moxie [13]	sim	exe	u	N	N	Y	N	scc	N
MPTRACE [23]	atr	asm	u	N	Y$_=$	S	N	aug	N
MSHADE [65]	sim/db/atr	exe	usd	Y	Y$_+$	Y	Y	dcc	Y

Table 1 (*continued*) Summary of some related systems.

Name	Purpose	Input Rep.	Detail	MD	MP	Sig.	SMC OK	Technology	Bugs OK
MX/Vest [69]	sim	exe	u	N	$Y_=$	Y	Y	scc+gi	Y
Pixie [13]	atr	exe*	u	Y	N	Y	N	aug	N
Pixie-II [47]	atr/otr/db	exe*	us	Y	N	Y	S	scc	N
Proteus [9]	atr	hll	u	N	Y_1	N	S	aug	N
Purify [33]	db	exe*	u	N	N	Y	N	aug	Y
qp/qpt [49]	atr/otr	exe	u	N	N	N	N	aug	N
RPPT [18]	atr	hll	u	N	Y_1	Y	N	aug	N
SELF [12, 35]	sim	exe	u	N	N	Y	Y	dcc	Y
SmICS [50, 51, 52, 53]	sim/db/atr/otr/tbc	exe	usd	Y	Y_1	Y	Y	tci+dcc	Y
Simon [26]	atr	asm	u	N	N	N	N	aug	N
SoftPC [57]	sim	exe	u(s)d	N	N	N	Y	dcc	Y
Spa [40]	atr	exe	u	N	N	S	Y	ddi	N
SPIM [34]	sim/atr	exe	u	N	N	Y	N	pdi	Y
ST-80 [21]	sim	exe	u	N	N	Y	Y	dcc	Y
Tango Lite [20, 32]	atr	asm	u	N	Y_1	N	S	aug	N
Tapeworm II [81]	atr	exe	us	Y	N	Y	Y	emu	Y
Titan [6, 7]	atr	exe	us	Y	N	Y	N	aug	N
TRAPEDS [77, 78]	atr	asm	us	Y	$Y_=$	S	N	aug	N
WWT [63]	atr/otr	exe	u	Y	Y_+	Y	N	emu+aug+ddi	Y
Z80MU [3]	sim	exe	u(s)	N	N	Y	Y	ddi	Y
Shade [16, 17]	sim/atr/otr/tbc	exe	u	N	N	Y	Y	dcc	N

Input Rep. describes the input to the tool. Each tool is a translator that processes an input form; the input affects the tool's portability and also the performance and accuracy (faithfulness) of the resulting code. Processing a high-level language input (*hll*) can have the best portability and best optimization but the tool can only be used for source programs written in the supported languages [83] and cannot generally analyze the effects of other translation tools (compilers, etc.). Consuming assembly code (*asm*) is less portable than a high-level language but can provide more detailed information and allows processing of output from a variety of compilers. To the extent that assembly languages are similar, such tools may be relatively easy to retarget, though detailed information may still be obscured. Finally, using executable code as input (*exe*) eliminates the need for access to the source and the (possibly complex) build process. However, information is usually reported in machine units, not source constructs. Some tools use symbol table information to report information symbolically. Others need symbolic information in order to perform translation (*exe**).

Detail describes how much of the machine is simulated. Most tools work with only user-level code (*u*); some also run system-level code (*s*); and system-mode simulation generally requires device emulation (*d*). Some target machines have no system mode, so simulation can avoid the costs of address translation and protection checks; these machines have the system mode marked in parenthesis.

MD reports whether the tool supports multiple protection domains and multitasking (multiple processes per target processor). This usually implies support for system-mode operation and address translation. Target systems that multitask in a single protection domain are listed as *N*. *MP* tells whether the tool supports multiple processor execution; Y_1 indicates that the tool uses a single host processor, $Y_=$ indicates that the tool runs as many target processors as host processors, and Y_+ that it uses multiple host processors and simulates more target processors than host processors. Simulating a multiprocessor generally introduces additional slowdown at least as big as the number of target processors divided by the number of host processors.

Supporting signals is often difficult since execution can be interrupted at any instruction and resumed at any other instruction, yet analysis and instrumentation may use groups of instructions to improve simulation efficiency. The *Sig.* column is *Y* for tools that can handle asynchronous and exceptional events. *S* indicates that the tool is able to deal with some but not all aspects; for example, signals may be processed so the program's results are correct, but no address trace information is generated.

SMC OK describes whether the tool is able to operate on programs where the instruction space changes dynamically. Dynamic linking is the most common reason, but there are a number of other uses [45]. Static rewrite tools can sometimes (*S*) dynamically link to statically-rewritten code, but the dynamically-formed link cannot be rewritten statically and thus may go untraced.

Technology describes the general implementation techniques used in each tool [61]. An "obvious" implementation executes programs by fetching, decoding, and then interpreting each instruction in isolation. Most of the implementations optimize by predecoding and then caching the decoded result; by translating to host code to make direct use of the host's prefetch and decode hardware [21]; and by executing target instructions in the context of their neighbors so that target state (e.g. simulated registers) can be accessed efficiently (e.g. from host registers) across target instruction boundaries. The implementations are:

☐ Hardware emulation, including dedicated hardware and microcode (*emu*).

☐ The "obvious" implementation, a decode and dispatch interpreter (*ddi*).

☐ Predecode interpreters (*pdi*) that pre-convert to a quick-to-decode *intermediate representation* or *IR*. The IR can take many forms; a particularly fast, simple, and common form is threaded code (*tci*).

☐ Static cross-compilation (*scc*) which decodes *and dispatches* during cross-compilation, avoiding essentially all run-time dispatch costs. Note that conversion is limited by what the tool can see statically. For example, dynamic linking may be hard to instrument statically. Limited static information also limits optimization. For example, a given instruction may *in practice* never be a branch target. Proving that is often hard [49, 55], so the static compiler may be forced to produce overly-conservative code. As a special case, where the host and target are the same, the static compiler merely annotates or *augments* (*aug*) the original program with code to save trace data or emulate missing instructions.

☐ Dynamic cross-compilation (*dcc*) is performed at run time and thus can work with any code including dynamically-linked libraries. Also, dynamic cross-compilers can perform optimistic optimizations and recompile if the assumptions were too strong [16, 35, 36, 42, 55, 52, 66]. However, since the compiler is used at run time, translation must be fast enough that the improved performance more than pays for the overhead of dynamic compilation [16]; in addition, code quality may be worse than that of a static cross-compiler [2, 36, 69] since dynamic code analysis may need to "cut corners" in order to minimize the compiler's running time.

Where interpreter specifics are unavailable the tool is listed as using a general interpreter (*gi*). Tools listed as *aug* and *emu* execute most target instructions using host hardware. Checkpointing and rollback (*cr*) can be used to simulate speculative execution, in order to trace it's effects [67].

Note that input forms lacking symbolic information – *exe* especially – can be hard to process statically because static tools have trouble determining what is code and what is data and also have trouble optimizing over multiple host instructions [49, 55]. By contrast, tools that perform dynamic analysis (including both interpreters and dynamic cross-compilers) can discover the program's structure during execution. Translation techniques can be mixed by using one technique optimistically for good performance and another as a fallback when the first fails. However, such implementations have added complexity because they rely on having two translators [2, 51, 52, 69, 82, 83].

Bugs OK describes whether the tool is robust in the face of application errors such as memory addressing errors or divide-by-zero errors. For example, application stores to random addresses may clobber Shade data structures. Typically, checking for addressing errors requires extra checks for every instruction that writes memory. In some systems the checks are simple range checks; tools that support multiple address spaces and sparse address spaces generally require full address translation [4, 53, 65]. Y^* indicates that checking can be turned on but performance is worse.

2.2   Cross-Architecture Simulation

Table 2 summarizes features of *cross-architecture* simulation tools that use different host and target instruction sets. The *Translation Units* column shows translation-time tradeoffs between analysis complexity and performance. *Assumptions* shows assumptions about the relationship between the host and target machines; these assumptions are usually used to simplify and speed up the simulator. *Perf.* shows the approximate performance as the slowdown of each tool compared to native execution. *Notes* shows special or missing features of each simulator. The columns are described in detail below.

Translation Units shows the number of (target) instructions that are analyzed and translated at a time. Using bigger chunks reduces dispatching costs and increases opportunities for optimization between target instructions. Larger translation units also typically require better analysis or dynamic flexibility in order to ensure that the program jumps always take a valid path or can

Table 2 Summary of some systems that perform cross-architecture simulation

Name	Translation Units	Host/Target Assumptions	Perf. (est.)	Notes
Accelerator [2]	proc–ip/proc	nr, bo, pg., ... ph, regs	1.5	targ. pg. ... mixed
Cerberus [10]	i-i/i		100	
Cygnus [30]	i-i/i	nr	10	same
			20	different
dis+mod+run [27]	bb-bb/bb	nr	10	
Executor [37, 54]	proc-proc/bb	nr	3-10	targ. pg.
FlashPort [28]	ip-ip/ip		1	hand
g88 [4]	i-bb/i	nr, bo	30	targ. pg.
GNU Simulators [11, 29]	i-i/i		40	
IMS [39]	i-i/i		1	
Kx10 [31]	i-i/i		200	targ. pg., ws.
Mable [19]	i-i/i		20-80	
mg88 [5]	i-bb/i	nr, bo	80	targ. pg.
Migrant [68]	ebb-ip/ebb	nr, bo	–	
Mimic [55]	ebb-ib/ib	nr, bo, regs	4	↓fp, ↓align, ... +dcc
Moxie [13]	bb-bb/bb	nr	2	
MSHADE [65]	bb-ebb/ebb	nr, bo	5-10	same, targ. pg.
MX/Vest [69]	ip-ip/ip	bo	2	mixed
SELF [12]	ip-ip/ip	none	N/A	VM
SiMICS [50, 51, 52, 53]	i-bb/i	nr, bo	15-30	targ. pg.
SoftPC [57]			–	
SPIM [34]	i-i/i	nr, bo	25	
ST-80 [21]	proc-proc/proc	none	N/A	VM
Z80MU [3]	i-i/i	nr, bo, regs	–	mixed
Shade [16, 17]	ebb-ib/ebb	nr, bo	1.9-4.9	same
			3.3-13.0	different (tracing off)

gracefully handle unexpected cases that arise from unwarranted optimism [16, 55, 49, 69]. Many tools use larger units for analysis than for translation. This keeps much of the simplicity of smaller translation units but enables optimizations that require broader analysis. Translation units are thus reported as *typ.-max./gen.*, where *typ.* is the typical unit of analysis, *max.* is the largest unit of analysis, and *gen.* is the largest target unit for which host code is generated. For example, Shade mostly uses small units, but analyzes larger units for condition codes, which otherwise become a simulation bottleneck. Shade then uses the results of the sophisticated analysis to generate one of two simple translations: either do or do not save condition codes at the end of a simulated basic block. Translation units include: individual instructions (i), basic blocks (bb), extended basic blocks with a single entry but many exits (ebb), inter-block (ib), procedural ($proc$), or interprocedural (ip).

Host/Target Assumptions describes assumptions that a tool makes about the similarity of the host and target machines. Assumptions can be used to reduce both the complexity of analysis and the detail of rewriting (translation) and thus the run-time cost. Assumptions include byte ordering (bo); numeric representation (nr), including size and format; the number of registers on the host and target machines ($regs$), and access to the host machine's privileged hardware (ph) in order to implement system-level simulation.

Perf. is a performance **estimate**, expressed as the number of (simple) instructions executed per (simple) simulated or traced instruction. A variety of other metrics, such as run-time dilation, might be reasonable, but are typically more dependent on the host and target machine implementations and are thus harder to use when comparing tools [50, 52]. The performance estimates here are necessarily inexact, as they are based on values reported using various metrics and target applications. Note that performance also depends on simulation detail; for example, Shade would be slower if it simulated both user and kernel address spaces. The entry *N/A* indicates "not applicable" because the target is a virtual machine. A dash (–) indicates unknown or unreported performance. Shade figures are the minimum and maximum over the SPEC92 [22] benchmarks.

Notes describes particular features of the tools: *targ. pg.* for detailed memory simulation including simulation of target machine pages; *ws.* for simulation between machines with incompatible word sizes (e.g. simulating a machine with 9-bit bytes on a machine with 8-bit bytes); $\downarrow fp$ for simulation that omits floating-point numbers; *fp+* for simulation that can be set either to run fast or to faithfully emulate the target machine; $\downarrow align$ for tools that omit simulation of unaligned accesses; *+dcc* for dynamic compilers where compile time is not included in the performance but where it would likely have a large effect; *VM* for emulation of a virtual machine that has been designed carefully to improve portability and simulation speed; *mixed* for simulators that can call between host and target code so that the application can, e.g., dynamically link to fast-running host-code libraries; *same* for figures reported on the same host and target; *different* for figures reported for cross-execution; and *hand* for tools that require some human intervention to perform cross-execution.

2.3 Comparison to Shade

Shade improves over many other tools by providing their individual features together in one tool, and by providing both detailed control and efficiency that is competitive with the other tools.

Most tools avoid cross-architecture execution or omit some machine features. These choices improve execution efficiency but limit the tool's applicability. Some exceptions are g88 and it's derivatives [4, 5, 50, 51, 52] and SimOS's MSHADE [65], which are somewhat less efficient than Shade and less flexible at tracing, and also Accelerator [2] and MX/Vest [69] which do not perform tracing and which use two translators, one optimistic and one conservative, to achieve high efficiency. Shade supports cross-architecture execution, and faithfully executes important machine features such as signals and self-modifying code (and thus dynamic linking), so it can be used on a wide variety of applications.

Simulators that use dynamic compilation are typically flexible and the compiled code performs well. However, many previous dynamic compilation systems have imposed limitations that Shade eliminates. For example, Mimic's compiler [55] produces high-quality code, but at such expense that overall performance is worse than Shade; Shade reduces compilation overhead by allowing multiple implementations of each application instruction, only optimizing the most common branches, and using a different data structure to minimize the space overhead of branches. MINT [83] is unable to simulate changing code and never reclaims space used by inactive code.

Tracing tools typically produce only address traces, and often run only on the machine for which the trace is desired. Even tools that allow cross-architecture simulation tend to limit the generality of the machine simulation or of the tracing facilities in order to maintain efficiency [27, 34]. Shade supports cross-architecture tracing and simulates user-mode operation in detail. It currently lacks system-mode tracing facilities provided by some other tools though some of these tools limit machine features and/or require hand-instrumentation of key kernel code. Shade collects more trace information than most other tools, though it lacks the timing-level simulation of mg88 [5] and the simulation and tracing of speculative execution provided by Mime [67]. With Shade, analyzers select the amount of trace data that Shade collects, and analyzers that consume little trace data pay little tracing overhead. Thus, it is typically the analysis tools that limit overall performance.

All of the listed tool building tools permit extended tracing. Shade provides the most efficient yet variable extensibility, and only Shade also inlines common trace operations. Shade analyzers have used both C and C++ as the extension language [58, 59]. We note also that although Shade is not designed for debugging, Shade-V9.V8 has been used as the back end of a debugger [25].

Shade's flexibility and performance does come at a penalty. For example, Shade performs inter-instruction analysis and host code generation; this makes Shade more complex and less portable than, e.g., g88. Shade does not presently simulate multiprocessors or system-mode operation. Though both are limits of the implementation not of the technique, supporting them would make Shade slower since they complicate simulation and enlarge the translated code size in order to, e.g., translate addresses on loads, stores, and so on [4, 53, 65].

3 ANALYZER INTERFACE

The remainder of this chapter focuses on Shade. This section describes the interface that an analyzer uses to manipulate Shade and the program being traced. Shade can also be used for pure simulation, which is simply a degenerate case where the analyzer asks for no trace data and does no work.

A Shade *analyzer* is a program (or that part of a program) which utilizes the simulation and tracing capabilities provided by Shade. Analyzers typically use Shade to collect raw trace data and then summarize that data to provide specific performance metrics. Shade analyzers have been used for pure simulation (no tracing), to generate memory address traces for use by other tools, provide a debugger interface to a simulated target machine for compiler cross-development [25], observe instruction operand values [64], analyze memory cache performance, analyze microprocessor pipeline performance, and analyze Shade's own performance.

Analyzers use Shade as a collection of library functions [14, 15]. Analyzers call these functions to identify the application program to be simulated, specify the level of tracing detail, and simulate one or more application instructions while collecting the specified trace information.

Shade "knows" how to efficiently collect common trace information such as the instruction address and text, data addresses for memory operations, and the contents of registers used by an instruction. Other information may be collected by analyzer-supplied trace functions. These functions have access to the application's simulated registers and memory and may thus collect arbitrary state information. Shade arranges for the analyzer-supplied functions to be called before and/or after simulating an application instruction.

Analyzers may specify what trace information to collect and what trace functions to call on a per-opcode or per-instruction-address basis. For example, an analyzer which wishes to analyze memory systems might request tracing of just instruction and data addresses. Tracing selections may change during the course of the simulation. Thus, an analyzer can skip tracing during application initialization, or can trace only in particularly interesting application or library code. The less trace data the analyzer requests, the faster Shade runs.

4 IMPLEMENTATION

This section describes the basic implementation techniques used in Shade. Section 4.1 first describes the overall structure of Shade. Section 4.2 describes dynamic compilation of *translations* that directly simulate and trace the application program. Sections 4.3 through 4.7 discuss a variety of details: caching and reusing translations to reduce compilation overhead, reducing the cost of dispatching between translations, the handling of condition codes and signals, and the translation of application references into references into simulated memory. Finally, Section 4.8 concludes with some special problems and considerations and the general techniques used in Shade.

4.1 Simulating and Tracing

The heart of Shade is a small main loop that repeatedly maps the current target (application) PC to a corresponding fragment of Shade host (simulator) code, called a *translation*. Each translation simulates one or more target in-

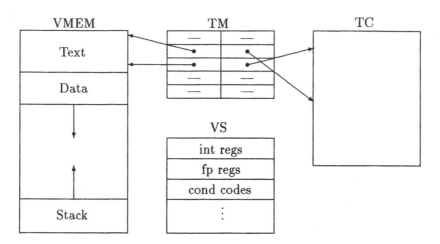

Figure 1   Shade data structures (not to scale).

structions, optionally saves trace data, updates the target PC and returns to the main loop. Shade builds translations by cross-compiling target instructions into host machine code. Shade translates application memory references to refer to simulated memory and, similarly, translates updates of target registers into updates of simulated registers. Figure 1 summarizes the primary data structures used by Shade.

The main loop, translations, and most utility functions called by translations all share a common register window and stack frame. Several host registers are reserved for special purposes. Register **vs** is a pointer to the application's *virtual state* structure which holds the simulated registers; **vpc** is the application's virtual program counter (this is part of the virtual state, but is used enough to warrant its own host register); **vmem** is the base address of the application's memory; **tr** points to the current trace buffer entry; **ntr** is the number of unused trace buffer entries; and **tm** points to the *translation map*, described below.

Shade maps the target PC to its corresponding translation using a data structure called the *translation map* (TM). The main loop does a fast, partial TM lookup. If that fails, a function is called to do a slower, full TM lookup. If that fails, the translation compiler is invoked to generate a new translation in the *translation cache* (TC) and update the TM.

4.2 Translations

Shade cross-compiles groups of target instructions to groups of host instructions called *translations*. Application instructions are typically translated in chunks which extend from the current instruction through the next control transfer instruction and accompanying delay slot. Translation also stops at tricky instructions such as software trap and memory synchronization instructions. Shade arbitrarily limits the number of application instructions per translation in order to simplify storage allocation, and the user's trace buffer size also limits translation size. Therefore, a translation may represent more or less than one basic block of application code. A given straight-line code fragment may have several entry points, and Shade generates separate translations for each entry point. Thus one fragment of application code may be simultaneously represented by more than one translation. Each translation consists of a prologue, a body with a fragment for each application instruction, and an epilogue.

Translation Prologue

The translation prologue (see Figure 2) allocates trace buffer space for the translation. If there is not enough space, the translation returns control to the main loop, which then returns to the analyzer, which consumes trace data and thus empties the buffer. Prologues are generated only for translations that collect trace information for at least one target instruction.

```
prologue:
      subcc    %ntr, count, %ntr      !  alloc., check trace space
      bge      body                   !  if enough space, run body
      add      %ntr, count, %ntr      !  dealloc. trace space
      return to main loop             !  return full buffer
body:
```

Figure 2   Translation prologue.

The trace space requirements for each translation could be stored in a data structure and tested by the main loop. That would save the code space now used for translation prologues, but would require executing additional instructions to address and load *count*, and would be inconsistent with translation chaining (see below, Section 4.4) in which translations branch directly to each other, bypassing the main simulator loop.

Translation Body

The translation body contains code to simulate and optionally trace application instructions. Simulation consists of updating the virtual state (registers plus memory) of the application program. Tracing consists of filling in the current trace buffer entry and advancing to the next.

```
add     %r1, %r2, %r3
```

Figure 3   Sample application code.

Figure 3 shows a sample application instruction, and Figure 4 shows code that simulates it. The translation body first loads the contents of application registers r1 and r2 from the application's virtual state structure into host scratch registers s1 and s2. Next, the translation performs the add operation. Then, the translation writes the result in host scratch register s3 back to the virtual state structure location for application register r3. Finally, the translation updates the application's virtual PC.

```
ld      [%vs + vs_r1], %s1
ld      [%vs + vs_r2], %s2
add     %s1, %s2, %s3
st      %s3, [%vs + vs_r3]
```

Figure 4   Translation body (no tracing).

The target code that is generated to actually perform the application operation is very often the same as the host code, but with different register numbers. Where the host machine is a poor match to the virtual target machine, or where we wish to virtualize the target machine operations, several instructions or a call to a simulation function may be used. At the other extreme, no instructions need be generated to simulate useless application instructions (e.g. nop).

Shade allocates host registers to represent target registers; allocation is on a per-translation basis and can thus span several target instructions. Host registers can thus hold (cache) values from one translated application instruction to the next in order to reduce memory traffic to and from the virtual state structure. Host registers are lazily loaded from the virtual state structure, then later lazily stored back, but no later than the translation epilogue.

Conceptually, Shade updates the virtual PC for each application instruction. In practice, the virtual PC is only updated in the translation epilogue, or as needed in the translation body for tracing application instruction addresses.

```
st      %vpc, [%tr + tr_pc]   ! trace instr addr
set     0x86004002, %o0
st      %o0, [%tr + tr_iw]    ! trace instr text
ld      [%vs + vs_r1], %s1    ! load 1st src reg
ld      [%vs + vs_r2], %s2    ! load 2nd src reg
st      %s1, [%tr + tr_rs1]   ! trace 1st src reg
st      %s2, [%tr + tr_rs2]   ! trace 2nd src reg

mov     %tr, %o0              ! arg1: trace buf
mov     %vs, %o1              ! arg2: virt. state
call pre-instruction trace function

add     %s1, %s2, %s3         ! simulate add
st      %s3, [%vs + vs_r3]    ! save dst reg
st      %s3, [%tr + tr_rd]    ! trace dst reg

mov     %tr, %o0              ! arg1: trace buf
mov     %vs, %o1              ! arg2: virt. state
call post-instruction trace function
```

Figure 5   Translation body (some tracing).

Tracing

Since saving trace data is typically expensive, Shade minimizes the amount of tracing code by giving analyzers precise control over which application instructions should be traced and what information should be collected for each instruction. For example, when an analyzer requests tracing for only data addresses of load instructions in a particular library (an address range), then Shade translates the library's load instructions to directly save the memory address in the trace record. No other trace information is saved for load instructions, and no trace information is saved for other instructions or for load instructions outside of the library.

Shade compiles the simulation and tracing code together. For example, Figure 5 shows code that simulates the sample application code, and, as instructed by the analyzer, traces the instruction address, instruction text, source and destination registers, and calls both pre- and post-instruction trace functions supplied by the analyzer. Whenever a translation calls an analyzer-supplied trace function, it first returns live application state to the virtual state structure for use by the trace function.

```
epilogue:
    update virtual state structure
    update virtual PC
    inc       count × trsize, %tr
    set pred and go to main loop, or go to next translation
```

Figure 6   Translation epilogue.

Translation Epilogue

The translation epilogue (see Figure 6) returns cached values to the virtual state structure, including the virtual condition codes, if they have been modified. The epilogue also updates the trace buffer registers **tr** and **ntr** if necessary. The virtual PC remains in a host register across translation calls. Upon leaving a translation, it contains the address of the next application instruction to be executed. Finally, the epilogue either returns control to the main simulator loop or jumps directly to the next translation.

4.3   Translation Caching

The *translation cache* (TC) is the memory where translations are stored. Shade simply compiles translations into the TC one after the other, and the *translation map* (TM) associates application code addresses with the corresponding translations (see Figure 1, pg. 18).

When more TC space is needed than is available, Shade frees all entries in the TC and clears the TM. Full flushing is used because translation chaining makes most other freeing strategies tedious [16]. Since full flushing deletes useful translations, the TC is made large so that freeing is rare [16]. Shade also flushes the TC and TM when the analyzer changes the tracing strategy (typically rare), since tracing is hardcoded into the translations.

If an application uses self-modifying code, the TC and TM entries for the modified code become invalid and must be flushed. SPARC systems provide the **flush** instruction to identify code that has changed; many other systems provide equivalent primitives [44]. When the application executes the modified instructions, Shade compiles new translations for the changed code.

The TM is implemented as an array of lists of <*target, host*> address pairs. Each pair associates an application instruction address with the corresponding translation. To find a translation, Shade hashes the **vpc** to produce a TM array index, then searches the address pair list for the given target address. If the search fails, a translation is generated, and a new address pair is placed at the head of the list.

Lists are actually implemented as fixed-length arrays, which makes the TM simply a two-dimensional array of address pairs. The TM may also be thought of as N-way set associative, where N is the list length. TM references have good locality, so each TM hit is moved to the front of the list to reduce the average search length and so that a fast, partial lookup typically hits [16]. Thus, inlining the first iteration of the TM lookup into the main loop is particularly effective, yielding good performance for common cases.

Since address pair lists are of fixed length, address pairs can be pushed off the end of a list and lost, which makes the corresponding translations inaccessible via the TM. The TM is large enough that this is not usually a problem [16]. In addition, translations are also likely to still be accessible via chaining from other translations, as described below.

4.4 Translation Chaining

If a target basic block ends with an unconditional branch to a second block, then any time that Shade executes a translation for the first block, it will always follow that by executing a translation for the second block. In such situations, the two translations, predecessor and successor, can be directly connected or *chained* so that the predecessor translation jumps directly to the successor, thus saving a pass through the main simulator loop.[1]

The predecessor and successor can be compiled in any order. If the successor is compiled first, the predecessor is compiled to branch directly to the successor. If the predecessor is compiled first, then at the time it returns to the main simulator loop, the return is overwritten with a branch to the successor. Translations for conditional branches are compiled with two separate exits instead of a single common exit, so that both legs may be chained.

Not all translations are chainable: register indirect jumps and software traps (which can cause control transfers) cannot be chained since the successor translation may vary. For efficiency, the main loop (Figure 7) has two entry points,

---

[1] Put another way, all translations end with a jump to code that dispatches to the next translation. Where dispatching is particularly simple, it is simply inlined in the translation.

```
unchainable:
    succ = fast_lookup (vpc);    ! check first tm entry
    if (succ)                    ! if fast lookup succeeds ..
       goto run;                 ! .. run the successor
    pred = dummy;                ! do not chain predecessor
chainable:
    succ = shade_trans (vpc);    ! find or compile successor
    pred->chain = succ;          ! chain predecessor or dummy
run:
    if (pending_signals)         ! if signal got queued ..
       succ = signal_vpc;        ! .. run instead of succ
    jump (succ);                 ! run successor translation
```

Figure 7 Simulator main loop.

chainable and **unchainable**. Translations with statically-known branch targets, such as most branch instructions, are compiled to jump to **chainable**, while translations with register-indirect jumps, traps, and so forth use the **unchainable** entry point. Using two entry points avoids a test in the main loop to see if the predecessor should be chained, and is similar in philosophy to compiling in the trace space check in the translation prologue (see Section 2).

Every time an unchainable translation is executed, it ends with a jump to the main loop. In contrast, a chainable translation's exit jumps to the main loop only once, to get chained. Thus, most invocations of the main loop are from unchainable translations [16].

4.5 Condition Codes

Simulating target machine condition codes can be difficult because there are several condition code bits and each bit can be a complex function of an instruction and its operands. Instead of simulating each condition code bit explicitly [27, 52], Shade uses the host machine hardware to set many *host* condition codes, all at once. Shade then simulates target conditional branches by executing host branches that read the target condition codes directly from the host condition code register. Since the host condition codes are also used by Shade and the analyzer, Shade also saves the host condition codes to the condition code region in the virtual state structure.

Unfortunately, Version 8 SPARC hosts cannot directly read and write the integer condition codes. Shade uses multi-instruction sequences to interpolate condition code values [16], at an added cost of several instructions each time the condition codes are saved to or restored from the virtual state structure.

Shade saves and restores condition codes across calls to analyzer-supplied trace functions, which may either read the target condition codes or set the host condition codes. Shade must also save the condition codes at the end of each block because it does not "know" whether they will be used in a subsequent block. However, condition codes are usually set and used together in one block and reset in a subsequent block before being used again. Shade analyzes condition codes across block boundaries and omits the condition code save whenever it can show that doing so is safe [16]. In practice, Shade cannot perform such analysis across, e.g., register-indirect jumps, but still on average[2] needs to save condition codes for only 7% of the integer benchmark instructions that set them and only 0.4% of the floating-point benchmark instructions that set them.

Although a variety of other techniques can reduce the cost of condition code saves [16, 69], reducing the number of saves via inter-block analysis eliminates most of the overhead of even expensive save/restore schemes.

4.6   Signals and Traps

A *signal* changes the program counter and thus the program's control flow, but without an explicit control transfer instruction. *Asynchronous* signals arise from external events such as timer expiration and keystrokes; *synchronous* signals, also known as *traps*, arise from internal events such as arithmetic overflow or invalid memory references.

Asynchronous signals can arise for a variety of reasons, and may arrive at any time, during execution of Shade, the translations, or the analyzer. Shade does not directly use or reserve any signals, but applications and analyzers may contend for signals. For example, both the analyzer and the application may wish to make use of signals for hangup, user interrupt and alarm clock. Shade resolves the contention by delivering signals according to ownership, rather than time of delivery. Shade also prevents applications from interfering with the analyzer's signal handling [16].

---

[2] In this chapter, "on average" means the geometric mean of dynamically weighted values over the SPEC92 benchmarks. For Shade-MIPS.V8 (below), "on average" is the geometric mean over the SPEC89 benchmarks.

Asynchronous signals for the application may actually arrive during execution of Shade or the analyzer. These signals are queued and Shade then returns to the interrupted instruction. Eventually, control returns to the main loop (Figure 7, pg. 24), which checks for pending signals. When the main loop detects a signal, it invokes the first instruction of the signal handler instead of the next instruction; simulation and tracing proceed as normal. Chaining may cause cycles that never invoke the main loop. A run-time option disables chaining [16], but pure simulation runs 57% slower on average and traced code is slowed some, as well.

Synchronous signals, e.g., from loading or storing unaligned data or from division by zero, arise only during execution of the application. Synchronous signals are handled by queuing the signal, aborting the translation, and returning to the main simulator loop for handling as above. Note that abortable translations are more expensive to execute. For example, aborting an instruction in a branch delay slot requires that Shade maintain an additional *next program counter* [16]. Most applications run without synchronous signals, so Shade generates abortable translations only in response to a run-time option.

4.7   Address Translation

Shade manipulates two kinds of addresses: *target addresses*, used by the application, and *host addresses*, used by Shade and the analyzer. When the application issues an address, say, 53, it refers to application memory. Since Shade or the analyzer may have something at host memory location 53, Shade *translates* application addresses to reference memory that is set aside specifically for simulating target (application) memory.

Shade allocates memory that it uses to simulate the target memory. A *base address* within the region is defined as target address zero. Shade then forms host addresses by adding the base address to each target address. For example, suppose the base address is 4096 and the application loads from 53; then the load is simulated by performing a load from 4096+53. Code starts near address zero, data is beyond that and grows towards high memory, and stack data starts at high memory and grows down (Figure 1, pg. 18). As shown in Figure 8, Shade treats application addresses as signed so that references to high memory are translated to host memory below the base address.

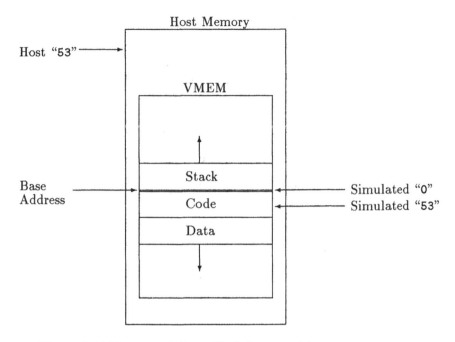

Figure 8 Address translation in Shade (not to scale).

As a special case (-benchmem=0), Shade can eliminate address translation overhead by loading the application code and data at their intended addresses, provided Shade and the analyzer are linked to avoid those addresses [16, 55, 69]. Eliminating address translation makes performance better than is reported here (Section 6), but special-case addressing conflicts may arise, and for some host operating systems, building and debugging analyzers may be harder.

Address translation is also necessary when the target address space is larger than the host address space or when multiple target address spaces or protection domains are multiplexed into fewer host domains [4, 53, 65]. Shade currently implements 64-bit addressing by ignoring the upper 32 bits of all addresses (see Section 9). More general translation would be slower but would prevent application addressing errors from clobbering Shade or analyzer data outside of VMEM [4, 53, 65].

4.8   Other Considerations

Simulating, tracing, and running the analyzer all in the same process improves Shade's efficiency but leads to conflicts over the use of per-process state and resources. Conflicts arise between the application program (e.g. the code generated by Shade to simulate the application), the analyzer, and Shade (translation compiler, etc.). The conflicts are resolved in various ways. For example, the host's memory is partitioned between Shade and the application, so that Shade uses one part of the memory, and the application another. Resource conflicts can also arise from sharing outside of the process. For example, Shade and the application use the same file system so files written by one can accidentally clobber files written by the other. In general, conflicts are resolved by partitioning the resource, by time-multiplexing it between contenders, or by simulating (virtualizing) the resource. Some conflicts are unresolved, usually due to an incomplete implementation [16].

Shade's target code parser is ad hoc, though machine code parsers can be built automatically [62]. Shade uses an ad hoc code generator which generates code in roughly one pass. Some minor backpatching is later performed to chain translations and replace nops in delay slots. The resulting code could no doubt be improved, but the time spent in the user-supplied analyzer usually dwarfs the time spent in Shade's code generation, simulation, and tracing combined.

Many of the implementation issues and choices, as well as some of the implementation alternatives, are described elsewhere [16], as are details of the signal and exception handling and implementation of the system call interface.

5   CROSS SHADES

The previous section focused on the Shade (subsequently referred to as Shade-V8.V8) for which the host and target architectures were both Version 8 SPARC, and for which the host and target operating systems were both SunOS 4.x [79]. Other Shades have been developed. The first, Shade-MIPS.V8, runs UMIPS-V [56], MIPS I [43] binaries. The second, Shade-V9.V8, runs SunOS 4.x, Version 9 SPARC [73] binaries. The host system for both is SunOS 4.x, Version 8 SPARC. There are also versions of Shade-V8.V8 and Shade-V9.V8 where both the host and target operating systems are Solaris 2.x [80]. All of these Shades are complete to the extent that they can at least run SPEC92 [22] binaries (SPEC89 [74] for Shade-MIPS.V8) compiled for the respective target systems.

5.1   Shade-MIPS.V8

Shade-MIPS.V8 provides Shade's custom tracing capabilities for MIPS binaries. Given Shade-V8.V8 and ready access to SPARC systems, SPARC was the natural choice for the host architecture. Most MIPS instructions are straightforward to simulate with just a few SPARC instructions, because both are RISC architectures, both support IEEE arithmetic, and the MIPS architecture lacks integer condition codes.

Little attention was paid to simulation efficiency, beyond the efficient simulation techniques already used in Shade. On average, Shade-MIPS.V8 executes about 10 SPARC instructions to simulate a MIPS instruction.

Some host/target differences make Shade-MIPS.V8 less faithful, slower, or more complicated. For example, MIPS systems support both big-endian and little-endian byte ordering [41], but V8 SPARC only supports the former. Shade-MIPS.V8 currently runs only code that has been compiled for MIPS systems running in big-endian mode. Shade thus avoids the more complicated simulation of little-endian access. Similarly, Shade-MIPS.V8 does not check for overflows that would cause exceptions on MIPS systems. Several MIPS features such as unaligned memory access instructions and details of floating-point rounding have no direct V8 SPARC counterparts, so Shade-MIPS.V8 simulates them, albeit more slowly. Many immediate fields are 16 bits on the MIPS and 13 bits on the SPARC; where target immediates do not fit in 13 bits, extra SPARC instructions are used to place the immediate value in a host scratch register. This difference complicates the translation compiler.

Some host/target differences help rather than hurt Shade-MIPS.V8 's efficiency. In particular, the MIPS architecture employs values stored in general purpose integer registers in place of integer condition codes. This reduces contention for the host condition codes [16].

5.2   Shade-V9.V8

Shade-V9.V8 simulates a V9 SPARC target and runs on a V8 SPARC host. The principal problems of simulating V9 applications on V8 hosts are wider integer registers and additional condition codes. Simulating a 64-bit address space would be a problem, but so far it has been avoided.

```
    ldd     [%vs + vs_r1], %s0  !  s0/s1: virt. r1
    ldd     [%vs + vs_r2], %s2  !  s2/s3: virt. r2
    addcc   %s1, %s3, %s5       !  add lower 32 bits
    addx    %s0, %s2, %s4       !  add upper 32 bits
    std     %s4, [%vs + vs_r3]  !  virt. r3: s4/s5
```

Figure 9   Shade-V9.V8 translation body.

The new V9 instructions present few new problems, but there are many new instructions. As a rough measure of relative simulation complexity, consider that, given Shade-V8.V8, it took about 3 weeks to develop Shade-MIPS.V8 and about 3 months to develop Shade-V9.V8 to the point where each ran SPEC89.

Shade usually generates a short sequence of V8 instructions for each V9 instruction. For example, Figure 9 shows the translation body fragment for a V9 **add**. Complicated instructions are compiled as calls to simulation functions.

The V9 target's 64-bit registers are simulated with register pairs on the V8 host. This doubles memory traffic for each register moved between the virtual state structure and the host registers. It also increases the number of such moves, since only half as many target registers can be cached in the host's registers.

V9 SPARC has two sets of condition codes. One set is based on the low 32 bits of the result, just as in V8; the other is set on the full 64 bits of the result. The host integer condition codes are often required to simulate 64-bit operations which themselves do not involve condition codes, as in the **add** example above. This increases the number of contenders for the host condition codes [16].

Shade-V9.V8 's performance is likely to degrade as compilers take advantage of more V9 features. For example, V9 supports more floating point registers and floating point condition codes than V8. V9 compilers that make better use of these registers will increase register pressure on the V8 host. Also, under Shade-V9.V8, applications are only allowed access to the lower 4GB of virtual memory. Thus, although programs manipulate 64-bit pointers, Shade-V9.V8 ignores the upper 32-bits of addresses during the actual accesses (load, store, register indirect jump, system call). Shade-V9.V8 will run slower if and when it needs to simulate a full 64-bit address space.

6   PERFORMANCE

This section reports on the performance of Shade. For Shade-V8.V8, performance is reported relative to native execution. Since SPARC V9 platforms are not available at the time of this writing, Shade-V9.V8 figures do not include relative performance. The standard Shade configuration used in these tests is a 4MB TC that holds 2^{20} host instructions, and a 256KB TM that holds 2^{13} (8K) lines, each with 4 address pairs.

This section reports Shade's performance when running the *008.espresso* and *015.doduc* SPEC92 [22] benchmarks.[3] These benchmarks are among the integer and floating-point benchmarks with the worst Shade performance. Shade-V8.V8 benchmarks are compiled for SuperSPARC and Solaris 2.3 using SPARC-compilers 3.0.1; native and profiled times are for execution on a SPARCcenter 2000. For Shade-V9.V8, the benchmarks are compiled for UltraSPARC and SunOS 4.x with a preliminary compiler that emits V9-only predicted branches and references to the V9-only floating-point registers and condition codes.

The measurements use six Shade analyzers, each performing a different amount of tracing. The analyzers use Shade to record varying amounts of information, but everything Shade records is then ignored. This "null analysis" was done to show the breakdown of time in Shade. With real analyzers, analysis typically dominates the run time and Shade is not the bottleneck. The analyzers are:

icount0: no tracing, just application simulation.

icount1: no tracing, just update the traced instruction counter (ntr) to permit instruction counting.

icount2: trace PC for all instructions (including annulled); trace effective memory address for non-annulled loads and stores. This corresponds to the tracing required for cache simulation.

icount3: same as icount2 plus instruction text, decoded opcode value, and, where appropriate, annulled instruction flag and taken branch flag.

icount4: same as icount3 plus values of all integer and floating point registers used in instruction.

---

[3] Instruction counts were gathered by running Shade on itself: the superior Shades ran the icount1 analyzer while the subordinate Shades ran the indicated analyzers and benchmarks. Percentage time distributions were measured using conventional profiling with cc -p and prof. Overall running times were collected by running each program ten times, adding reported user and system times, discarding results more than 1.96 sigma from the mean, and then averaging the remainder.

`icount5`: same as `icount4` plus call an empty user trace function before and after each application instruction.

Table 4 shows how much slower applications run under Shade compared to native execution. The *inst* column shows the average number of instructions that were executed per application instruction. The *time* column shows the CPU (user + system) time; for Shade-V8.V8 as a ratio to native time, for Shade-V9.V8 as absolute time in seconds. *N/A* indicates "not applicable". On average, Shade-V8.V8 simulates SPECint92 3.9 times slower than native and SPECfp92 1.9 times slower.

Shade is usually more efficient on floating-point code (*doduc*) than on integer code (*espresso*). There are various factors. For example, floating-point code has larger basic blocks, which improves host register allocation, including the condition code register, and also reduces the number of branches and thus the number of lookup operations to map the target PC to the corresponding translation. Floating-point benchmarks other than *doduc* typically have yet longer basic blocks and better performance under Shade. Floating-point code also uses more expensive operations, so relatively more time is spent doing useful work. The relative costs are closer for higher levels of tracing, since the overhead of tracing is nearly independent of the instruction type.

Shade-V9.V8 is less efficient than Shade-V8.V8, and less efficient for integer than floating point applications. The wider V9 words cause more memory traffic and more contention for host registers. V9 also has more condition codes and is thus more work to simulate. On average, Shade-V9.V8 simulates SPECint92 for V8 (*sic*) 11.0 times slower than they run native, and SPECfp92 benchmarks for V8 3.5 times slower. Shade-V8.V8 simulates these same benchmarks 3.9 and 1.9 times slower than they run native, respectively.

Table 3 shows how much larger a translation is than the application code it represents. *Input size* is the dynamically-weighted average size of a target basic block. *Output size* is the dynamically-weighted average number of instructions in a translation and the code space expansion over the input size. Output sizes do not directly correlate to instruction counts, since portions of most translations are conditionally executed, and since some instructions are executed outside of the TC in the translation compiler, simulation functions, and the analyzer.

Table 3 Code translation expansion, dynamically weighted.

Shade	App.	native		icount0		icount1		icount2		icount3		icount4		icount5	
		inst	time	inst	time	inst	time	inst	time	inst	time	inst	time	inst	time
V8.V8	espresso	1.0	1.0	3.6	4.3	4.1	4.9	6.7	8.5	11.1	12.2	13.4	20.5	38.8	60.7
	doduc	1.0	1.0	3.0	2.8	3.2	2.9	6.0	7.3	9.8	12.3	12.4	18.0	37.5	56.4
V9.V8	espresso	1.0	N/A	10.0	680	10.4	720	12.1	800	16.1	1.0K	18.6	1.3K	42.3	3.2K
	doduc	1.0	N/A	6.5	210	6.7	220	8.6	350	12.3	490	15	690	39.6	2.0K

Table 4 Slowdown: instruction count and CPU time dilation for Shade-V8.V8, instruction count dilation and absolute time in seconds for Shade-V9.V8.

Shade	App.	Input size	Output size												
			icount0		icount1		icount2		icount3		icount4		icount5	
V8.V8	espresso	5.4	20	3.6x	25	4.7x	41	7.6x	67	12.5x	78	14.5x	199	37x
	doduc	11.7	32	2.7x	38	3.2x	72	6.1x	120	10.3x	146	12.5x	401	34x
V9.V8	espresso	5.6	44	7.8x	49	8.7x	60	10.7x	87	15.5x	99	17.7x	229	41x
	doduc	11.2	63	5.7x	68	6.1x	90	8.1x	136	12.2x	161	14.5x	407	37x

For both *espresso* and *doduc*, and for all tracing levels, both versions of Shade spend most of their time executing code from the TC and simulation libraries. For pure simulation and low levels of tracing, Shade-V8.V8 typically spends 65-80% of the execution in the TC and 20-30% in library code that is called from the TC to help with the simulation; most of the time in the library is spent saving and restoring host condition codes (Section 4.5), with the rest spent simulating **save** and **restore** instructions and executing the main loop, etc. Shade-V9.V8 spends relatively more time saving and restoring condition codes and simulating instructions, so it typically spends only 55-70% of the running time in the TC, with 30-45% of the time spent in the simulation library. For higher levels of tracing, both versions of Shade spend more time in the TC, executing code that saves trace data, as much as 95% for Shade-V8.V8 and as much as 90% for Shade-V9.V8. For **icount5** tracing, the analyzer-supplied pre- and post-instruction tracing routines take 5-9% of the execution time, even though they are empty; for **icount4** and below, the (null) analyzer is less than 1% of the of the execution time. Shade also spends less than 1% of its running time in the compiler. Better optimization would take longer and produce faster code, both of which would increase the percentage of time spent in the compiler.

A small TC increases the frequency with which useful translations are discarded. A small or ineffective TM increases the frequency with which useful translations are lost. Translations that collect a lot of information take longer to run, and thus reduce the percentage of time spent in simulation functions, even though their absolute running time is unchanged. All of the analyzers used in these tests are trivial; **icount5** uses null functions that are called before and after each application instruction.

Table 5 shows the average number of instructions that are executed by the code generator to translate one host instruction. The number of instructions executed by the code generator is a function of the instruction set architecture of the host and target machines and the level of tracing. Note that without translation caching, the compiler would be invoked every time a target instruction was run and applications would run hundreds or thousands of times slower. Measurements of the TC and TM effectiveness are reported elsewhere [16].

Table 5 Code generator instructions per application instruction translated.

Shade	App.	icount0	icount1	icount2	icount3	icount4	icount5
V8.V8	espresso	745	949	1581	1762	3958	4514
	doduc	632	813	1549	1720	4550	5100
V9.V8	espresso	1045	1244	1883	2030	4903	5494
	doduc	769	939	1669	1818	5597	6327

7 CONCLUSIONS

Shade is a custom trace generator that is both fast and flexible, providing the individual features of other tracing tools together in one tool. Shade achieves its flexibility by using dynamic compilation and caching, and by giving analyzers detailed control over data collection. Thus analyzers pay for only the data they use. Since Shade is fast, analyzers can recreate traces on demand instead of using large stored traces. Shade's speed also enables the collection and analysis of realistically long traces. Finally, Shade simulates many machine details including dynamic linking, asynchronous signals and synchronous exceptions. By providing a detailed simulation and by freeing the user from preprocessing steps that require source code and complicated build procedures, Shade satisfies a wide variety of analysis needs in a single tool.

8 ACKNOWLEDGEMENTS

Shade owes much to its predecessors, particularly its immediate predecessor Shadow, which was created by Peter Hsu [38]. Robert Cmelik developed Shade, with numerous suggestions from David Keppel. Steve Richardson, Malcolm Wing, and other members of the Shade user community provided useful user interface feedback and helped debug Shade. Robert Bedichek, Alex Klaiber, Peter Magnusson and the anonymous SIGMETRICS referees gave helpful comments on previous papers about Shade, and Tom Conte, Peter Magnusson and Rich Uhlig helped improve drafts of this chapter. Finally, authors of many of the systems in the related work section went out of their way to help us understand their tools; we apologize for errors and omissions. This work was supported by Sun Microsystems, NSF #CDA-8619-663 and NSF PYI #MIP-9058-439.

Exercises

2.1 Shade includes a dynamic compiler.

(a) What source language do the lexer and parser recognize?

(b) What target language does the code generator emit?

(c) What operations does Shade perform that are performed by a conventional compiler?

(d) What operations does Shade perform that aren't performed by a conventional compiler?

(e) What operations does a conventional compiler perform that aren't performed by Shade?

2.2 Shade examines and translates application instructions whenever the translation compiler is invoked at run time (on each translation cache miss). In principle, Shade can also analyze instructions statically, before the program is run. Could Shade perform all instruction analysis statically? Would it help if the tracing level was set statically and never changed? Why or why not?

2.3 Shade creates translations only for straight-line code sequences. Shade could instead analyze larger input units and generate larger translations for, e.g., loops, conditionals, etc. Why does Shade stop translating at branches? Why might it be good to use larger input units?

2.4 Suppose the tracing level can change dynamically and that instrumentation is dispatched (selected) every time an instruction is executed, instead of being hard-coded into translations. What extra overhead would there be?

2.5 Translations always invoke user-supplied tracing routines using procedure calls. Other tracing code, however, is simply inlined in the translations. For example, the code that traces the destination register for each instruction appears in each translation, instead of being called as a separate routine. Why doesn't Shade inline user-supplied routines?

2.6 The threaded-code simulator SimICS [50, 51, 52, 53] checks after every instruction whether there are any interrupts that need service. In contrast, Shade checks only occasionally, when the main loop is invoked. What are the advantages and disadvantages of each approach?

2.7 Currently, Shade implements (simulates) the **exec** system call ("use the current process to run a new program") so that the new program is executed directly by the host. What are advantages and disadvantages of running the new program native vs. "following" **exec** and having the new program run under Shade as well?

2.8 Shade currently implements (simulates) a **fork** system call ("duplicate the parent process, give the new child process a new process identifier") by executing a host machine **fork**. Thus, after a target **fork**, both the parent and child processes are being simulated and traced. Where does trace data go? What are some alternatives?

2.9 In Shade, all cached target registers are saved back to the simulated register file (virtual state structure) before calling per-instruction, user-supplied tracing routines. Why? What change would make this unnecessary?

2.10 When the translation cache (TC) is full and Shade needs space for new translations, Shade simply clears the TC. The text of this chapter mentions only that other methods are "tedious." What are some other methods, why would they be better, and why are they "tedious"? *Hint:* consider deleting a translation that is chained to by another translation.

2.11 Applications that modify instructions use the **flush** instruction to invalidate the target machine's instruction cache; Shade uses the target's **flush** to invalidate the corresponding translations from the TC and TM.

   (a) TM entries are tagged with just the address of the first target instruction in the block. When the **flush**ed address is in the middle of a block, the TM tag may not match. How does Shade determine what blocks to flush?

   (b) Deleting translations from the TM still leaves some translations accessible via chaining. How does Shade find translations that are accessible only via chaining?

2.12 Shade currently supports a wide variety of options for controlling application execution. One option is a "breakpoint" mechanism that causes the application to halt and return control to the analyzer, so that, for example, the analyzer can change the tracing level after a particular instruction is executed.

   (a) Describe how tracing control **TC_STOPA** could be implemented, where **TC_STOPA** stops the application and restarts the analyzer immediately after a particular instruction is executed.

   (b) Describe how **TC_STOPB** could be implemented, where **TC_STOPB** halts the application *before* the **TC_STOPB**'d instruction is executed. When the application is restarted at that same instruction, the **TC_STOPB** must be skipped once, or else the application will never execute past the **TC_STOPB**'d instruction. In addition, when execution halts at one **TC_STOPB**'d instruction, the application may be restarted at some other instruction. Execution should then halt at the next **TC_STOPB**'d instruction, whether or not that instruction is the one that caused the last halt.

2.13 Some systems, including most of Shade's targets, support shared memory between processes. Shade's host system also supports shared memory, so most of the target machine's shared memory operations are implemented simply as host machine operations.

   (a) What extra work does Shade need to do to simulate shared memory?

   (b) Does it matter if the other processes that share memory are being run under Shade?

   (c) What if the shared memory contains code?

   Hint: the basic shared memory operations create a shared segment, map it into the application's address space at either an application-selected address or at a system-selected address, and unmap a shared segment.

2.14 Shade emulates condition codes exactly and saves them away in the virtual state structure if necessary. Shade could instead save the data values and operation code that would set the condition codes, and create the condition code bits lazily. For example, Shade currently saves the condition codes produced by "addcc r3,#7, r0", but it could instead save r3, #7, and the addcc opcode value, then perform an "addcc" to set the condition codes only when necessary. What factors increase or decrease the profitability of setting the condition codes lazily?

2.15 Suppose that the host supported segmented addressing, where each reference to a virtual address is converted to a "long address" by concatenating with a segment base address (a contemporary example of this is the Intel 80x86, which uses both paging and segmentation). How could Shade take advantage of segmentation?

2.16 Shade currently supports a fixed operating system interface. For example, one version of Shade-V9.V8 emulates the Solaris ABI (Application Binary Interface). Sometimes it would be useful to experiment with new system calls without rewriting Shade. One way to make Shade extensible this way is to allow the analyzer to dynamically bind kernel emulation code that Shade would call when the application executes a system call instruction. Would this be simple or hard? What parts of Shade would need to be changed?

2.17 Shade currently executes only user-mode code. What are some implementation issues in extending Shade to execute system-mode code?

2.18 Shade currently simulates only uniprocessor applications. What are some implementation issues in extending Shade to execute multiprocessor applications with concurrent access to shared data?

2.19 If Shade is extended to trace multiprocessors, should there be separate trace data streams, one per processor, or interleaved traces such that traces from all processors appear in a single stream?

2.20 Shade translates application references by simply adding an offset. Although simple translation usually works well, application errors that cause stray memory references can clobber values in both Shade and the analyzer. What changes would be needed to have Shade detect such erroneous memory references? How would performance be affected?

2.21 What if the address checking mechanism described above is also used to enforce protection so that a target address space cannot, e.g., read from another target address space?

REFERENCES

[1] Anant Agarwal, Richard L. Sites and Mark Horowitz, "ATUM: A New Technique for Capturing Address Traces Using Microcode," Proceedings of the 13th International Symposium on Computer Architecture (ISCA-14), June 1986, pp. 119-127.

[2] Kristy Andrews and Duane Sand, "Migrating a CISC Computer Family onto RISC via Object Code Translation," Proceedings of the Fifth International Conference on Architectural Support for Programming Languages and Operating Systems (ASPLOS-V), October 1992, pp. 213-222.

[3] Robert A. Baumann, "Z80MU," Byte Magazine, October 1986, pp. 203-216.

[4] Robert Bedichek, "Some Efficient Architecture Simulation Techniques," Winter 1990 USENIX Conference, January 1990, pp. 53-63.

[5] Robert Bedichek, "The Meerkat Multicomputer: Tradeoffs in Multicomputer Architecture," Doctoral Dissertation, University of Washington Department of Computer Science and Engineering technical report 94-06-06, 1994.

[6] Anita Borg, R. E. Kessler, Georgia Lazana and David W. Wall, "Long Address Traces from RISC Machines: Generation and Analysis," Digital Equipment Western Research Laboratory Research Report 89/14, (appears in shorter form as [7]) September 1989.

[7] Anita Borg, R. E. Kessler and David W. Wall, "Generation and Analysis of Very Long Address Traces," Proceedings of the 17th Annual Symposium on Computer Architecture (ISCA-17), May 1990, pp. 270-279.

[8] Bob Boothe, "Fast Accurate Simulation of Large Shared Memory Multiprocessors," technical report UCB/CSD 92/682, University of California, Berkeley, Computer Science Division, April 1992.

[9] Eric A. Brewer, Chrysanthos N. Dellarocas, Adrian Colbrook and William E. Weihl, "Proteus: A High-Performance Parallel-Architecture Simulator," Massachusetts Institute of Technology technical report MIT/LCS/TR-516, 1991.

[10] Eugene D. Brooks III, Timothy S. Axelrod and Gregory A. Darmohray, "The Cerberus Multiprocessor," Lawrence Livermore National Laboratory technical report, Preprint UCRL-94914, 1987.

[11] Steve Chamberlain, Personal communication, 1994.

[12] Craig Chambers, David Ungar and Elgin Lee, "An Efficient Implementation of SELF, a Dynamically-Typed Object-Oriented Language Based on Prototypes," OOPSLA '89 Proceedings, October 1989, pp. 49-70.

[13] Fred Chow, A. M. Himelstein, Earl Killian and L. Weber, "Engineering a RISC Compiler System," IEEE COMPCON, March 1986.

[14] Robert F. Cmelik, "Introduction to Shade," Sun Microsystems Laboratories, Incorporated, February 1993.

[15] Robert F. Cmelik, "The Shade User's Manual," Sun Microsystems Laboratories, Incorporated, February 1993.

[16] Robert F. Cmelik and David Keppel, "Shade: A Fast Instruction-Set Simulator for Execution Profiling," Sun Microsystems Laboratories, Incorporated, and the University of Washington, technical report SMLI 93-12 and UWCSE 93-06-06, 1993.

[17] Robert F. Cmelik and David Keppel, "Shade: A Fast Instruction-Set Simulator for Execution Profiling," Proceedings of the 1994 ACM SIGMETRICS Conference on Measurement and Modeling of Computer Systems May 1994, pp. 128-137.

[18] R. C. Covington, S. Madala, V. Mehta, J. R. Jump and J. B. Sinclair, "The Rice Parallel Processing Testbed," Proceedings of the 1988 ACM SIGMETRICS Conference on Measurement and Modeling of Computer Systems, 1988, pp. 4-11.

[19] Peter Davies, Philippe LaCroute, John Heinlein and Mark Horowitz, "Mable: A Technique for Efficient Machine Simulation," Quantum Effect Design, Incorporated, and Stanford University technical report CSL-TR-94-636, 1994.

[20] Helen Davis, Stephen R. Goldschmidt and John Hennessy, "Multiprocessor Simulation and Tracing Using Tango," Proceedings of the 1991 International Conference on Parallel Processing (ICPP, Vol. II, Software), August 1991, pp. II 99-107.

[21] Peter Deutsch and Alan M. Schiffman, "Efficient Implementation of the Smalltalk-80 System," 11th Annual Symposium on Principles of Programming Languages (POPL-11), January 1984, pp. 297-302.

[22] K. M. Dixit, "New CPU Benchmark Suites from SPEC," Digest of Papers, COMPCON February 1992, pp. 305–310.

[23] Susan J. Eggers, David Keppel, Eric J. Koldinger and Henry M. Levy, "Techniques for Efficient Inline Tracing on a Shared-Memory Multiprocessor," Proceedings of the 1990 ACM SIGMETRICS Conference on Measurement and Modeling of Computer Systems, May 1990, pp. 37-47.

[24] Alan Eustace and Amitabh Srivastava, "ATOM: A Flexible Interface for Building High Performance Program Analysis Tools," Proceedings of the USENIX 1995 Technical Conference on UNIX and Advanced Computing Systems, New Orleans, Louisiana, January 16-20, 1995, pp. 303-314.

[25] Doug Evans, Personal communications, December 1992.

[26] Richard M. Fujimoto, "Simon: A Simulator of Multicomputer Networks" technical report UCB/CSD 83/137, ERL, University of California, Berkeley, 1983.

[27] Richard M. Fujimoto and William B. Campbell, "Efficient Instruction Level Simulation of Computers," Transactions of The Society for Computer Simulation 5(2), April 1988, pp. 109-123.

[28] FlashPort product literature, AT&T Bell Laboratories, August 1994.

[29] GNU debugger and simulator, Internet Universal Resource Locator `ftp://prep.ai.mit.edu/pub/gnu`, GDB distribution, `sim` subdirectory.

[30] Torbjörn Granlund, "The Cygnus Simulator Proposal," Cygnus Support, Mountain View, California, March 1994.

[31] Stu Grossman, Personal communication, November 1994.

[32] Stephen R. Goldschmidt and John L. Hennessy, "The Accuracy of Trace-Driven Simulations of Multiprocessors," Stanford University Computer Systems Laboratory, technical report CSL-TR-92-546, Septemeber 1992.

[33] Reed Hastings and Bob Joyce, "Purify: Fast Detection of Memory Leaks and Access Errors," Proceedings of the Winter USENIX Conference, January 1992, pp. 125-136.

[34] John Hennessy and David Patterson, "Computer Organization and Design: The Hardware-Software Interface" (Appendix A, by James R. Larus), Morgan Kaufman, 1993.

[35] Urs Hölzle, Craig Chambers and David Ungar, "Optimizing Dynamically-Typed Object-Oriented Languages With Polymorphic Inline Caches," Proceedings of the European Conference on Object-Oriented Programming (ECOOP), July 1991, pp. 21-38.

[36] Urs Hölzle and David Ungar, "Optimizing Dynamically-Dispatched Calls with Run-Time Type Feedback," Proceedings of the 1994 ACM Conference on Programming Language Design and Implementation (PLDI), June, 1994, pp. 326-335.

[37] Mat Hostetter, Personal communication, July 1993.

[38] Peter Hsu, "Introduction to Shadow," Sun Microsystems, Incorporated, July 1989.

[39] "IMS Demonstrates x86 Emulation Chip," Microprocessor Report, 9 May 1994, pp. 5 and 15.

[40] Gordon Irlam, Personal communication, February 1993.

[41] David James, "Multiplexed Busses: The Endian Wars Continue," IEEE Micro Magazine, June 1990, pp. 9-22.

[42] Ronald L. Johnston, "The Dynamic Incremental Compiler of APL\3000," APL Quote Quad 9(4), Association for Computing Machinery (ACM), June 1979, pp. 82-87.

[43] Gerry Kane, "MIPS R2000 RISC Architecture," Prentice-Hall, Englewood Cliffs, New Jersey, 1987.

[44] David Keppel, "A Portable Interface for On-The-Fly Instruction Space Modification," Proceedings of the 1991 Symposium on Architectural Support for Programming Languages and Operating Systems (ASPLOS-IV), April 1991, pp. 86-95.

[45] David Keppel, Susan J. Eggers and Robert R. Henry, "A Case for Runtime Code Generation," University of Washington Computer Science and Engineering technical report UWCSE TR 91-11-04, November 1991.

[46] David Keppel, Susan J. Eggers and Robert R. Henry, "Evaluating Runtime-Compiled Value-Specific Optimizations," University of Washington Computer Science and Engineering technical report 93-11-02, November 1993.

[47] Earl Killian, Personal communication, February 1994.

[48] James R. Larus, "Efficient Program Tracing," IEEE Computer 26(5), May 1993, pp. 52-61.

[49] James R. Larus and Thomas Ball, "Rewriting Executable Files to Measure Program Behavior," Software – Practice and Experience 24(1), February 1994, pp. 197-218.

[50] Peter S. Magnusson, "A Design For Efficient Simulation of a Multiprocessor," Proceedings of the First International Workshop on Modeling, Analysis, and Simulation of Computer and Telecommunication Systems (MASCOTS), La Jolla, California, January 1993, pp. 69-78.

[51] Peter Magnusson, "Partial Translation," Swedish Institute for Computer Science technical report T93:05, 1993.

[52] Peter S. Magnusson and David Samuelsson, "A Compact Intermediate Format for SIMICS," Swedish Institute of Computer Science technical report R94:17, September 1994.

[53] Peter Magnusson and Bengt Werner, "Some Efficient Techniques for Simulating Memory," Swedish Institute of Computer Science technical report R94:16, September 1994.

[54] Clifford T. Matthews, "680x0 emulation on x86 (ARDI's syn68k used in Executor)" USENET `comp.emulators.misc` posting, 3 November, 1994.

[55] Cathy May, "Mimic: A Fast S/370 Simulator," Proceedings of the ACM SIGPLAN 1987 Symposium on Interpreters and Interpretive Techniques; SIGPLAN Notices 22(6), June 1987, pp. 1-13.

[56] "UMIPS-V Reference Manual," MIPS Computer Systems, Incorporated, 1990.

[57] Robert D. Nielsen, "DOS on the Dock," NeXTWorld, March/April 1991, pp. 50-51.

[58] David Notkin and William G. Griswold, "Enhancement through Extension: The Extension Interpreter," Proceedings of the ACM SIGPLAN '87 Symposium on Interpreters and Interpretive Techniques, June 1987, pp. 45-55.

[59] David Notkin and William G. Griswold, "Extension and Software Development," Proceedings of the 10th International Conference on Software Engineering, Singapore, April 1988, pp. 274-283.

[60] Jim Pierce and Trevor Mudge, "IDtrace – A Tracing Tool for i486 Simulation," Proceedings of the International Workshop on Modeling, Analysis and Simulation of Computer and Telecommunication Systems (MASCOTS), January 1994.

[61] Thomas Pittman, "Two-Level Hybrid Interpreter/Native Code Execution for Combined Space-Time Program Efficiency," Proceedings of the 1987 ACM SIGPLAN Symposium on Interpreters and Interpretive Techniques, June 1987, pp. 150-152.

[62] Norman Ramsey and Mary F. Fernandez, "The New Jersey Machine-Code Toolkit," Proceedings of the Winter 1995 USENIX Conference, New Orleans, Louisiana, January, 1995.

[63] Steven K. Reinhardt, Mark D. Hill, James R. Larus, A. R. Lebeck, J. C. Lewis and David A. Wood, "The Wisconsin Wind Tunnel: Virtual Prototyping of Parallel Computers," Proceedings of the 1993 ACM SIGMETRICS Conference on Measurement and Modeling of Computer Systems, June 1993 pp. 48-60.

[64] Stephen E. Richardson, "Caching Function Results: Faster Arithmetic by Avoiding Unnecessary Computation," Sun Microsystems Laboratories, Incorporated technical report SMLI TR92-1, Septemeber 1992.

[65] Mendel Rosenblum and Emmett Witchel, "SimOS: A Platform for Complete Workload Studies," Personal communication (submitted for publication), November 1994.

[66] H. J. Saal and Z. Weiss, "A Software High Performance APL Interpreter," APL Quote Quad 9(4), June 1979, pp. 74-81.

[67] Sumedh W. Sathaye, "Mime: A Tool for Random Emulation and Feedback Trace Collection," Masters thesis, Department of Electrical and Computer Engineering, University of South Carolina, Columbia, South Carolina, 1994.

[68] Gabriel M. Silberman and Kemal Ebcioğlu "An Architectural Framework for Supporting Heterogeneous Instruction-Set Architectures," IEEE Computer, June 1993, pp. 39-56.

[69] Richard L. Sites, Anton Chernoff, Matthew B. Kerk, Maurice P. Marks and Scott G. Robinson, "Binary Translation," Communications of The ACM (CACM) 36(2), February 1993, pp. 69-81.

[70] Rok Sosič, "Dynascope: A Tool for Program Directing," Proceedings of the 1992 ACM Conference on Programming Language Design and Implementation (PLDI), June 1992, pp. 12-21.

[71] Rok Sosič. "Design and Implementation of Dynascope, a Directing Platform for Compiled Programs," technical report CIT-94-7, School of Computing and Information Technology, Griffith University, 1994.

[72] The SPARC Architecture Manual, Version Eight, SPARC International, Incorporated. 1992.

[73] The SPARC Architecture Manual, Version Nine, SPARC International, Incorporated, 1992.

[74] "SPEC Newsletter," Standard Performance Evaluation Corporation.

[75] Amitabh Srivastava, Personal communication, January 1995.

[76] Amitabh Srivastava and Alan Eustace, "ATOM: A System for Building Customized Program Analysis Tools," Proceedings of the 1994 ACM Conference on Programming Language Design and Implementation (PLDI), June 1994, pp. 196-205.

[77] Craig B. Stunkel and W. Kent Fuchs, "TRAPEDS: Producing Traces for Multicomputers via Execution Driven Simulation," ACM Performance Evaluation Review, May 1989, pp. 70-78.

[78] Craig B. Stunkel, Bob Janssens and W. Kent Fuchs, "Address Tracing for Parallel Machines," IEEE Computer 24(1), January 1991, pp. 31-38.

[79] "SunOS Reference Manual," Sun Microsystems, Incorporated, March 1990.

[80] "SunOS 5.0 Reference Manual," SunSoft, Incorporated, June 1992.

[81] Richard Uhlig, David Nagle, Trevor Mudge and Stuart Sechrest, "Trap-driven Simulation with Tapeworm II," Sixth International Conference on Architectural Support for Programming Languages and Operating Systems (ASPLOS-VI), San Jose, California, October 5-7, 1994.

[82] Jack E. Veenstra, "Mint Tutorial and User Manual," University of Rochester Computer Science Department, technical report 452, May 1993.

[83] Jack E. Veenstra and Robert J. Fowler, "MINT: A Front End for Efficient Simulation of Shared-Memory Multiprocessors," Proceedings of the Second International Workshop on Modeling, Analysis, and Simulation of Computer and Telecommunication Systems (MASCOTS), January 1994, pp. 201-207.

3

INSTRUMENTATION TOOLS

Jim Pierce*, Michael D. Smith†, Trevor Mudge*

Department of Electrical Engineering and Computer Science
University of Michigan, Ann Arbor
† Division of Applied Sciences
Harvard University, Massachusetts

1 INTRODUCTION

The instrumentation of applications to generate run-time information and statistics is an important enabling technology for the development of tools that support the fast and accurate simulation of computer architectures. In addition, instrumentation tools play an equally important role in the optimization of applications, in the evaluation of new compilation algorithms, and in the analysis of operating system overhead. An instrumentation tool is capable of modifying a program under study so that essential dynamic information of interest is recorded while the program executes. The instrumentation process should not affect the original functionality of the test program, although it will slow down its operation. In a typical situation, a computer architect uses an instrumentation tool to produce an instruction or data trace of an application. The architect then feeds that trace to a trace-driven simulation program. The usefulness of instrumentation tools is obvious from a quick glance at current research publications in the area, where a significant number of authors use traces generated by two of the most popular instrumentation tools: pixie [23] and spixtools [6]. These tools are popular because of their applicability to many architectures and programs, their relatively low overhead, and their simplicity of use.

This chapter's focus is the design of instrumentation tools. Section 1 describes how instrumentation tools fit into the broad range of techniques available for the collection of run-time information. Section 2 lists the points in the compilation process at which we can instrument an application. It goes on to discuss the advantages and disadvantages of performing instrumentation at these points, noting that the basic structure of an instrumentation tool and the problems faced are common to all of the approaches. Section 3 then discusses the specifics of instrumentation tool design, and Section 4 presents the important characteristics of some existing instrumentation tools. Finally, an appendix is included to illustrate the use of two existing instrumentation tools.

1.1   Methods for collecting run-time information

Before we discuss the design of instrumentation tools in detail, we first describe other approaches that provide the ability to collect run-time information. In general, we can classify a run-time data collection method as either a hardware-assisted or a software-only collection scheme. Each type of approach has advantages and disadvantages to consider.

A hardware-assisted collection scheme involves the use of hardware devices that are added to a system solely for the purpose of data collection. These monitoring devices are not necessary for the proper functioning of the computer system under test. Many different hardware methods exist for unobtrusively monitoring system-wide events. They include: 1) specially designed hardware boards, such as the BACH system [9], which observe and record bus activity; 2) off-computer logic analyzers, such as the University of Michigan's Monster system [21], that monitor the activity of the system bus; and 3) special on-chip logic, such as the performance monitoring counters on the DEC ALPHA 21064 microprocessor chip, which summarize specific run- time events [7]. The two main advantages of a hardware-assisted collection scheme are that one can build hardware to capture almost any type of event and that a hardware monitor can theoretically collect dynamic information without slowing down the application under test. Unfortunately, there are a number of disadvantages to these schemes too. First, since a huge amount of data can be gathered in a short time, the monitoring hardware is built either to summarize events (e.g., a counter that only counts the number of cache misses and not their addresses) or to record disjoint segments of program operation (e.g., a hardware monitor with a large memory that accepts the run-time information at the full execution rate and then later dumps this data to a backing store). In either case, less than the full amount of information is gathered which could lead to a distorted picture. To minimize the amount of unwanted data collected, researchers have combined hardware-assisted approaches with software instrumentation of applications to signal when the hardware should start and stop monitoring [21]– another compelling reason to understand software instrumentation methods. Finally, hardware-assisted collection schemes are costly and highly dependent upon the characteristics of the monitored machine; thus, they are not a practical alternative for many users.

Software-only collection schemes, on the other hand, are relatively inexpensive and more portable than hardware-assisted collection schemes because the software schemes use only the existing hardware to gather the desired run-time information. In general, we can divide the software-only schemes into two approaches: 1) those which simulate, emulate, or translate the application code and 2) those which instrument the application code. Chapter 2 presented a detailed description of the first approach. Briefly, a code emulation tool is a program that simulates the hardware execution of the test program by fetching, decoding, and emulating the operation of each instruction in the test program. SPIM [12] and Shade [5] are examples of tools in this category. One of the major advantages of emulation tools is that they support cross-simulation and the ability to execute code on hardware that may not yet exist. Compared to instrumentation tools though, an emulated binary, even with sophisticated techniques such as dynamic cross-compilation [5], is noticeably slower than an instrumented binary when capturing the same run-time information.

An instrumentation tool works by rewriting the program that is the target of the study so that the desired run-time information is collected during its execution. The logical behavior of the target program is the same as it was without instrumentation, and the native hardware of the original application still executes the program, but data collection routines are invoked at the appropriate points in the target program's execution to record run-time information. Overall, researchers have proposed the following three distinct mechanisms to invoke the run-time data collection routines: microcode instrumentation, operating system (OS) trapping, and code instrumentation.

Agarwal, Sites, and Horowitz [1] describe a microcode-instrumentation technique called ATUM (Address Tracing Using Microcode) that supports the capture of application, operating system, interrupt routine, and multiprogramming address activity. Instead of instrumenting the individual applications, their technique "instruments" the microcode of the underlying machine so that the microcode routines record, in a reserved portion of main memory, each memory address touched by the processor. This approach is effective because, typically, only a small number of the microcode routines are responsible for the generation of all memory references. This approach is general because it is independent of the compiler, object code format, and operating system– as Agarwal states [2], ATUM is "tracing below the operating system." In fact, any information visible to the microcode can be instrumented. Agarwal, Sites, and Horowitz report that the overhead of this approach causes applications to run about ten times slower than normal when used to collect address traces [1]. Of course, microcode instrumentation is only applicable to hardware platforms using microcode and even then the user must have the ability to modify the code. Furthermore, since most processors today have hardwired control, this approach has limited applicability.

A more widely applicable approach is to collect run-time information using OS traps. For instance, data address traces can be collected by replacing each memory operation in the target program with a breakpoint instruction which traps to a routine that records the effective address. A disadvantage of using OS traps is that, if many events must be recorded, the cumulative OS overhead of handling all the traps is significant. However, there are a number of exception mechanisms in operating systems that can be utilized to improve the efficiency of this method. Tapeworm II [28] is an example of an efficient software-based tool that drives cache and TLB simulations using information from kernel traps. It utilizes low-overhead exceptions and traps of relatively few events. The applicability and efficiency of the OS-trap approach depends upon the accessibility of certain OS primitives. With proprietary operating systems, this can be a problem.

The most generally applicable approach is the direct modification of the program's code. This approach, called instrumentation, inserts extra instructions into the target program to collect the desired run-time information. Data collection occurs with minimal overhead because the application runs in native mode with, at most, the overhead of a procedure call to invoke a data collection routine. Most instrumentation tools can create instrumented binaries that run at less than a ten-times slowdown in execution time when collecting an address trace. Some instrumentation tools such as QPT [18] rely on sophisticated analysis routines and post-processing tools to reduce this overhead even more. This approach is generally applicable because it is independent of the operating system and underlying hardware, it has been implemented on systems ranging from Intel architectures [22] to the DEC ALPHA architecture [18][24]. Furthermore, most code instrumentation tools require only the executables, not the sources files, so a user can instrument a wide range of programs.

There are a number of shortcomings to code instrumentation, however. It is most suited to the instrumentation of application programs. Furthermore, most code instrumentation tools only instrument single-process programs; kernel code references and multiple process interactions are not typically included. Therefore, address traces generated by these tools are often incomplete and of limited utility for TLB or cache simulations that require the monitoring of system-wide events. Recently however, there have been tools written that do instrument kernel code and multitasking applications [4][8][19].

Overall, software-only collection schemes are less expensive to implement and easier to port from system to system than hardware-assisted schemes. Software-only schemes, however, do impose some overhead on the system under test and often are restricted in the type of runtime information that they can gather. Even so, the robustness and simplicity of code instrumentation tools makes them a popular choice by today's computer architects. The remainder of this chapter focuses on the design of code instrumentation tools.

2 WHEN TO INSTRUMENT CODE

Code instrumentation can be performed at any one of three points in the compilation process: after the executable is generated, during object linking, or during some stage of the source compilation process. Although different problems arise depending upon when the code is instrumented, the general procedure of instrumentation is the same at all levels. In general, code instrumentation involves four steps:

1. preparing the code for instrumentation - code extraction, disassembly, and/or structure analysis,

2. adding instrumentation code - selecting instrumentation points and inserting code to perform the run-time data collection,

3. updating the original code to reflect new code addition - reassembly, relocation information update, or control instruction target translation,

4. constructing the new executable.

We now turn to the issues involved in instrumenting code at the different stages in the compilation process.

2.1 Executable instrumentation

Instrumenting the executable or late code modification is of the greatest utility to the user. However, it is also the most difficult for the instrumentation tool since code structure information is not available. The tool is responsible for recognizing and disassembling the code sections, instrumenting the code, and then relocating the code while rebuilding the executable. The missing information affects the tool's ability to perform all three actions. Without the structure information, the tool must invoke compiler knowledge or code structure heuristics to accomplish the tasks which can result in both performance and reliability problems. When the tool cannot accurately predict code behavior statically, runtime overhead is incurred to adjust the behavior during execution. In addition, instrumentation can fail or worse, produce incorrect code, due to invalid code structure assumptions. These issues will be discussed more fully in the next section.

Sophisticated tools which can overcome these obstacles present many advantages to the user such as the following:

☐   Source code independence - This makes to a wide range of programs available for tracing.

☐   Program generation independence - Binaries produced by different compilers of various languages can be instrumented.

☐   Automatic library module instrumentation - Full tracing of user-level execution is easy since statically linked library code is included in the executable.

☐   Fast and efficient - No source code recompilation or assembly is required. The user is not required to maintain instrumented library modules.

☐   Code creation details hidden - The user need not be familiar with the compile-assembly-link process needed to create the application. In particular, details such as the necessary library modules or flags, non-standard linking directives, or intermediate assembly code generation are of no concern.

Late code modification tools have various requirements for the information necessary in the binary file. The most general tools can instrument a stripped binary- a binary without a symbol table. At the other extreme are tools which require the compiler to include additional symbol table information. These tools usually require the source to have been compiled with the -g option which includes profile and debugging information in the symbol table. Late code modification tools exist for many microprocessors and several of them are discussed in Section 4.

2.2 Link-time instrumentation

If one is willing to give up source code independence, a convenient time to instrument a program is after the objects have been compiled but before the single executable has been created and the relocation and module information has been removed. Instrumentation can be done by a sophisticated linker which includes an object rewriter. During the linking process each object is passed to the rewriter which performs the necessary code modifications. It handles code and data relocation by just noting location changes in the object's relocation dictionary and symbol table. The modified objects are then passed back to the linker proper and are combined into one executable in the normal manner. Recompilation of the source code is unnecessary. The presence of the relocation information and the symbol table make relocation straightforward. Postponing modification until the executable stage when this information is missing makes relocation much more difficult and sometimes impossible.

There are several tools which perform link-time modification. Mahler is a backend code generator and linker for Titan, a DECWRL experimental workstation [30]. The module rewrite linker can perform intermodule register allocation, instruction pipeline scheduling, and the insertion of code for basic block counting and address trace generation. Code and data relocation is done as described above. Another tool, epoxie, relies on incremental linking which produces an executable containing a combined relocation dictionary and symbol table [29]. Its advantages over Mahler are that the standard linker can be used and data sections remain fixed so data relocation is not necessary. Epoxie produces address traces and block statistics. An extension of epoxie has been created by Chen which can instrument kernel-level code [4]. It is described in Section 4.8.

Link-time instrumentation is not automatic like late code modification and requires input from the user. The user must have the application object files and know the application's linking requirements. In addition, the source files are probably necessary to generate the object files.

2.3 Source code modification

The earliest time to instrument the code is while it is being compiled. This is also perhaps the most straightforward time since the tool has maximal knowledge about the code. Unfortunately, it has several drawbacks from the user perspective:

□   Source files are required.

□   Compiler limited - Most tools are either incorporated into one compiler or based upon a particular language or intermediate level generated by one compiler. This further restricts the traceable applications.

□   Instrumentation speed - Each time the application is instrumented the source must be recompiled. This also implies that the user must be familiar with the application's compilation procedure.

□   Limited code instrumentation - Library modules are not instrumented automatically because they are not included in the source files. It is possible to create separate instrumented copies of all library modules and link them to the instrumented source objects but this requires obtaining the module source code and maintaining multiple versions of modules. Kernel code is difficult if not impossible to instrument with this method.

A major advantage of source-level instrumentation is that the binary creation phase of the instrumentation is greatly simplified. Often the unmodified system assembler and linker can be used to create the binary. Furthermore, the large amount of information available at this stage permits types of instrumentation to be done which are not feasible at later times. For instance, most source-level tools take advantage of compiler control-flow knowledge to reduce the amount of instrumentation code. This reduces both the execution time and resulting trace size.

AE (Abstract Execution) is a tracing system developed by Larus and Ball which is incorporated as part of the Gnu C compiler [3]. Its goal is to generate very small traces which can be saved and then reused for multiple simulation runs. The modified compiler actually produces two executable programs. The first is the modified application. In addition to normal compilation, the compiler uses the notion of abstract execution to insert tracing code in the application code. Abstract execution is based upon control-flow tracing to reduce the amount of trace code necessary. The resulting trace produced by the modified application is only a tiny part of the full trace. This allows traces representing long execution runs to be saved on disk. The compiler also produces an application specific trace regeneration program. The regeneration program is a post-processing tool which accepts the compacted trace and outputs the full execution trace. The tracing overhead, including the cost of saving the compacted trace to disk, is 1-12 times the unmodified program's execution time [17].

MPtrace is a source-level instrumentation tool developed by Eggers et al. to generate shared-memory multiprocessor traces [8]. Their goals were to develop a tool which was highly portable, caused minimal trace dilation, and generated accurate traces, i.e., complete traces which closely resemble those gathered using non-intrusive techniques. Dilation describes the increases in execution time that result from code expansion due to instrumentation. Minimizing program dilation is critical in multiprocessor tracing since a change in execution time effects the coordination of multiple processes and thus the overall execution behavior of the program. Source-level instrumentation allows MPtrace to achieve those goals. MPtrace is more closely tied to a parallel C compiler than to an architecture. Thus, its portability depends upon the compiler's portability. MPtrace was initially created for Sequent ix86-based shared-memory systems and only twenty five percent of the tracing system was machine dependent, most of that being a description of the instruction set.

MPtrace attempts to limit execution time dilation by employing compiler flow analysis techniques to reduce the amount of added instrumentation code. It instruments the code by adding assembly instructions to the assembly-level output of the compiler which will produce a skeletal trace. At the same time, program details are encoded in a roadmap file used for later trace expansion. The modified assembly-level sources are assembled and linked using the respective unmodified system tools. A compacted trace is produced upon the execution of the instrumented application. Using a post-processing program and the roadmap file, the full multiprocessor trace can later be generated. MPtrace can achieve a time dilation of less than a factor of 3 but the usual execution time increase is around a factor of 10 [8]. Library module code is not traced.

In summary, there are three times at which code instrumentation can take place. Late code modification does not require source files, library code is automatically instrumented, and the binary creation details are hidden from the user. However, due to the lack of information available in the binary file, late code modification tools are the most complex and the resulting binaries can suffer performance and reliability problems. Link-time modification takes advantage of some code information to simplify binary creation. It retains use of the system linker, can instrument module code, but the application source is likely to be required. Finally, source-level instrumentation utilizes substantial code information to simplify the code instrumentation process and to produce complex traces. It requires application sources and usually more information from the user. Library module code is not easily instrumented. The remainder of the chapter will focus on late code modification tools.

3   HOW LATE CODE MODIFICATION TOOLS ARE BUILT

An instrumentation tool must insert tracing instructions into the executable without altering the logical behavior of the program. At no point can the added instructions change the program state. For trace generation, the events which need to be recorded are the execution of basic blocks and all data memory references. With this information, an execution profile, memory reference, or full execution trace can efficiently be produced. The usual way these events are recorded is by adding code segments prior to each event. The code stores the information in a trace buffer which is periodically checked during program execution and flushed to backing store when full. The four tasks of the instrumentation tool are to:

1. Find the section(s) of the executable file which contain code and disassemble them to obtain program structure information,

2. Insert instructions to record events thereby expanding the original code section,

3. Translate all addresses which were changed because of the code expansion,

4. Put parts back together to make a new executable.

The next four subsections describe the problems faced and the specific actions required of the tool during each of the above stages. The final subsection discusses some architectural properties which facilitate or frustrate late code instrumentation. To assist in describing problems and the methods used to overcome them, we use several existing instrumentation tools as examples: IDtrace for the Intel architecture, pixie for the MIPS architecture, and QPT for both MIPS and SPARC architectures. These tools will be discussed in detail in Section 4. IDtrace is used most often as an example due to the authors' familiarity with the tool. However, it should be noted that all late code instrumentation tools encounter similar instrumentation problems and rely on similar solutions.

3.1   Code extraction and disassembly

The first steps of the instrumentation tool are to locate and then disassemble the code sections of the executable. Unix executables come in a variety of flavors: ELF, COFF, ECOFF and the BSD a.out format [10][14], but their structure is basically the same. They all begin with tables containing information such as the number, type and location of sections in the file, if and where the sections are to be loaded into memory, and where to begin program execution. Most executables contain one text section, one data section, and one BSS section. The text section contains code. The BSS section allocates space for uninitiated data and is actually empty in the file. Once the text section is located, it must be disassembled. During disassembly the code is split into basic blocks and a relocation table is created which stores the locations of these blocks. This table will be needed later to instrument the code and update the target addresses of control instructions. Since instructions will be inserted into the code, almost all instructions will have their location shifted in memory and so the branch and jump instruction targets must be translated to reflect this. For most instructions this is straightforward since the targets are known at instrumentation time. For data objects, however, address translation is difficult, and without the symbol table, impossible. It is important that all data locations remain unchanged during instrumentation. Therefore, data sections are not modified and are loaded into memory in their original positions.

In some cases, data can be found within the code segment, and this can present several problems for disassembly. There are two reasons a compiler might put non-instruction bytes in the text section. One is to insure constant data cannot be written and to allow the data to be shared by multiple processes. The other source of non-instruction bytes are in-lined indirect jump tables which are created by the compiler for switch or case statements. The obvious problem associated with data in the text section is that, without additional information, the disassembler treats the data words as instructions and tries to disassemble them. These "non-instructions" could mistakenly define basic blocks, be instrumented, or even be modified. Even if the data were not mistakenly modified by instrumentation, earlier code expansion would cause it to be moved within the section. As stated before, data addresses cannot be relocated so this cannot be allowed to happen. The solution is to create a new text section which contains the instrumented code and to treat the complete original text section as a data section. It might be thought that modifying or adding erroneous instructions would lead to incorrect execution. This will not happen because these "bogus" instructions will never be executed. Since control was never passed to data in the text section in the original program, control will not pass to the instrumented data in the new program.

Another, more subtle, problem is more serious and affects ISAs with variable-length instruction. It is highly likely that after a disassembler blindly disassembles through non-instruction bytes, it will be out of alignment with the following real instruction bytes. For instance, suppose a disassembler creates meaningless instructions from a block of constant data and it needs one byte past the end of the data block to complete the last instruction. Again, these bogus instructions are of no concern because they will never get executed. However, because of the one byte used earlier, disassembly will be out of alignment with the beginning of the true instruction bytes after the constant data and will continue to generate meaningless instructions. To combat this problem, the disassembler must know where non-instruction bytes are located in the text section and skip over them. Constant data locations can be found in the symbol table but locations and sizes of jump tables can only be deduced by knowing compiler code generation behavior. Thus, instrumentation tools like IDtrace which run on ISAs with variable-length instruction must be compiler dependent and could require the executable to contain the symbol table to assist in disassembly. Fortunately for IDtrace, most compilers for the Intel architecture put constant data in the data section and the symbol table is not necessary. However, IDtrace's disassembler is compiler dependent and will not properly instrument programs with unrecognizable jump table code.

3.2   Code insertion

Once the code is disassembled, the instrumentation code is added in binary form since there is no later assembly phase. Actual code insertion is not difficult. The only requirement is that the added code cannot alter the functionality of the program. Most instrumentation tools add short code sequences at the beginning of each basic block. If a memory reference trace is required, instruction sequences are also added prior to each memory referencing instruction.

For instance, during profile instrumentation, IDtrace labels each basic block with a unique number. Instrumentation produces two new files: the new executable and a .blk file. The latter holds information about each block such as its size, beginning address, and label number. During runtime, an array exists in memory which holds the execution count of each block. A code sequence is inserted before each basic block which will increment the proper array position for that block. When the program exits, this array is dumped to the .cnt file. Figure 1 is an example of IDtrace basic block instrumentation code. The block count array variable that is incremented is checked for overflow, and the trace buffer is checked and emptied if close to full. Even though each count array entry is a 32-bit unsigned integer value, it could still overflow if the program were sufficiently long. Using a command line option, IDtrace adds code to check for

```
        push status_flag_reg         ; save status flag register
        push temp_reg                ; save temp register
        temp_reg <- block_number     ; put block label in register
        M[ctab+(4*temp_reg)]         ; update basic block execution
            <- M[ctab+(4*temp_reg)] + 1  ;  count table
        temp_reg <- tbuf_ptr
        (temp_reg > tbuf_near_full)   ; check if trace buffer is
        if not goto END               ;   nearly full
        call flush_buffer             ; if full, flush trace buffer

END:    pop temp_reg                  ; restore temp register
        pop status_flag_reg           ; restore status flag register
```

Figure 1 Instrumentation code inserted before each basic block by IDtrace in profile mode.

overflow and do sequential saves to the `.cnt` file. This adds extra instructions to each basic block sequence and will slow execution.

Original Instruction

```
    reg1 <- reg1 + M[reg2+100]
```

Instrumented Instruction

```
        push status_flag_reg          ; save status flag register
        push temp_reg1                ; save temp registers
        push temp_reg2
        temp_reg1 <- reg2+100         ; compute effective address
        temp_reg2 <- trc_buf_ptr      ; load trace buffer pointer
        M[temp_reg2] <- load_tag      ; record reference type tag
        M[temp_reg2+1] <- temp_reg1   ; record reference address
        trc_buf_ptr <- trc_buf_ptr + 5 ; step trace buffer pointer
        pop temp_reg2                 ; restore registers
        pop temp_reg1
        pop status_flag_reg           ; restore status flag register
        reg1 <- reg1 + M[reg2+100]    ; original instruction
```

Figure 2 Instrumentation code inserted before a data reference instruction by IDtrace in memory reference mode.

Memory reference code is similar. It calculates the effective address of the data reference and sends it to a trace buffer. Figure 2 shows the code added by IDtrace to record a data reference.

3.3   Address translation

As the new code is added to the instrumented text section, the control instruction targets must be translated. This is easy for conditional branches and most jump and call instructions because they contain either the absolute target address or its relative offset. Most tools create a relocation table to perform address translations during instrumentation. The table holds the original and corresponding new addresses of all control instructions and their targets. IDtrace accomplishes address translation using two code passes. During the first pass through the code, the original locations of all control instructions and their targets are entered into the table. During the second pass, instrumentation instructions are inserted in the code and the new addresses of the targets are added in the table. When a control instruction is encountered and the new location of target is already in the table (this would occur for a backward branch), the new relative distance can be calculated and entered in the instrumented code immediately. When a forward branch is encountered the new location of the target will not be in the table and the new location of the branch must be noted in the table. Later, when the target instruction is instrumented and its new location is known, the relative offset in the earlier branch instruction is adjusted.

Unfortunately, there are some control instructions for which the target cannot be calculated at instrumentation time. The most difficult ones to handle are indirect call instructions where the target address is found in a register or memory location. Since the data values are unknown during instrumentation, the target cannot be calculated. Furthermore, instrumentation does not affect data values, so execution of the unaltered instruction will produce the original target address rather than the new address. To maintain correct program behavior the address translation must be performed at runtime. As the code is being instrumented, a *translation table* is created which is a list of original and new address pairs corresponding to the beginning of each procedure. This table is included in the instrumented file and is loaded into memory at runtime. Each indirect call instruction is replaced by a group of instructions that computes the original target address and then passes this address to a *call-handling routine*. This routine performs a translation table lookup using the original target address to find the associated new address. If a target translation is found, control is passed to the translated address and the indirect call works as intended. If, however, the target is not found, an error message is reported and execution halts.

Without the use of the symbol table, some heuristic is necessary to detect procedure beginnings. For example, IDtrace marks all instructions following a return or nop instruction as potential procedure beginnings. If the code contains procedures with other instructions endings or if the target of an indirect call is the middle of a procedure, the table lookup scheme will fail. Even if execution progresses correctly, this method incurs substantial runtime overhead for each indirect call executed and significant memory space is required to hold the table.

Indirect jump instructions also pose a translation problem but can be handled in a similar manner to indirect calls. The jump instruction is replaced by code which computes the original target address and passes the address to the runtime lookup routine. This scheme has two drawbacks however. One disadvantage is the increase in overhead due to more runtime translations. The other is that the translation table requires more entries. Not only procedure beginning addresses but all basic block beginning addresses must be included in the table. This increased table size requires more space and increases address lookup time.

If instrumentation can be based upon compiler code generation knowledge, indirect jumps can be handled in a more efficient manner. In compiled code, indirect jumps are used in two situations. One is in conjunction with a jump table produced for switch or case statements. A jump table is a list of absolute addresses and the target of the indirect jump is found by using a register value as an index into the table. If the jump table can be identified, the absolute addresses can be translated at instrumentation time and the unaltered indirect jump instruction will work correctly at runtime. IDtrace translates the jump table addresses during instrumentation since it can find the location and size of the jump tables during disassembly. The other use of indirect jumps is for procedure returns in many RISC processors, such as the MIPS and ALPHA architectures. These too can be translated during instrumentation if assumptions about the compiler are utilized. The discussion of nixie in Section 4.2 describes how this can be done.

QPT cleverly stores the translation table in the location of the original text section [18]. Instead of being an opcode, the word at the original instruction address is the translated address. This allows QPT to load a complete translation table, one which holds the translation for every original instruction address, without using any additional memory or file space. This succeeds only because 1) there is not constant data in the text section, and 2) instructions are a fixed 4-byte length.

A final issue in branch translation is branch target distances. Some ISAs such as the Intel architecture, include both short and long target length branch instructions. Usually, code expansion moves the targets out of range of the original short branch instructions. The simplest solution is to convert all short branches to long branches. In MIPS code, all branches targets are 24 bit long but it is still possible for code expansion to push target distances beyond this distance. Pixie can adjust for this if -branchcounts is given as a command-line option.

3.4   Rebuilding the executable

After the code has been instrumented and target translation is completed, the file sections must be combined to make a new executable. There are now the original text, data, and BSS sections, a new text section, and some tables and buffer space. The original sections must be loaded into memory in their original locations since they contain data. The optimal solution would be to either extend the text section to include the new text and translation table or to create a new text section. Space would be added to the BSS section to include the trace and block count buffers. The executable file format tables would be updated to reflect these changes and to point to the new text section as the location to begin execution. For various reasons, the optimal solution is not possible on many platforms.

The main problem encountered is that many OS loaders do not make full use of the information found in the load format tables. Most formats allow the user to specify the number of text and data sections, the location of where they are to be loaded into memory, and at what address execution is to begin. Unfortunately, to facilitate faster loading, most OS loaders load an application's sections into memory in the same positions in which they reside in the file, ignoring the position information in the format tables. Furthermore, Unix System V loaders only accept one file structure. It must contain one text section, one data section, and one BSS section, in that order. Execution must begin at a fixed address in the text section. The data section must immediately follow the text section. Obviously, special tricks are required to create the new, instrumented binary.

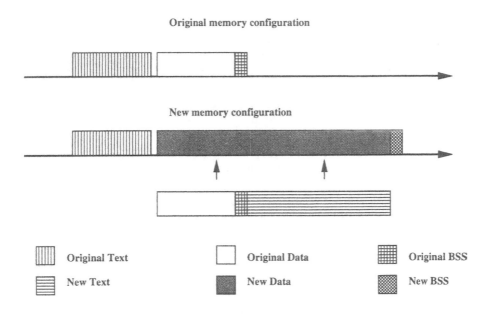

Figure 3   Original and new binary file configuration.

The solution used by IDtrace is illustrated in Figure 3. It combines the original data and the zero-filled BSS sections along with the new text section, trace buffer, and other tables into one big data section. Execution must begin in the original text section so the first few instructions there are modified to transfer control to the beginning of the new code found in the middle of the expanded data section. Another dummy BSS section is added to the end to satisfy the loader's requirement of one BSS section. Note that if the first instructions of the text section were not changed the program would run exactly as before since the original text and data sections are unmodified.

QPT has similar problems on SPARC processors because the text and data sections abut one another leaving no room to expand the text section. In this case, the QPT designers had two choices: add a new text section after the BSS section, which would require explicitly represent zero-filled data in the binary file; or, add a new text section between the data and BSS sections, which would create relocation problems with BSS data since the addresses of BSS data would then point to new text code. They compromised. The new text section is added between the data and BSS sections. Then, immediately upon execution, the new text copies itself to a location above the BSS data and zero fills the uninitialized memory space.

Rebuilding methods which expand the data space must allow for correct dynamic memory allocation (i.e., malloc). For example, on Intel platforms, the last address of the data space is stored in the _curbrk variable found in the application program. It is accessed by sbrk, a routine called by C's malloc function to position dynamically allocated memory. The _curbrk value must be updated with the last address of the expanded data space so that memory will not be allocated over top of the new code. IDtrace must know the location of _curbrk to make this change. Since IDtrace does not depend upon the symbol table, it finds the location of _curbrk by pattern matching disassembled instructions with the known sbrk instruction sequence. From those instructions, it extracts the location and updates _curbrk to reflect the data section's expanded size. If IDtrace cannot find _curbrk a warning message is produced. This is not always an error, however, since _curbrk is not included in all programs.

There are several other small issues which must be handled before the new binary will run correctly. First, the exit call must be modified so that the trace and basic block count buffers can be dumped to a file before control is returned to the OS. Most instrumentation tools modify the exit routine to call a new routine which performs these cleanup functions and then exits. The address of the exit procedure can be found in several ways:

☐   Lookup up the address in the symbol table. This method, of course, requires the binary to contain the symbol table.

☐   Pattern matching the disassembled code for the known sequence of exit procedure instructions. This method relies upon code knowledge.

☐   Knowing the location of a call to the exit procedure in the program and extracting the address from the instruction bytes. This is not too difficult because the initialization library code, crt0.o, contains an exit call and this code is always positioned at the beginning of the text section. This method also relies upon code knowledge.

The start code must also be modified to initialize instrumentation buffers and perhaps open trace files. If the OS loader cannot be told to begin execution at a non-default location, the original start code must also jump to the beginning of the new code section.

As the above sections have described, many problems are encountered when trying to modify an application at the executable stage. Actually inserting the trace code is not nearly as difficult as translating control instruction targets and rebuilding the binary. Some tools rely on compiler-based assumptions to overcome these problems. Others require significant information in the symbol table. Still other tools, such as pixie, sacrifice execution efficiency in order to be almost compiler independent.

3.5   ISA properties

Some inherent architectural features simplify instrumentation. Others pose difficulties or add complexity to the resulting code. Some of these properties are discussed below. In general, RISC processor code is more easily instrumented and the resulting code is shorter and faster. However, some instrumentation problems are unique to RISC code.

Load-store vs. Memory-to-memory architectures

The major factor in the size and consequently the execution time of a program instrumented to trace memory references is the number of instructions requiring tracing code. Thus an instruction set that includes memory-to-memory operations such as the Intel architecture will have many more instructions to instrument than does a load-store architecture which usually retrieves operands from the register file. Memory-to-memory architectures often have a smaller register set which forces local variables to be stored in memory locations. Furthermore, memory operands can often be used as a source and destination in the same instruction thereby generating two trace entries from one instruction. All of these properties of memory-to-memory architectures contribute to the large size and runtime dilation of instrumented code. The i486 has approximately 180 instructions which can address memory. In addition, many of these instructions can perform both a load and a store and some non-string instructions reference two different addresses [13]. In contrast, the MIPS R3000 has only 14 instructions which can reference memory. Each can only perform a single read or write and no instruction can access more than one memory address [15].

Multi-reference instructions

Some processor instruction sets such as the i486 and the RS/6000 include string operations which can perform an indeterminate number of references per instruction. One example in the i486 ISA is the **rep** instruction prefix which can cause one string instruction to repeatedly access sequential memory addresses until a condition is satisfied. It is impossible to ascertain the number of iterations at instrumentation time. To record an accurate reference trace, the single instruction must be replaced by a sequence of instructions which output the reference, perform the string operation, check the condition, and loop back if the condition is not satisfied. This emulation code adds to the size and execution time of the instrumented binary.

Register allocation

As seen in the sample code in Figure 1 and Figure 2, registers used in the trace code segments must be first saved and then restored so that the inserted trace code will not alter the current state of the application. If the processor has a large register set, tricks can be performed to eliminate these time consuming operations. For instance, pixie scans the original code prior to instrumentation and utilizes the three least referenced registers as dedicated instrumentation registers. The original code instructions which referenced these registers are replaced with memory referencing instructions. Pixie then uses the registers exclusively as instrumentation registers holding buffer pointers and effective address calculations. They are used in instrumentation segments throughout the program without having to continually save and restore their values [29]. QPT relies on the caller-save procedure register convention to scavenge instrumentation registers. QPT finds registers which were saved by the calling procedure but unused in the current procedure. This assumes that the program obeys the calling convention, and QPT tries to use symbol table information and optional command-line arguments to verify this. If it cannot be assured, the register values are saved and restored as described earlier. Because their target processors have 32 registers, pixie and QPT are able to contain code expansion.

Condition codes

Condition code values are part of the state of the computer and so should not be altered by actions in the tracing code. The Intel architecture has special instructions which push and pop the status flag register and these instructions are used by IDtrace to hide any effect the tracing code might have on the flags. The SPARC processor has four condition code registers. While the processor does not have user mode instructions which save and restore the registers, two types of arithmetic instructions are implemented: one which affects condition codes and one which does not. QPT's tracing code uses the non-affecting arithmetic instructions in all places except for the trace buffer overflow check.

In this case, it either inserts the check instructions where the condition codes are not live or performs the check with a more expensive code sequence which does not affect the codes.

Variable instruction lengths

Variable length instructions in combination with data located within the text section can wreak havoc with code disassembly. The disassembler must use information in the symbol table to skip constant data and use compiler specific knowledge to recognize and pass over jump tables. This was an unexpected and serious problem with IDtrace. Instruction length also affects the length of the output trace. When instructions are of uniform length, the trace need not contain the address of each instruction in order to quickly derive an execution trace. It is sufficient only to output each executed basic block beginning and data reference addresses. The position of data references relative to instruction references can be denoted using only a small integer offset. The offset represents the number of instructions executed since the last basic block beginning or data reference.

Delayed branches

Delayed branches in some RISC processors necessitate careful instrumentation. An instruction in a delayed branch slot succeeds a branch instruction in assembly code order but will get executed regardless of the branch direction. It is important that no instrumentation code get inserted between the branch and the delay slot instruction. The easiest way to handle this situation is to move any delay slot instruction which requires instrumentation to a location prior to the branch. It must be verified that this movement does not affect the outcome of the branch.

Indirect addressing

Finally, ISAs with heavy dependence upon indirect addressing will suffer from the overhead caused by the runtime address translation. In the MIPS architecture for instance, procedure returns are done with the jump register instruction (jr). The call instruction stores the return address in a general purpose register (usually r31) and jr indirectly finds the return address in that register. Thus, every return causes an address table lookup thereby adding to the execution time of the instrumented program. A method to avoid this overhead which is based upon compiler knowledge is described in Section 4.2.

4 CURRENT INSTRUMENTATION TOOLS

Late code instrumentation tools can be found for most of the popular current microprocessor. The following is a description of a selection of tools for use on various platforms.

4.1 IDtrace

IDtrace is an instrumentation tool for Intel architecture Unix platforms [22]. It instruments SysV R4 ELF binaries compiled using Intel/AT&T C, USL CCS C, and gcc compilers. Currently, it cannot automatically process code compiled by Intel's Proton compiler developed for the Pentium. IDtrace can produce a variety of trace types including profile, memory reference, and full execution traces. Primitive post-processing tools which read output files, view traces, and compute basic profile data are included in the IDtrace package. IDtrace can instrument stripped binaries, i.e., the symbol table is not needed. However, the executable must be statically linked and kernel code references are not included in the trace. Using full execution trace instrumentation, IDtrace will produce a executable which is about 5 times larger and runs 10-12 times slower than the original.

Primarily due to the need to recognize jump table code for disassembly purposes, IDtrace is compiler-dependent. To help alleviate problems due to non-compiler generated code, IDtrace can accept hints from the user on how to instrument a binary. The location or size of a jump table or the location of the beginning of a procedure are examples of such hints. IDtrace reads the hint information from an input file and uses it to assist in disassembling the code and translating addresses. As an example, execution of an instrumented program might abort with a message stating that a particular indirect call target address could not be translated at runtime. This could occur if IDtrace did not recognize the address as a procedure beginning and add it to the runtime transition table. The user could add this address to the hint file and reinstrument the program. IDtrace will then include the address and its translation in the translation table so that runtime lookup can occur during re-execution. While this process is tedious, it does allow the execution of handwritten or other non-compiled assembly code.

4.2 pixie and nixie

Pixie was the first binary instrumentation tool which received widespread use. Pixie is a full execution trace generation tool which runs on MIPS R2000, R3000 and R4000 based systems [23]. The tool is included in the performance/debugging software package of most systems based upon the MIPS architecture. Versions are available which instrument ECOFF and ELF file formats. With newer versions of pixie, if pixified dynamic libraries exist, they can be linked into the instrumented application to generate traces of dynamically-linked as well as statically linked code. Pixie does not, however, record kernel activity.

The default instrumentation option is to record only basic block execution counts. An informative post-processing tool, pixstats, can interpret the output to present a wide-array of runtime statistics. Using command line arguments, pixie will also instrument the application to produce an instruction and/or data trace. The reference trace output is written to a file descriptor. Using another tool called makepipe, the trace can be piped directory to a trace consumer program such as a memory simulator. Program expansion and time dilation depend upon the type of instrumentation used. When tracing both instruction and data references, the new executable is roughly 3 times larger and 4 to 5 times slower. The time dilation does not count the time required to save or pipe the trace.

Pixie is virtually compiler-independent. Constant data in the text section does not cause disassembly problems because the MIPS architecture has fixed-length instructions. It avoids having to recognize and decipher jump tables by performing all indirect jump address translations at runtime. Thus, switch generated indirect jumps, procedure returns effected by jump-to-register-value instructions, and indirect calls, all incur the overhead of a runtime table lookup to perform the target address translation. While pixie is not as restrictive as IDtrace, it does have some limitations. Like, IDtrace, it must use some heuristic to decide upon basic block separation. These heuristics are based upon MIPS compiler generated code. Hand assembled code could cause errors in separation and lead to inaccurate results. In addition, pixie cannot trace past fork calls and will fail on some special library routines.

In an attempt to lower the runtime overhead of pixie, another tool called nixie was created [29]. At the cost of becoming compiler-dependent and operating on a smaller set of application binaries, it makes assumptions about the binary code structure in order reduce runtime address translations. One of the main sources of these translations is the use of indirect jump instruction, jr, to perform procedure returns in MIPS code. The compiler convention for a procedure call is to use jal or jalr and put the return address in r31. The return code convention is to use jr r31. Nixie avoids the runtime translation for the return by translating during instrumentation the return address found in the jal instruction. Then, nixie assumes that jr via r31 is a return and the value in r31 has already been translated. The jalr instructions are treated as indirect calls and are translated using the runtime lookup table as before. When the new address is found, the new return address is put in r31. The remaining jr instructions (the ones not using r31) are assumed to be indirect jumps produced by case or switch statements. Nixie recognizes the code patterns the compiler uses to begin a jump table and deciphers the size and memory location of the jump table. The entries in the table are translated at instrumentation time so they do not require runtime translation. The developers found about two dozen places in standard library code where the above assumptions were incorrect. Fixes for these exceptions were built into nixie so that most code can be instrumented without error.

Because nixie makes compiler-based assumptions about code structure, it can only instrument a subset of the pixie instrumentable applications. However, results from benchmark tests showed that the runtime of nixie instrumented binaries were up to 30% faster than pixie-instrumented ones [29].

4.3   Goblin

Goblin is a trace generation tool which instruments IBM RS/6000 applications [26]. It annotates code on the basic block level, i.e., code is added prior to each basic block to report block execution. Goblin has characteristics of both a late code and link-time modification tool. It accepts as input an executable with a detailed symbol table yet performs instrumentation separately on each object. The instrumented objects are reassembled and linked into a new executable by the system's assembler and linker programs. Goblin's first step is to use the descriptive symbol table to separate and disassemble the executable into assembly code objects. It then annotates the assembly code, records static data about the blocks in the objects, and updates the symbol table to reflect the instrumentation changes in each object. The regular system assembler and linker are then used to create an instrumented executable from the instrumented objects. The profile routines are introduced at the link stage as a profile library to be included in the image. The user can select different kinds output traces by linking in different trace libraries. Several libraries exist. One generates a complete basic block trace. Another allows the generation of a full memory reference trace. Finally, since storage of large traces is difficult, there is library which performs on-the-fly basic block statistic calculations so that the whole trace need not be saved.

4.4   SpixTools

SpixTools comprises several programs that implement late-code modification of SPARC application binaries to produce instruction-level statistics [6]. The two main tools in the SpixTools distribution are spix and spixstats. Spix accepts an executable program and generates an instrumented executable. When run, this instrumented executable produces, in addition to its normal output, information indicating the number of times that each basic block in the original program was executed. By default, this information is directed to file descriptor 3, but the user can change this default through the use of the -fd option in spix. Unlike pixie, spix does not generate instruction or data traces; it only generates basic block counts[1]

Spixstats uses the basic block counts to summarize the behavior of the instrumented program. This tool creates tables of (static and dynamic) opcode usage, branch and delay slot statistics, register and addressing mode usage, distribution of constants in immediate and displacement fields, and gprof-like per-function information. The ranking of functions is based on the total number of instructions executed in that function and not on the total number of cycles spent in that function. Exact cycle counts would require specific pipeline and memory system information which is not available to spixstats.

Spix handles the problems with executable instrumentation in similar fashion to the tools already discussed. For instance, when spix cannot correctly identify the targets of a register-indirect jump instruction, it simply has the instrumented executable print a diagnostic message indicating the address of the undiscovered target instruction and then terminate abnormally. Through the use of the -jaddr option in spix, the user then re-instruments the executable with this extra piece of information. This method is not unlike the hint information in the IDtrace approach. Furthermore, like the previous tools, spix works only with static code (no support for self-modifying code or dynamic libraries), and it is not capable of instrumenting the kernel.

---

[1] Older versions of spix were capable of generating instruction and data traces. These capabilities have been removed since other SPARC tools (such as *Shade*) replaced them.

For the SPEC89 benchmarks, spix roughly quadruples the size of the executables. For the integer benchmarks where the average basic block size is small, the spix-instrumented executables run approximately 2.5-times slower. On the floating-point intensive benchmarks where instrumentation code execution can be overlapped with long latency floating-point operations and the basic block size is larger, the spix-instrumented executables run anywhere from 5% to 50% slower [6].

4.5 QPT

Like its predecessor AE [16], the design goal of QPT is to produce compact traces which can be stored for later simulations [18]. The difference between the two tools is that QPT instruments the executable while AE is part of a C compiler. This allows QPT to be applicable to many applications created by various compilers. As noted in the last section, QPT must overcome the disassembly and relocation obstacles common to all late code modification tools. In addition, QPT performs control flow analysis to reduce the amount of inserted tracing code. Therefore, it must rely heavily on symbol table information and code structure knowledge in order to reconstruct the exact code structure. QPT processes the code on a procedure basis. The address of each procedure is found in the symbol table and a control flow graph (CFG) is constructed with a basic block at each node. Using heuristics to decide the likeliest execution path, optimal code insertion points are located on CFG edges rather than nodes (blocks) and trace instructions are added to the original code.

The trace regeneration process is another unique feature of QPT. The trace output by the instrumented program is a compact trace which needs expansion before it can be used by a trace consumer program. Most tools supply statically created information files which can be read by a post-processor program to expand the trace. The AE system creates an application-dependent trace regeneration tool for each instrumented application. In both these cases the expanded trace would then be piped to the consumer program. QPT instead creates a regeneration program object file which can be linked into the compiled consumer program. Thus, the consumer program can read the compacted trace directly from disk [17].

The performance of the abstract execution instrumentation depends upon the regularity of the program's control flow and memory reference patterns. Numeric programs with sequential access patterns and few conditional branches require less instrumentation and therefore produce a more compact trace than do non-numeric programs with more irregular behavior. Statistics reported by Larus in [17] show that the runtime of traced programs ranges from 1.4 to 12.3 times that of the non-traced program. These numbers include the time to store the trace to disk. The compact traces are between 13 and 250 times smaller than the expanded full execution trace. Larus states that regeneration costs are insignificant since the regeneration routine can produce the full trace at a rate of 200,000 to 500,000 addresses per second while most memory simulators consume addresses at the rate of tens of thousands per second. QPT does not currently instrument dynamically-linked shared libraries but could be modified to do so.

4.6 ATOM

ATOM [24] is a tool that allows the user to build his/her own customized instrumentation and analysis tools. For example, using ATOM, a few small C routines can be written to emulate the functionality of pixie and pixstats on a DEC ALPHA machine. On the other hand, if the trace information generated by pixie is not adequate, ATOM can be directed to gather and analyze a customized set of trace information.

Within ATOM, the authors have defined a set of instrumentation primitives common to all instrumentation programs. These primitives separate the tool-specific part of an instrumentation program from the common infrastructure required by all instrumentation tools. As a user, you write C routines using ATOM's instrumentation library which indicate the parts of the application program that interest you. For instance, ATOM provides library routines that allow you to have access to each procedure in an application, each basic block in that procedure, and each instruction in that basic block. By appropriately indicating where instrumentation code should go (e.g., before or after a particular set of program structures) and by indicating the particular information to be gathered at this instrumentation point, you can use ATOM to access all of the dynamic information in an application.

In addition to instrumentation routines, an ATOM user can also write analysis routines (e.g., cache simulation routines that use the instrumentation data) that become part of instrumented program. In this way, both the instrumented code and the analysis code run in the same address space and thus experience lower communication overhead of a simple procedure call rather necessitating context switching, file piping, or inter-process communication. The ATOM system guarantees correct operation by ensuring that the instrumented routines and the analysis routines do not share library procedures or data. Still, incorporation of the analysis routines into a single executable with the instrumented application program can perturb the output trace. For instance, if an analysis routine dynamically allocates memory, the trace of the heap addresses in an instrumented application will be different from the addresses used in the uninstrumented version of that application. ATOM employs several techniques and urges the user to avoid certain programming constructs to make certain that the behavior of the application is unchanged by the instrumentation and analysis routines.

ATOM is implemented on top of a link-time modification system called OM [25]. ATOM works by translating an ALPHA executable into OM's RISC-like symbolic intermediate representation. Through some extensions to OM, ATOM inserts instrumentation procedure calls at the appropriate points in the application code, optimizes the instrumentation interface, and translates the symbolic intermediate representation back into an ALPHA executable.

Since ATOM starts with an executable file, it can be considered a late-code modification tool. It, however, is not as robust an approach as a tool such as pixie, since ATOM requires relocation information in the executable image in order to work. This relocation information simplifies the work required to adjust branch targets due to the insertion of instrumentation code.

Another advantage of the ATOM approach is that the underlying OM system can efficiently support an approach that does not steal registers from the application program. ATOM (like QPT and unlike pixie) uses the typical register save and restore mechanisms of a procedure call at each instrumentation site. This approach is desirable because it means that ATOM works on programs that use signals and setjmp-program features which are difficult to correctly handle under an approach that steals registers. The downside of a procedure call approach is that it incurs a greater overhead for each instrumentation action, especially if one does not have exact information on the register requirements of the instrumentation routines. Since the instrumentation routines can be quite complex in the ATOM system (remember that ATOM allows the user to use the instrumentation information immediately in an analysis routine), ATOM relies on sophisticated heuristics and techniques to reduce the procedure call overhead.

The performance of ATOM is related to the granularity of instrumentation and the complexity of the analysis routines. Srivastava and Eustace [24] report performance numbers for several different analysis tools built with ATOM. To summarize, for an analysis tool that instruments each memory reference and simulates a direct-mapped 8 kilobyte cache, Srivastava and Eustace found that it took an average of approximately 120 seconds to instrument each program in the SPEC92 benchmark suite and that each instrumented program ran an average of nearly 12-times slower than the uninstrumented version. On the other hand, for an analysis tool that simply instrumented each system call site and summarized this information, they found that it still took only 120 seconds on average to Instrument the SPEC92 suite but each instrumented program now ran only 1.01-times slower. Overall, ATOM is a powerful tool for building customized analysis programs.

4.7   Spike

Spike is an instrumentation tool which, like AE, was built into a compiler (GNU CC) [11]. Unlike AE, it is optimized for on-the-fly trace consumption rather than trace storage. This is performed by linking the original program with an instrumentation library. The library contains a procedure that is invoked for every trace event. This procedure can implement any kind of simulator or trace collector. In many ways, this is similar to ATOM.

Spike can trace data, instruction addresses, and an instruction behavior trace used for processor simulation. This last kind of trace is a dynamic list of *abstract machine architecture instructions*, or *amai*. Each *amai* is described by a type (e.g., integer add, floating-point multiply), and a list of source and destination operands. Any memory accessing instruction includes the memory address as well. The format and content of the *amai* are based on the RTL intermediate code language of the GNU C compiler.

Spike causes execution time dilation from a factor of 3–9 times. Because Spike operates on the compiler's intermediate representation of a program, it is largely machine-independent. Spike has been implemented for the Motorola 68000 family, the SPARC, and the HP PA-RISC instruction set architectures.

4.8   Multitasking and kernel tracing tools

Most code instrumentation tools simply record user-level events within a single thread of control. Recently though, researchers have implemented tracing systems that extend existing code instrumentation tools so that they are able to capture multitasking traces and kernel actions. We briefly describe two such systems that illustrate the key issues related to the gathering of an accurate interleaving of application and operating system reference traces within a multitasking environment. As will be seen, one could further extend these tools so that they could record other types of dynamic information.

The basic action of any multitasking tool is the sequenced collection of trace data from each instrumented application into a single global trace buffer. Recall that the act of instrumenting an individual application involves the placement of instrumentation code around the points of interest in the program and the inclusion of extra support routines which provide initialization, trace buffer management, and other support functions. In general, the instrumentation of each program in a multitasking workload is identical to the instrumentation of a single program except that the support routines change to reflect the management of the shared trace buffer. On the other hand, the trace of a multitasking workload is slightly different than the trace produced by a single application because the multitasking trace must include extra process information to distinguish the trace items of one process from the trace items of another process. For efficiency and practicality reasons, the existing multitasking tracing tools add extra support code into the operating system kernel to help gather this process information and ensure the consistent writing of the global trace buffer.

For the most part, the operating system is just another instrumented application. However, the portions of the operating system that are required to support the tracing system must be runnable with tracing turned off. The dumping of the global trace buffer to disk, for instance, is not part of the normal operation of the system and thus should not be traced. Furthermore, several portions of the operating system are too delicate to instrument automatically. For example, standard basic block instrumentation techniques will fail to instrument properly an operating system routine which flushes the CPU write buffer.

Chen [4] describes one such multitasking tracing tool based on the epoxie instrumentation tool [29] that modifies executables prior to linking. Chen's modified epoxie tool instruments code written for the MIPS instruction set architecture and thus, like pixie [23], uses register scavenging to select registers for use by the instrumentation code. Ideally, one would like to share the pointer into the global trace buffer indicating where the last trace item was written among all of the instrumented applications. Unfortunately, register scavenging precludes the direct mapping of a single global buffer into each application, since it is impossible to guarantee that one single register is available in all instrumented applications at all times. As a result, Chen's system maintains a trace buffer for each traced process, and at every entry into the kernel, the kernel copies the contents of the current process's trace buffer into the global trace buffer.

The tracing of system activity is more sensitive to software trace distortion than the user-level tracing of a single application. Chen's tool illustrates how one can minimize the problems of memory and time dilation. Even though epoxie creates instrumented executables with very little code expansion due to its link-time optimizations, these instrumented executables are approximately 2-times larger and run approximately 15-times slower than the uninstrumented versions of the executables [4].

Compensation for memory dilation in epixie is accomplished in two ways. First, traces are collected on a system with a large amount of physical memory so that page misses due to limited memory capacity do not occur, and second, the traces are used to simulate the TLB behavior of an uninstrumented system. Time dilation is only partially compensated for; in particular, the rate of the system clock interrupt is reduced by 1/15, and the idle activity– the time spent in the operating system idle loop– is scaled by a factor of 15. These rough compensations are adequate because the research focus is on memory system behavior, and Chen claims that memory system behavior is largely unaffected by errors in these areas. The other operating system entity affected by time dilation is the process scheduler, and the effects of time dilation on scheduler policy is minimized by focusing on single-process and client-server workloads where context switches are driven by the applications and not by the scheduler policy. Similar techniques were employed by Agarwal [2] and Mogul and Borg [20].

Mazieres and Smith [19] describe another multitasking tracing tool based on the QPT instrumentation tool [18] that performs late code modification. Unlike Chen [4], their research is interested in the analysis and evaluation of I/O-bound applications such as network applications. Therefore, they organized their multitasking tool to reduce the effects of time dilation. Essentially, Mazieres and Smith attack the problem of time dilation in two ways. First, they chose QPT as their base instrumentation tools since it uses abstract execution [3] to minimize the amount of instrumentation overhead that occurs during the execution of an instrumented application. Second, they implemented their tool on a SPARC architecture where they could take advantage of several unused registers that are reserved by the SPARC ABI [27]. They use one of these reserved registers as the single, global, register-based, trace-buffer pointer that is shared by all instrumented executables. This decision removes the need for the copying of the per-process trace buffers into the global trace buffer as seen in Chen's system. They also describe a few other optimizations that have the potential to further reduce instrumentation overhead.

Overall, the systems by Chen and by Mazieres and Smith prove that it is possible to gather useful multitasking traces using code instrumentation techniques. However, there are several problems that make the gathering of accurate multitasking traces significantly more difficult that the gathering of a single application trace.

Exercises

3.1 Different computer architectures will schedule the same event at differing times. One goal of simulation is to determine the bottlenecks in this schedule. Based on this observation, consider the following statement: hardware-collected traces are more valuable than software-collected traces for simulation. Is this correct? Why or why not?

3.2 Many architectures provide a "block move" multi-reference instruction that copies one block of memory to another. An example would be:

```
copy.w R1, R2, R3          ; copy R3 words from M[R1] to M[R2]
```

This instruction poses a serious problem when creating a data trace (as described in Section 3.5: *Multi-reference instructions*). Only the starting addresses are found in the registers specified by the **copy** instruction, but this single instruction accesses the data cache many times. This chapter proposed changing the **copy** into a small loop to solve the problem.

Suggest an instrumentation method that does not require replacing the **copy** instruction. Put your answer in the form of pseudo code, such as Figures 1 and 2. (*Hint*: You may consider assigning some of the work to the simulator, instead of the instrumentation tool.)

3.3 Instrumented code runs slower than non-instrumented code. The slowdown is due to many factors. One is the execution time of the additional instructions. Explain two other, additional reasons for slowdown.

3.4 There are many solutions to the **_curbrk** dynamic memory allocation problem that IDtrace must face. Describe another solution besides the one that the designers of IDtrace developed. Compare your solution with theirs.

3.5 There are several reasons that gathering a trace in a multitasking environment is more difficult than in a normal, single-threaded environment. List two such reasons. Give an example for each where the normal, single-threaded approach breaks down.

3.6 Should compiler-based tools such as AE and Spike use the same solution to the address translation problem (see Section 3.3) as do late code modification tools? Explain why or why not.

3.7 IDtrace labels each basic block with a unique number. Explain how these numbers can be used to generate a trace of instruction addresses.

3.8 Operating system calls reveal much about a program: its I/O behavior, its use of system resources, etc. One method to obtain a system call trace is by use of OS traps. It is also possible to use software techniques alone.

   (a) Develop a software-only instrumentation technique to record system call events. (One detail that may help: Unix I/O system calls return the number of bytes read/written by the call in a pre-specified register.)

   (b) Using the trace obtained in part (a), along with a trace of data and instruction address references, describe a technique to measure all I/O activity generated by a program. Be sure to consider *all* activity. (For simplicity, you may assume that only one process is executing on the system at a given time.)

3.9 Obtaining a trace of a real-time application, such as an interactive database or the kernel, is difficult with late code modification instrumentation techniques. One reason is the slowdown that these techniques incur interferes with the time-critical nature of the application. Explain how trace sampling can be incorporated to solve these problems (see Chapter 6: *Sampling for cache and processor simulation*). Be specific about the modifications to inserted instrumentation code that are required to implement sampling.

3.10 This chapter concerns itself with tracing compiled languages such as C and FORTRAN. Interpreted languages such as LISP or BASIC can also be traced by instrumenting the interpreter. Unfortunately, the same program will have considerably different traces when used with different interpreters. Develop an instrumentation technique that measures the data references due to the interpreted-language program itself, without measuring the extra data references generated by the interpreter.

REFERENCES

[1] A. Agarwal, R. Sites, and M. Horowitz, "ATUM: A new technique for capturing address traces using microcode," Proceedings of 13th Annual Symposium on Computer Architecture, (Tokyo, Japan), Jun. 1986, pp. 119-127.

[2] A. Agarwal, *Analysis of Cache Performance for Operating Systems and Multiprogramming.* Kluwer Academic Publishers: Norwell, MA, 1989.

[3] T. Ball and J. Larus, "Optimally profiling and tracing programs," Proceedings of the 19th Annual Symposium on Principles of Programming Languages, Jan. 1992.

[4] J. Chen, "The Impact of Software Structure and Policy on CPU and Memory System Performance," Technical Report CMU-CS-94-145, School of Computer Science, Carnegie Mellon University, Pittsburgh, PA, May 1994.

[5] B. Cmelik and D. Keppel, "Shade: A fast instruction-set simulator for execution profiling," Proceedings of 1994 SIGMETRICS Conference on Measurement and Modeling of Computer Systems, (Nashville, TN), May 1994, pp. 128-137.

[6] B. Cmelik, "SpixTools Introduction and User's Manual," Technical Report SMLI TR-93-6, Sun Microsystems Laboratory, Mountain View, CA, Feb. 1993.

[7] Digital Equipment Corp., *Alpha Architecture Handbook*, 1992.

[8] S. Eggers, D. Keppel, E. Koldinger, and H. Levy, "Techniques for efficient inline tracing on a shared-memory multiprocessor," Proceedings of 1990 SIGMETRICS Conference on Measurement and Modeling of Computer Systems, (Boulder, CO), May 1990, pp. 37-47.

[9] K. Flanagan, K. Grimsrud, J. Archibald, B. Nelson, "BACH: BYU Address Collection Hardware," Technical Report TR-A150-92.1, Department of Electrical and Computer Engineering, Brigham Young University, Provo, UT, Jan. 1992.

[10] G. Gircys, *Understanding and Using COFF*, O'Reilly & Associates, Sebastopol, CA.

[11] M. Golden, "Issues in Trace Collection Through Program Instrumentation," MS Thesis, Department of Electrical and Computer Engineering, The University of Illinois, Urbana-Champaign, 1991.

[12] J. Hennessy and D. Patterson, *Computer Organization and Design: The Hardware/Software Interface*, Morgan Kaufmann Publishers: San Mateo, CA, 1993.

[13] Intel Corp., *i486 Microprocessor Programmer's Reference Manual*, 1990.

[14] Intel Corp., *UNIX System V Rel. 4.0 Programmer's Guide*, Order #465800-001, 1990.

[15] Kane, Gerry, *MIPS R2000 RISC Architecture*, Prentice Hall: Englewood Cliffs, NJ, 1987.

[16] J. Larus, "Abstract execution: A technique for efficiently tracing programs," *Software Practice and Experience*, Volume 20, Number 12, Dec. 1990, pp. 1241-1258.

[17] J. Larus, "Efficient program tracing," *IEEE Computer*, Volume 26, Number 5, May 1993, pp. 52-60.

[18] J. Larus and T. Ball, "Rewriting executable files to measure program behavior," *Software Practice and Experience*, Volume 24, Number 2, Feb. 1994, pp. 197-218.

[19] D. Mazieres and M. Smith, "Abstract Execution in a Multitasking Environment," Technical Report 31-94, Center for Research in Computing Technology, Harvard University, Cambridge, MA, Nov. 1994.

[20] J. C. Mogul and A. Borg, "The effect of context switches on cache performance," Proceedings of the International Conference on Architectural Support for Programming Languages and Operating Systems, (Santa Clara, CA), 1991, pp. 75-84.

[21] R. Uhlig, D. Nagle, T. Stanley, T. Mudge, S. Sechrest and R. Brown, "Design tradeoff for software-managed TLBs," *ACM Transactions on Computer Systems*, Volume 12, Number 3, Aug. 1995, pp. 206–235.

[22] J. Pierce and T. Mudge, "IDtrace: A Tracing Tool for i486 Simulation," Technical Report CSE-TR-203-94, Dept. of Electrical Engineering. and Computer Science, University of Michigan, Jan. 1994.

[23] M. Smith, "Tracing with Pixie," Technical Report CSL-TR-91-497, Center for Integrated Systems, Stanford University, Nov. 1991.

[24] A. Srivastava and A. Eustace. "ATOM: A system for building customized program analysis tools," Proceedings of the SIGPLAN 1994 Conference on Programming Language Design and Implementation, (Orlando, FL), Jun. 1994, pp. 196–205.

[25] A. Srivastava and D. Wall, "A Practical System for Intermodular Code Optimization at Link-Time," Research Report 92/6, DEC Western Research Laboratory, Palo Alto, CA, Dec. 1992.

[26] C. Stephens, B. Cogswell, J. Heinlein, G. Palmer, and J. Shen, "Instruction level profiling and evaluation of the IBM RS/6000," Proceedings of 18th Annual International Symposium on Computer Architecture, (Toronto, Canada), May 1991, pp. 180-189.

[27] Sun Microsystems, *The Sparc Architecture Manual*, 1989.

[28] R. Uhlig, D. Nagle, T. Mudge, and S. Sechrest, "Trap-driven simulation with Tapeworm II," Proceedings of the 6th International Conference on Architectural Support for. Programming Languages and Operating Systems, (San Jose, CA), Oct. 1994.

[29] D. Wall, "Systems for late code modification," In *Code Generation-Concepts, Tools, Techniques*, Springer-Verlag, 1992, pp. 275-293.

[30] D. Wall, "Link-Time Code Modification," Research Report 89/17, DEC Western Research Laboratory, Palo Alto, CA, Sept. 1989.

Appendix: Instrumentation Tool Use Examples

This appendix gives two examples of how late code modification tools can be used to gather dynamic information. We assume that the user is familiar with Unix and can create a statically-linked executable on a Unix system.

Runtime statistics

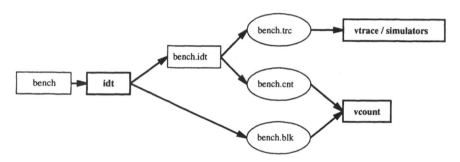

Figure 4   IDtrace programs and files – Rectangles are executables, ovals are data files produced by IDtrace, boldface names are IDtrace tools.

Suppose one wanted to compare to frequency of usage of certain instructions between several architectures. In particular, suppose one wanted to compare the most frequently used instructions in a typical RISC processor (R3000) with that of a CISC-like processor (i486). This could easily be done using two instrumentation tools: pixie on a MIPS R3000-based DECstation running Ultrix and IDtrace on a i486-based SysV Unix system. Suppose cc1, the major part of the C compiler gcc, is used as a benchmark program. The program cc1 must be statically linked but neither the symbol table in the binary nor the sources are necessary. The steps required to use IDtrace are show in Figure 4. The use of pixie is similar. First, we instrument the i486 version of cc1 by typing

```
idt cc1
```

The will produce the instrumented binary **cc1.idt**, and the basic block information file **cc1.blk**. Then typing

```
cc1.idt stmt.i
```

will execute the instrumented version of cc1 and also produce the basic block execution count file **cc1.cnt**. The post-processing tool vcount can then be run,

```
vcount cc1
```

to produce some basic runtime statistics. Part of the list of statistics is shown in Table 1.

Table 1   i486 profile information gathered using IDtrace and vcount.

Instruction Usage Percentage			Other Information	
mov	19,306,218	29.7%	Dynamic instruction count:	65,081,680
cmp	9,642,978	14.8%	Dunamic block count:	17,257,218
push	4,211,418	6.5%	Average inst. per block:	3.8
je	4,166,722	6.4%	Static block count:	41,807
jne	3,309,404	5.1%	Largest block (# of inst.):	95

Pixie works in a similar manner. First the executable is instrumented by typing

```
pixie cc1
```

which creates the files **cc1.pixie** and **cc1.Addrs**. Then the new program is run,

```
cc1.pixie stmt.i
```

to produce the **cc1.Counts** file. Finally, pixstats reads the output files to calculate an extensive list of runtime information part of which is shown in Table 2.

Memory simulation trace

Now suppose one needs memory reference traces for some type of memory system simulation. The method to generate the trace is similar to that explained above. To create a reference trace using pixie, type

```
pixie -idtrace cc1
```

Table 2   MIPS R3000 profile information gathered using pixie and pixstats
on cc1.

Instruction Usage Percentage			Other Information
spec	27,615,307	33.19%	84,450,624 (1.015) cycles (3.38s @ 25.0MHz)
lw	13,027,613	15.66%	83,199,619 (1.000) instructions
addu	7,676,940	9.23%	17,272,839 (0.208) basic blocks
addiu	7,363,426	8.85%	13,217,812 (0.159) branches
sw	7,357,767	8.84%	4.8 instructions per basic block
			6.3 instructions per branch

which modifies the binary to record both instruction and data references. Using
-itrace or -dtrace will give just instructions or just data respectively. Typing

idt -c cc1

will instrument an Intel architecture binary to record a cache line trace. In
this trace, all data references will be output, but only one instruction reference
will be output per cache line. This reduces the number of instruction reference
entries which must be recorded. The cache line size can be adjusted using the
-l option. When cc1.pixie is executed, the trace is sent to a file descriptor.
Using a program called makepipe, the trace can be piped directly to a cache
simulator. IDtrace will send the output trace to a file, in this case cc1.trc.
The trace can be send directly to a simulator by using standard csh pipe com-
mands. Technical reports for both tools give trace format descriptions as well
as complete descriptions of command-line options and trace piping methods
[22][23].

4

STACK-BASED SINGLE-PASS
CACHE SIMULATION
Thomas M. Conte

Department of Electrical and Computer Engineering
University of South Carolina, Columbia, South Carolina

1 INTRODUCTION

Memory systems composed of cache memories are so crucial to high-performance computer architecture design that performance evaluation of cache memories has received phenomenal attention. In 1991, Smith catalogued 487 technical papers and reports that dealt with some aspect of caching [11]. This chapter and the following chapter address the problem of simulating cache-based memory systems. To do this optimally requires measurement of the performance of a large number of cache designs. This process is called *memory system prototyping* here, since this process uses software to construct a prototype memory system. The performance of the prototype is then tested for a set of benchmarks. This software performance evaluation process must be fast yet accurate. A fast method is important so that memory address traces from long-running benchmarks can be used to explore a large design space of potential prototypes.

Researchers have devised analytic models and novel simulation approaches to measure cache performance [9],[1],[6]. Analytic cache models achieve moderate accuracy and are useful for qualitative comparisons. Of the simulation approaches, the direct approach is to simulate the cache at the register-transfer level. This approach is called the *traditional cache simulation* approach throughout this chapter. Prototyping demands simulation of a large number of cache designs, limiting the usefulness of traditional cache simulation. To eliminate the number of required simulations, *single-pass cache simulation* is often used. Such methods simulate multiple cache designs in a single pass through the benchmark traces by exploiting the inclusion property of stacking replacement algorithms (*least-recently used* is the most common member of this class of replacement algorithms [9]). This method has been extended to include rigid placement/replacement algorithms used in direct-mapped caches [13]. Single-pass cache simulation is ideally suited for prototyping.

This chapter focuses on single-pass cache simulation. The key concepts are introduced using the recurrence/conflict single-pass variation, described in [6],[7]. Several extensions to the basic single-pass technique are discussed. One technique, an extension to capture multiprogramming effects, is discussed in detail. Multiprogramming degrades memory system performance since context switching reduces the effectiveness of cache memories. For the memory system prototypes to be correct, multiprogramming effects must be taken into account.

2   SINGLE-PASS CACHE SIMULATION

A traditional cache simulator uses a data structure that is a replica of the tag store of the cache being simulated. The simulation involves updating this data structure at each reference. When an address in the trace is not present in the tag store structure, the corresponding cache miss is recorded. The advantages of such a technique are its efficiency and simplicity. A simple array can be used for the tag store of a direct-mapped cache. The time complexity for such an algorithm is $O(N)$ in N inputs. Since the tag store does not change in size during simulation, the space complexity is $O(1)$.

The disadvantage of the traditional cache simulator is its lack of generality. A simulation must be performed for each configuration of cache under study. Hence the term *multiple-pass* cache simulator can be used to describe the traditional simulator since it requires multiple passes over the trace.

Single-pass cache simulation relies on the inclusion property of stacking replacement algorithms. Exploitation of this property allows this class of simulators to find the miss ratios for an entire design space of cache dimensions with one pass over the trace. The space complexity of these algorithms is directly proportional to the *static* program size. Hence, it is $O(1)$. The disadvantage of these approaches is their time complexity, which is $O(N \times d)$, where d is the average stack depth [6]. However, this asymptotic complexity can be misleading. If there are K designs to simulate, the single-pass technique can capture all K designs in one run, whereas the traditional simulator required K runs. Due to this, there exist many situations where the single-pass technique is more effective.

The particular single-pass simulation approach presented in this paper is based on the recurrence/conflict model of the miss ratio. The model is introduced below followed by a description of the simulation method.

2.1 Recurrences and conflicts

The metric used in many memory system studies is the miss ratio. This is the ratio of the number of references that are not satisfied (i.e., that *miss*) for a cache at a level of the memory system hierarchy over the total number of references made at that level. The miss ratio has served as a good metric for memory systems since it is a characteristic of the workload (e.g., the memory trace) yet independent of the access time of the memory elements. A given miss ratio can be used to decide whether a potential memory element technology will meet the required access time for the memory system [8]. The recurrence/conflict model of the miss ratio is best illustrated with an example. Consider the trace of Figure 1. The *recurrences* in the trace are accesses e, f, g and h. In the ideal case of an infinite cache, the miss ratio, ρ, may be expressed

Reference	a	b	c	d	e	f	g	h
Address	0	1	2	3	1	2	1	0

Figure 1 An example trace of addresses.

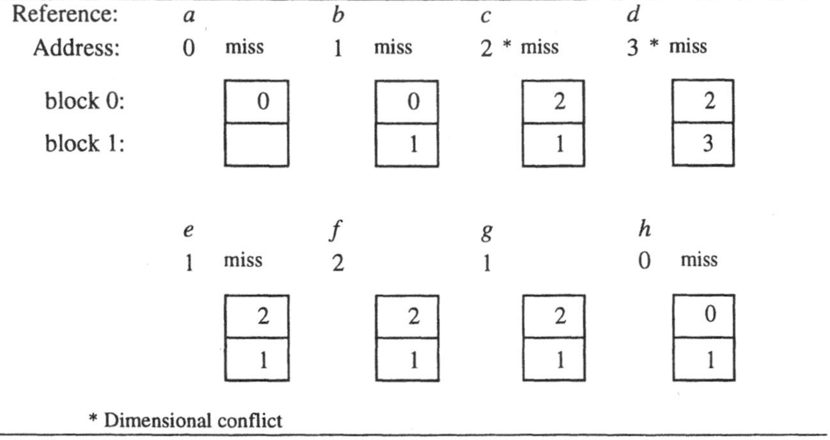

Figure 2 An example two-block direct-mapped cache behavior.

as

$$\text{miss ratio} = \rho = \frac{N - R}{N}, \tag{4.1}$$

where R is the total number of recurrences and N is the total number of references. Non-ideal cache behavior occurs due to *conflicts*. A *dimensional conflict* is defined as an event which converts a recurrence into a miss due to limited cache capacity or mapping inflexibility.

For illustration, consider a direct-mapped cache composed of two, one-byte blocks. The behavior of this "toy" cache for the example trace (Figure 1) is shown in Figure 2. A miss occurs for the recurring reference e because reference d purges address 1 from the cache due to insufficient cache capacity. Similarly, a miss occurs for recurring reference h due to reference c. References d and c represent a dimensional conflict for the recurrences e and h, respectively. The other misses, a, b, c and d, occur because these are the first references to addresses $0, 1, 2$ and 3, respectively.

The following formula can be used for deriving cache miss ratio, ρ, for a given trace, a given cache dimension:

$$\rho = \frac{N - (R - D)}{N}, \tag{4.2}$$

where D the total number of dimensional conflicts. (For the example, $\rho = (8 - (4 - 2))/8 = 0.75$.) This is a general model and can be extended to account for other effects, such as conflicts due to multiprocessor cache coherence [12] and context switching (explained in Section 3.1).

2.2   Reference streams and cache dimensions

For memory system design, the behavior of a benchmark (or any program) can be captured by tracing the memory accesses during the benchmark's execution. A formal abstraction of a benchmark's trace is termed a *reference stream*. This is a sequence of references to addresses, $w(k)$, of length N ($0 \leq k < N$). When required, the addresses are represented by lower-case Greek letters, such as α, β, γ. The reference stream is assumed to be generated by a single process in a multiprogramming system. Note that a reference at $w(k)$ occurs later than $w(k + 1)$ in time, but the parameter k does not represent parameterized time since it does not take into account the difference in service times between cache hits and cache misses. For this reason, k is referred to as the *reference count*. The trace also contains information about voluntary context switching. A reference is called a *voluntary context switch event* if the benchmark relinquished the CPU after the reference (e.g., a system call was performed).

The dimension of a cache is expressed using the notation, (C, B, S), for a cache of size 2^C bytes, with block size 2^B bytes, and 2^S blocks contained in each associativity set. The term *set size* is used to mean associativity level, or the number of blocks per set. *Cache size* is the total number of bytes per cache. *Block size* has been called *line size* elsewhere [10]. Note that $C \geq B + S$. The notation (C, B, ∞) is an abbreviation for the dimension of a fully associative cache ($S = C - B$). For example, a cache of dimension $(10, 6, 0)$ is a 1KB direct-mapped cache with a block size of 64 bytes; and, a cache of dimension $(21, 10, 11)$ (alternately, $(21, 10, \infty)$) is of size 2MB with 1KB-length blocks and it is fully associative. For the purposes of the discussions that follow, caches are assumed to use LRU replacement and map addresses into sets using bit selection [6].

It is useful to partition the reference stream by setting the block offset portion of all addresses in the stream to zero. This produces a *block reference stream*, $w_B(k)$, which is defined such that

$$w_B(k) = 2^B \left\lfloor \frac{w(k)}{2^B} \right\rfloor.$$

In binary, this is equivalent to setting the least-significant B bits to zero.

2.3 Least-recently used (LRU) stack operation

Least-recently used (LRU) stacks were first introduced by Mattson et al. in [9] as a way to model the behavior of paging systems. An LRU stack operates as follows: when an address, $w_B(k) = \alpha$, is encountered in the block reference stream, the LRU stack is checked to see if α is present on the stack. If α is not present, it is pushed onto the stack. However, if α is present (e.g, it is a recurring reference), it is removed from the stack, then repushed onto the stack. This is illustrated in Figure 3 for the example reference stream at the beginning of this section (Figure 1).

A stack is represented as $S_B(k)$, maintained for a block size B at time k. The ith ordered item of $S_B(k)$ is expressed as, $S_B(k)[i]$. The stack may also be expressed as an ordered list, such that $S_B(k) = \{S_B(k)[0], S_B(k)[1], \ldots, S_B(k)[m]\}$ where m is the depth of the stack. The following operations are defined for

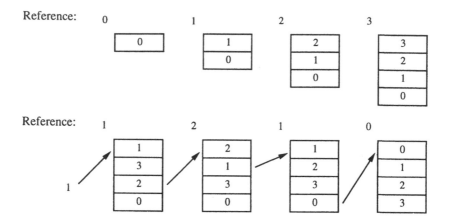

Figure 3   An example of LRU stack operation.

a stack:
the **push**($\cdot$) function,

$$\textbf{push}(S_B(k), \alpha) = \Big\{\alpha, S_B(k)[0], S_B(k)[1], \ldots, S_B(k)[m]\Big\},$$

the $\boldsymbol{\Delta}(\cdot)$ function,

$$\Delta(S_B(k), \alpha) = i, \qquad \text{if } S_B(k)[i] = \alpha,$$

and, the **repush**($\cdot$) function,

$$\textbf{repush}(S_B(k), \alpha) \;\; = \;\; \Big\{\alpha, S_B(k)[0], S_B(k)[1], \ldots, S_B(k)[\Delta(S_B(k), \alpha) - 1],$$
$$S_B(k)[\Delta(S_B(k), \alpha) + 1], \ldots, S_B(k)[m]\Big\}.$$

$\Delta(S_B(k), \alpha)$ and **repush**($S_B(k), \alpha$) are undefined when $\alpha \notin S_B(k)$. When $S_B(k)$ and α are understood, it is convenient to use $\boldsymbol{\Delta} = \boldsymbol{\Delta}(S_B(k), \alpha)$. Note that **push**($\cdot$) and **repush**($\cdot$) are defined as side-effect-free functions rather than procedures. This is to remove dependence on the time variable, k.

The least-recently used management policy for a stack is shown in Figure 4 for an address $\alpha = w_B(k)$. In Step 1.1, the references between the top of stack and the recurring reference are denoted by the set $\Gamma = \{\beta_i \mid \beta_i = S_B(k-1)[i], 0 \leq i \leq \boldsymbol{\Delta}\}$. Figure 4 is applied to $\alpha = w_B(k)$ for all k. The LRU policy is essentially a definition for calculating $S_B(k)$ from $S_B(k-1)$ and α. In most

1.   **if** $\alpha \in S_B(k-1)$ **then**
1.1   do_recurrence(α, Γ)
1.2 $S_B(k) \leftarrow$ **repush**($S_B(k-1), \alpha$),
2.   **else** $S_B(k) \leftarrow$ **push**($S_B(k-1), \alpha$)
3. $N \leftarrow N + 1$

Figure 4 The least-recently used management policy for a stack, $S_B(k)$ (adapted from Mattson *et al.*).

situations, $S_B(k)$ is calculated in order to obtain other statistics, such as the stack depth distribution.

The complexity of the algorithm of Figure 4 depends on the complexity of the do_recurrence() procedure. Assume for the moment that the complexity of this procedure is $O(d)$ on average, where d is the average stack depth (the validity of this assumption is justified below). The outer algorithm's complexity is also dependent on the efficiency of the set (stack) existence operator in Step 1. In Mattson *et al.* [9], the set-existence operation was determined by scanning the entire stack. This has an average complexity $O(d)$ for the set existence [6]. This results in a complexity of $O(N \times d)$ for the entire algorithm. This approach to calculating set existence can be replaced by using a hash table lookup, where each entry of the new table contains a pointer to the stack frame. Hash table lookup also has complexity of $O(d)$ on average [3]. However, there is a practical advantage to using hash table lookup. For the hash table implementation, only the hash conflict set for the block needs to be searched to determine whether the reference is first-time. This is a constant-time improvement and does not change the asymptotic behavior.

2.4   Recurrence/conflict-based single-pass simulation

The single-pass cache simulation algorithm for limited associativities ($S < C - B$) is created by expanding the do_recurrence procedure of Figure 4 [6],[6]. A single-pass algorithm that uses the recurrence/conflict model is presented in Figure 5 (notation used in Figure 5 is summarized in Table 1). This algorithm is similar to the original algorithm of Traiger and Slutz [13]. However, where Traiger and Slutz recorded temporal localities, this algorithm records recurrences and conflicts. Since temporal locality functions can occupy considerable space, using recurrences and conflicts is an advantage. In this respect, the recurrence/conflict approach is similar to the algorithm of Hill and Smith [6].

do_recurrence(α, Γ):
1          $R[B] \leftarrow R[B] + 1$
2   for $\beta_i \in \Gamma$ do
2.1 $u \leftarrow u + 1$
2.2 $d \leftarrow |\beta_i - \alpha|$
2.3 $z \leftarrow \text{ctz}(d)$
2.4 $p[z] \leftarrow p[z] + 1$
2.5 $z_{\max} \leftarrow \max(z, z_{\max})$
3          $C_\infty \leftarrow \lfloor \log_2 u \rfloor + B$
4   for $c \leftarrow B$ to C_∞
4.1 $D[c, B, \infty] \leftarrow D[c, B, \infty] + 1$
5          $z \leftarrow z_{\max}$
6          $S_{target} \leftarrow 1$
7          $nss \leftarrow 0$
8   for $s \leftarrow 0$ to $S_{\max}$
8.1 $C_{MC} \leftarrow B$
8.2   while $z \geq 0$ and $nss < S_{target}$
8.2.1 $nss \leftarrow p[z]$
8.2.2 $z \leftarrow z - 1$
8.3   if $nss \geq S_{target}$ then
8.3.1 $C_{MC} \leftarrow z + s + 1$
8.4   for $c \leftarrow B + s$ to C_{MC}
8.4.1 $D[c, B, s] \leftarrow D[c, B, s] + 1$
8.5 $S_{target} \leftarrow 2 \times S_{target}$

Figure 5   The recurrence/conflict single-pass cache simulation algorithm.

Whenever a reference is found on the stack in Figure 5, its presence indicates that it is a recurrence. The number of times this event occurs in Step 1 of Figure 5 is used to keep a count of the number of recurrences ($R[B]$). The remainder of the algorithm is devoted to calculating the dimensional conflicts ($D[C, B, S]$).

Table 1 Notation used in Figure 5.

Symbol	Definition
α	Current reference
β_i	Intervening references from Γ
u	Number of unique references
d	Address distance
$\text{ctz}(d)$	Counts trailing zeros (in binary) for d
z	Count of trailing zeros
$p[z]$	Histogram of counts of trailing zeros
$z_{\max}$	Maximum trailing zeros number
C_{∞}	largest fully-associative cache with a dimensional conflict
S_{target}	Target set size
nss	Number of references in the same set
C_{MC}	Largest cache with a dimensional conflict
N	Total number of references

The **for** statement that iterates for all intervening references in Step 2 of Figure 5 calculates the raw information for determining two classes of cache organizations. The maintenance of the number of unique references (u) in Step 2.1 is used to calculate the largest-sized fully associative cache with a dimensional conflict (C_infty). This calculation is done in Steps 3 and 4 by finding the $\log_2$ of this count. Unlike the algorithm of Mattson, *et al.*, only cache sizes that are multiples of powers of 2 are considered [9]. The remainder of Step 2 calculates a histogram, $p[z]$, of a function of the current reference (α) and each intervening reference (β_i) (Step 2.4). This function is the lowest power of two factor of the arithmetic difference between the two references (Steps 2.2 and 2.3). For a range of direct-mapped caches, this function is equivalent to the largest cache size in which a miss will still occur for α due to the intervening reference to β_i. (Mattson, *et al.* refer to $\text{ctz}(|\beta_i - \alpha|)$ as the *right-match* function, since it counts the maximum right-most bits that match between β_i and α.) The remainder of the procedure uses this information to calculate this cache size for all associativities (Steps 5–8).

The histogram ($p[z]$) is processed for all associativities by scanning the histogram from largest to smallest potential conflicting cache size. A set size can be thought of as a *conflict tolerance*. A conflict between α and β_i for a direct-mapped cache of dimension $(C, B, 0)$ is equivalent to α and β_i occupying the same set in caches (C, B, S) for $C - B \geq S > 0$. The larger the set size, S, is, the more numerous are the allowed same-set mappings between references to α before these mappings result in a miss.

In Steps 6 to 8, the set sizes are considered in increasing order to determine how many same-set mappings are tolerable. For each set, the largest cache size in which a miss will occur, C_{MC}, ($MC = maximum\ conflict$) is the product of the same cache size for a direct-mapped cache times the set size (Step 8.3.1, note that addition of these exponents of base 2 implies multiplication). If no same-set mappings remain in the histogram, the only conflicts accounted for are those that occur in caches containing a single block (Step 8.1).

The complexity of the inner-most **while** statement of Steps 8.2–8.2.2 is dependent on S_{target} and z. The initial value of z is z_{max}, which is bounded by the word size of the trace (e.g., 32 bits) since z_{max} is an indirect result of the $ctz(d)$ function of Step 2.3. Therefore, z has a constant upper bound. The other determiner of the **while** statement's execution is S_{target} which is 2^s due to Steps 6, and 8.5. Therefore, S_{target} also has a constant upper bound of $2^{S_{max}}$. The **while** statement therefore has a worst-case execution time of $\max(z_{max}, 2^{S_{max}})$, which results in a complexity of $O(1)$. The surrounding **for** statement also has a complexity of $O(1)$, resulting in a total complexity for Step 8 and all of its substeps of $O(1)$.

The complexity of the **do_recurrence()** procedure is $O(d)$ in the worst case due to the scanning of the stack in Steps 2.1–2.5. An input that elicits worst-case behavior is a cyclic referencing pattern of addresses, such as

$$\alpha, \beta, \gamma, \delta, \alpha, \beta, \gamma, \delta, \alpha, \ldots,$$

where each cycle consists of $\alpha, \beta, \gamma, \delta$. Consider a trace of such a pattern of length N having K cycles. In such a trace, any recurrence must traverse $d = N/K$ references in Steps 2.1–2.5. Hence, the complexity of this is $O(N/K)$, or simply $O(d)$.

3   EXTENSIONS TO SINGLE-PASS TECHNIQUES

This section discusses extensions to single-pass algorithms in detail. Several extensions have been proposed, including:

☐ **Multiprogramming**: In his Ph.D. thesis, Thompson extended fully-associative, stack-based, single-pass techniques to measure conflicts due to multiprogramming [12]. These extensions are valid for any MOESI cache coherence protocol. Thompson includes specific algorithms for the Berkeley, Dragon, Illinois, and Firefly protocols (see [2] for an overview of these protocols).

☐ **Write-back caches**: Thompson also studied the correct simulation of write-back traffic in a fully-associative cache using a stack-based, single-pass technique. Wang and Baer extended this work to caches with limited associativity [14]. Both schemes relie on keeping the *dirty level* for an entry in the stack: the smallest cache for which the block is still dirty (not yet written back).

☐ **Load-forwarding**: Sectored cache design (sometimes called *sub-blocking* is a common technique to reduce the traffic for a miss while maintaining a small cache tag store. Chen, *et al.* has developed a single-pass technique for measuring the effects of load-forwarding when used with a sectored instruction cache [15].

3.1 An example extension: Context switching

Single-pass algorithms have been extended to context switching by the author [7]. Context switching occurs due to two distinct events: (1) a *voluntary context switch*, where the benchmark relinquishes the processor and, (2) an *involuntary context switch*, where the benchmark's execution is suspended due to external interrupts. Voluntary context switches are a characteristic of the benchmark application. They occur at the same place in the execution between different benchmark runs. On the other hand, involuntary context switches are determined by the I/O system behavior (device interrupts), clock frequency (timer interrupts), etc. They do not occur at the same place between runs of the benchmark, and are not characteristic of the benchmark. Page faults are treated as involuntary context switches because page faults depend on the interaction of processes in the system, whose interaction is assumed to be pseudo-random in nature.

Since involuntary context switches occur at random, it is assumed that involuntary context switches can occur with equal probability for each reference in the reference stream [5]. This probability is denoted, q, and termed the involuntary *context switching intensity*. Separation of the system's characteristics from the characteristics of the benchmark allows many different systems to be considered without re-simulating the benchmark's behavior. This is the main goal of single-pass techniques in general [13]. Although the occurrence of involuntary context switches is not a characteristic of the benchmark, the benchmark's susceptibility to their occurrence is. This susceptibility can be measured as the expected number of multiprogramming conflicts due to random involuntary context switching. A method to measure this susceptibility is presented below that records the benchmark's susceptibility to all context-switching intensities in a single-pass through the trace. The empirical results discussed in [7] demonstrate the validity of this approach.

The working set of a process/benchmark may have been flushed from the cache before it re-enters the run state after a context switch. Let f_{CS} represent the *fraction of the cache's contents flushed between context switches*. The number of processes executed before a process returns from a context switch is a function of the system load and the operating system scheduling policy. Furthermore, the particular cache blocks flushed due to a context switch also depends on the reference patterns of the processes executing on the system. This makes f_{CS} highly dependent on several volatile variables and therefore difficult to measure. (Several empirical estimates of f_{CS} are presented in [7].) Some virtual memory system implementations force a cache flush to eliminate problems with page sharing of writable pages. Also, it has been shown that for small cache sizes, a context switch effectively flushes the cache, therefore $f_{CS} = 1$ [10]. For larger caches, this provides an upper bound for the effects of context switching.

The components of multiprogramming conflicts

Multiprogramming conflicts are defined in terms of *potential victims*. A recurring reference that is not removed from a cache by a dimensional conflict, yet that may be removed by a context switch, is a potential victim of the context switch. The numbers of each type of potential victims are defined as $X_V[C, B, S]$ and $X_I[C, B, S, q]$, for all voluntary and involuntary context switches, respectively. $X_V[C, B, S]$ is the total number of potential victims due to voluntary context switching for caches of dimension (C, B, S). $X_I[C, B, S, q]$ is the expected number of potential victims due to involuntary context switching of intensity q. The multiprogramming conflicts are expressed in terms of victims as,

$$M[C, B, S, q] \equiv f_{CS}\left(X_V[C, B, S] + X_I[C, B, S, q]\right). \qquad (4.3)$$

The equation for the miss ratio (Equation 4.2) can be modified to take into account the new conflicts,

$$\rho = \frac{N - (R - D - M)}{N} = \frac{N - (R - D - f_{CS}(X_V[C, B, S] + X_I[C, B, S, q]))}{N}.$$

$$(4.4)$$

Determining the multiprogramming conflicts involves measuring X_V and X_I from the reference stream. The measurement can be done by extending the recurrence/conflict single-pass technique. The miss ratio is then calculated by first calculating $M[C, B, S, q]$ using Equation 4.3 for a value of f_{CS}, then using the result to complete Equation 4.4.

Multiprogramming extensions to LRU stack operation

The extensions required to the recurrence/conflict single-pass technique measure X_V and X_I are shown in Figure 7. The procedure for determining X_V is illustrated in Figure 6. The procedure operates as follows: When α is processed, if it is not a recurring reference (i.e., the test of Step 1 of Figure 7 fails), then it cannot be a victim since it cannot produce a hit. However, if α is a voluntary context switch event, it is marked as such when it is pushed on the stack in Step 2 (marked references are shown using asterisks in Figure 6). If α is a recurring reference, X_V is conditionally incremented if a marked reference is encountered when the dimensional conflicts are calculated. X_V is only incremented for all dimensions in which α does not have a dimensional conflict. If X_V were incremented for all dimensions, a reference might be counted more than once as a conflict, once as a multiprogramming conflict and once as a dimensional conflict. Notice that the references immediately below a marked reference being repushed inherit the marking in Figure 6 (Step 1.6 and its substeps of Figure 7). This is done to insure all subsequent recurring references that cross the context switch event are subject to a voluntary context switch.

The procedure for determining $X_I[C, B, S, q]$ using an LRU stack is somewhat more complicated than that for determining $X_V[C, B, S]$. Recall that an involuntary context switch may occur between every reference. Let L, the *context switch distance*, be the number of potential involuntary context switch events for the recurring reference α at reference count k (i.e., $\alpha = w_B(k - L)$ and $w_B(k - L) = w_B(k)$). Let p_L be the probability that at least one involuntary context switch occurs between times $k - L$ and k. Then,

$$p_L = \sum_{j=1}^{L} \binom{L}{j} q^j (1 - q)^{L-j}.$$

$$(4.5)$$

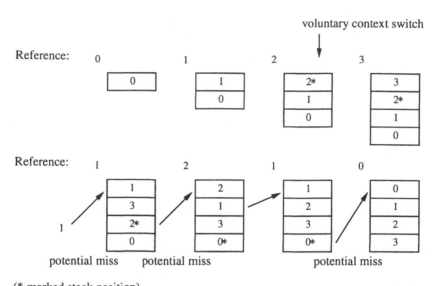

Figure 6   An example for voluntary context switch of the modified LRU stack operation.

Define $n_L[C, B, S]$ to be the number of recurrences not subject to dimensional conflicts that have a context switch distance of L. Therefore,

$$X_I[C, B, S, q] = E\left[n_L[C, B, S]\right] = \sum_L p_L n_L[C, B, S]. \qquad (4.6)$$

Equation 4.6 expresses the expected number of potential victims due to involuntary context switching. The equation fits naturally into a stack-based method. The new metric $n_L[C, B, S]$ can be recorded by annotating the references on the stack.   Figure 8 shows an example of calculating $X_I[C, B, S]$.   The figure shows that a counter of the number of context switch events affecting α is kept, defined as $c_I(\alpha)$. Initially and after a recurring reference is repushed, $c_I(\alpha) \leftarrow 1$ (Step 2.1 and 1.8 of Figure 7). In Step 1.3, its substeps, and Step 1.4, L is computed from one plus the sum of the counters of entries above α on the stack. (Notice that $c_I(\alpha)$ is not part of the calculation of L, Figure 8 illustrates this). In Step 1.5 and its substeps, $n_L[C, B, S]$ is incremented for all caches in which there are no dimensional conflicts. Let $S_B(k-1)[\Delta - 1] = \beta_0$, the address that is directly above α in the stack $S_B(k-1)$. As a bookkeeping step, $c_I(\beta_0)$ is incremented by $c_I(\alpha)$ (Step 1.7). In this way, all the references

1.	**if** $\alpha \in S_B(k-1)$ **then**
1.1	$vol\_cs \leftarrow$ **false**
1.2	$L \leftarrow 1$
1.3	**for** $i \leftarrow 0$ **to** Δ **do**
1.3.1	$\beta_i \leftarrow S_B(k-1)[i]$
1.3.2	**if** β_i *marked as a voluntary context switch event* **then**
1.3.2.1	$vol\_cs \leftarrow$ **true**
1.3.3	$L \leftarrow L + c_I(\beta_i)$
1.4	$L \leftarrow L + 1$
1.5	**for all** (C, B, S) *without a dimensional conflict* **do**
1.5.1	$n_L[C, B, S] \leftarrow n_L[C, B, S] + 1$
1.5.2	**if** vol_cs **then**
1.5.2.1	$X_V[C, B, S] \leftarrow X_V[C, B, S] + 1$
1.6	**if** α *marked as a voluntary context switch event* **then**
1.6.1	*mark* $S_B(k-1)[\Delta + 1]$
1.6.2	*unmark* α
1.7	$c_I(\beta_{\Delta-1}) \leftarrow c_I(\beta_{\Delta-1}) + c_I(\alpha)$
1.8	$c_I(\alpha) \leftarrow 1$
1.9	$S_B(k) \leftarrow$ **repush**$(S_B(k-1), \alpha)$,
2	**else**
2.1	$c_I(\alpha) \leftarrow 1$
2.2	$S_B(k) \leftarrow$ **push**$(S_B(k-1), \alpha)$

Figure 7 An LRU stack method modified for context switching.

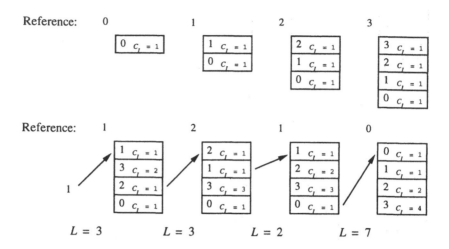

(C_I is stack counter-- see text)

Figure 8   An example for involuntary context switching of the modified LRU stack operation.

deeper in the stack than α in $S_B(k-1)$ will arrive at the correct context switch distance.

The algorithm shows $n_L[C, B, S]$ being maintained for all values of L. Not all values of L must be recorded using $n_L[C, B, S]$. Rather, power-of-two sized categories can be retained. The scheme used for the simulations that is presented below uses 14 categories. The first category contains $n_L[C, B, S]$ for $1 \le L < 4$, following this, the ith category contains $n_L[C, B, S]$ for $2^{(i+2)} \le L < 2^{i+3}$. This quantization scheme is based on observations of the distribution of $n_L[C, B, S]$ vs. L. The scheme does however produce error for small q, and this is commented on in the following section.

Notice that the calculation of $n_L[C, B, S]$ is independent of the context switching intensity distribution assumptions. The function used to calculate p_L in Equation 4.6 need not be Equation 4.5. It is possible to substitute other context switching intensity distributions into Equation 4.6 without altering the presented single-pass method. The impact of this observation is that the method is more general than the assumption of uniformly-distributed involuntary context switching of Equation 4.5. Empirical results of the method are presented in [7].

4 CONCLUDING REMARKS

This chapter has discussed techniques for capturing the performance of an entire space of cache designs in one run. These single-pass techniques have proven to be powerful methods for cache simulation. Their success is due to the inclusion property of cache replacement algorithms. Unfortunately, there has been little success in finding anologies to inclusion for processor and interconnection simulation.

The recurrence/conflict-based version of single-pass cache simulation has been implemented in the **recon** tool by the author and his students. Contact the author to obtain a copy.

Exercises

4.1 Show the LRU stack operation for the following block reference trace:

1, 2, 3, 4, 5, 1, 3, 4, 5, 2, 1, 7, 1, 3, 4, 5

How many recurrences occur? How many dimensional conflicts occur for a four-block fully-associative cache? For a six-block fully-associative cache?

4.2 *Least frequently used* (LFU) is a replacement algorithm that selects a block for replacement that has the lowest usage count of any block in the cache. Explain the operation of a single-pass algorithm for caches managed by LFU replacement.

4.3 FIFO is a replacement algorithm that selects the oldest block in the cache for replacement. Can FIFO be simulated using a stack? Explain why or why not using an example.

4.4 This chapter has talked about several kinds of conflicts: dimensional, and multiprogramming, for example. List two kinds of conflicts not discussed here. Determine the expression for the miss ratio, $\rho(C, B, S)$, taking these new conflict types into account.

4.5 Memory systems are often built in hierarchies of multiple levels of caches. Develop a single-pass technique to record the misses of a two-level cache hierarchy. Assume that the dimensions, (C, B, S), of the first-level cache are fixed.

4.6 Locality of reference is a common concept in cache analysis. There are two classes of locality, temporal and spatial. Temporal locality is the characteristic that an address referenced at time t has a high probability of being re-referenced at time $t + \tau$, for small values of τ. Although this definition captures the concept of temporal locality, it does not explain how to measure the amount of temporal locality in the reference stream. Explain how $n_L[C, B, S]$, developed for measuring involuntary context switching, can also be used to quantify the temporal locality of a reference stream.

4.7 An alternative to the context switching algorithm presented here is to empty the stack when a context switch event occurs in the reference stream (i.e., in the trace). Give two reasons why the algorithm presented in this chapter is superior to this "stack-emptying" approach.

4.8 The algorithm of Figure 5 uses one stack per block size. It is possible to use a unified stack across all block sizes as well. Develop a scheme for this that processes the input stream $w(t)$ instead of $w_B(t)$. (Hint: Consider a variation of $\text{ctz}(|\beta - \alpha|)$ that finds the smallest block size shared by address references α and β.)

4.9 The **for** loop of Figure 5 (Step 8.4) can be converted to a single

$$D[C_{MC}, B, s] \leftarrow D[C_{MC}, B, s] + 1$$

if the user is willing to post-process the $D[C, B, S]$ array. (The same is true for Step 4 as well.) Explain the required post-processing.

REFERENCES

[1] A. Agarwal, M. Horowitz, and J. Hennessy, "An analytical cache model," *ACM Trans. Computer Systems*, vol. 7, pp. 184–215, May 1989.

[2] J. Archibald and J.-L. Baer, "Cache coherence protocols: Evaluation using a multiprocessor simulation model," *ACM Trans. Comput. Sys.*, vol. 4, pp. 273–298, Nov. 1986.

[3] T. H. Cormen, C. E. Leiserson, and R. L. Rivest, *Introduction to Algorithms*. Cambridge, MA: McGraw-Hill (MIT Press), 1990.

[4] T. M. Conte, "Systematic computer archiecture prototyping," Ph.D. dissertation, Department of Electrical and Computer Engineering, University of Illinois, Urbana, IL, 1992.

[5] I. J. Haikala, "Cache hit ratios with geometric task switch intervals," in *Proc. 11th Ann. Int'l Symp. Computer Architecture*, (Ann Arbor, MI), pp. 364–371, June 1984.

[6] M. D. Hill and A. J. Smith, "Evaluating associativity in CPU caches," *IEEE Trans. Comput.*, vol. C-38, pp. 1612–1630, Dec. 1989.

[7] W. W. Hwu and T. M. Conte, "The susceptibility of programs to context switching," *IEEE Transactions on Computers*, vol. C-43, no. 9, pp. 993–1003, Sep. 1994.

[8] K. R. Kaplan and R. O. Winder, "Cache-based computer systems," *Computer*, vol. 6, pp. 30–36, Mar. 1973.

[9] R. L. Mattson, J. Gercsei, D. R. Slutz, and I. L. Traiger, "Evaluation techniques for storage hierarchies," *IBM Syst. J.*, vol. 9, no. 2, pp. 78–117, 1970.

[10] A. J. Smith, "Cache memories," *ACM Computing Surveys*, vol. 14, no. 3, pp. 473–530, 1982.

[11] A. J. Smith, "A second bibliography on cache memories," *Comput. Architecture News*, vol. 19, pp. 138–153, June 1991.

[12] J. G. Thompson, *Efficient analysis of caching systems*, Ph.D. dissertation, Computer Science Division, University of California, Berkeley, CA, Oct. 1987. Report No. UCB/CSD 87/374.

[13] I. L. Traiger and D. R. Slutz, "One-pass techniques for the evaluation of memory hierarchies," IBM Research Report RJ 892, IBM, San Jose, CA, July 1971.

[14] W.-H. Wang and J.-L. Baer, "Efficient trace-driven simulation methods for cache performance analysis," *ACM Trans. Comput. Sys.*, vol. 9, pp. 222–241, Aug. 1991.

[15] W. Y. Chen, P. P. Chang, T. M. Conte and W. W. Hwu, "The effect of code expanding optimizations on instruction cache design," *IEEE Transactions on Computers*, vol C-42, no. 9, pp. 1045–1057, Sep. 1993.

5

NON-STACK SINGLE-PASS SIMULATION

Rabin A. Sugumar, Santosh G. Abraham*

Cray Research Inc., Chippewa Falls, Wisconsin, USA

Hewlett-Packard Laboratories, Palo Alto, California, USA

1 INTRODUCTION

The previous chapter dealt with stack-based single-pass simulation. Stack-based single-pass simulation permits the simulation of a range of cache configurations in a time and space efficient manner. All stack-based simulation algorithms maintain multiple caches in a stack, exploiting inclusion properties between caches. During simulation they do a sequential search down the stack examining, modifying and moving entries as appropriate. Stack-based single-pass simulation is elegant and efficient relative to performing the simulations one at a time. However, taking a step back we see that the essential idea exploited in stack-based single-pass simulation is one of reducing simulation effort by simulating multiple configurations together and exploiting relations between the configurations to reduce simulation effort. This idea may be exploited to develop efficient single-pass algorithms in situations where stack simulation is not applicable. Even in situations where stack simulation is applicable non-stack single-pass simulation algorithms can be more efficient by avoiding the sequential search of the stack. In this chapter we discuss single-pass simulation algorithms that are not stack-based.

We illustrate some of the general principles of single-pass simulation using the algorithm presented in Section 4 that simulates multiple write buffers in a single-pass through a trace of time-stamped write addresses and generates the stall cycles for each simulated write buffer [13]. This algorithm is based on the inclusion property stating that a write buffer stalls only when a smaller write buffer stalls. Therefore, when a write does not stall one write buffer, it also does not stall all larger write buffers. The state of a write buffer is represented by the number of cycles to write out and retire all the current entries to memory. The write buffer algorithm exploits the additional property that between stalls, the state of a larger buffer may be derived from that of a smaller buffer. These properties hold under certain assumptions described in detail in Section 4. Write buffer simulation works as follows: The smallest write buffer is simulated for each write. When the write does not stall the buffer, no other buffer is examined. When a write does stall the buffer, larger write buffers are examined successively until the write does not stall a write buffer, or all the buffers are examined.

The goal of all architectural simulation is to measure performance metrics such as stall cycles or miss ratio of the simulated system. In order to determine performance metrics for several configurations efficiently in a single-pass simulation algorithm, conditions for no change or a regular change in the metric for a large fraction of the configurations need to be derived. In the running example of write buffer simulation, the metric, stall cycles, for any of the configurations changes only on a stall in the smallest buffer. The metric has to be updated only on a stall in the smallest buffer, which is not a frequent occurrence in most cases. In order to maintain metrics, state changes of the simulated system need to be tracked. In single-pass simulation, to maintain the state of several configurations efficiently, situations where there is no change or a regular change in the difference in state between two configurations need to be identified. As long as such conditions hold, the state of just one configuration is updated. Later, when the other configurations need to be examined, their states are derived and updated. In the running example, it is possible to accumulate the change in state of larger buffers between stalls of the smallest buffer, and to derive their state on a stall of the smallest buffer. In many cases, the efficiency with which state and metric values may be maintained depends on the data structure used to represent the configurations. For instance, in Mattson, et al.'s stack simulation algorithm a single stack is used to represent a range of fully-associative caches, and the states of all caches are implicitly updated through operations on the stack data structure. Some other novel data structures for state maintenance are presented in this chapter.

In the rest of the chapter several algorithms that exploit the general principles of single-pass simulation are presented. The algorithms are for the efficient simulation of important architectural features such as fully associative and set associative caches and write buffers, and are useful as such. In addition, each algorithm uses different kinds of properties to do single-pass simulation efficiently, and the methods used should prove helpful in the development of other single-pass algorithms. The chapter has four sections following this introduction. In Section 2 we go back to fully-associative cache simulation. We describe simulation algorithms that examine a range of cache sizes at each step in contrast to regular stack simulation, and are thus faster than stack simulation by an order of magnitude. In a similar vein, Section 3 deals with set-associative cache simulation, presenting algorithms that search the space of caches simulated more efficiently than the stack based algorithm. Section 4 deals with multi-configuration simulation of write-buffers; it is an example of the application of single-pass simulation ideas to something other than caches. In the concluding section, we discuss areas for future development and extension of single-pass simulation ideas.

Most of the algorithms described in this chapter have been implemented. Implementations of the algorithms are available either as part of the Cheetah tool available by anonymous ftp from **ftp.eecs.umich.edu** or directly from the authors. We also present experimental and theoretical performance comparisons between algorithms wherever possible. In addition to describing the theoretical foundations of the algorithms, we also present techniques for efficient implementation where they are not obvious.

This chapter is based on material that has appeared earlier in [12, 11, 13, 14].

2 FULLY-ASSOCIATIVE CACHE SIMULATION

In stack-based fully-associative cache simulation described in an earlier chapter, during the stack search each cache size starting at the smallest is examined until there is a hit. It would be more efficient to skip a bunch of cache sizes after each examination, and quickly identify the minimum cache size that is hit. This chapter describes some such algorithms that simulate fully-associative caches by examining a range of cache sizes at each step. All the algorithms share a common theme — the lines in the cache are maintained in an efficient search structure (e.g.) binary trees. A hash table is used to obtain information about when the current line was last accessed previously, and this information is used to look up the data structure. During the lookup the minimum cache that contains the line is determined. All the algorithms make use of the inclusion property used in stack simulation, and in fact maintain the stack implicitly; so they are applicable only for replacement policies that are stack algorithms. In addition, the algorithms work best with LRU, the most commonly used replacement policy, and we will assume LRU in most of the section.

We will describe three algorithms. The first one uses a binary tree as the search structure, the second uses m-ary trees and the last is a simple algorithm which uses a list and a hash table to determine miss-ratios for a few cache sizes of interest. As in stack simulation the input to the simulation is a trace of addresses, and the output of the simulation is the miss ratio for each cache size in the range of cache sizes simulated.

2.1   Binary Tree Algorithm

All the lines in the in the fully-associative caches simulated are maintained as a balanced binary tree. The key used is the most recent time of arrival (arrival time) of an address. The tree is formed such that an inorder traversal yields addresses in increasing order of their arrival time; i.e., it generates the stack of the conventional stack-based algorithm. Each node in the tree contains an address, its arrival time and the number of nodes in its right subtree (we assume arbitrarily that nodes in right subtrees have higher arrival times).

To process an address, its arrival time is obtained from a search structure such as a hash table. A path is traced in the binary tree from the root node to the node with that arrival time as follows. Starting from the root node, the arrival time of the address x_t is compared to the arrival time of the node in the tree. If the arrival time of x_t is greater, the right child is inspected next. If the arrival time of x_t is less, the current node and all nodes in its right subtree also have an arrival time that is greater. So these lines have displaced the searched for node from smaller caches (i.e. these lines are above the searched for line in the stack). Therefore the number of nodes to the right plus one for the node itself is added to a count and the left child is inspected. If the arrival time is equal, the node is found. The number of nodes to the right of the node is added to the count and the count now gives the number of lines in the smallest cache containing the line searched for (i.e. the stack depth). The node where the match occurs is deleted from the tree and is put back with the current time as the arrival time.

To ensure logarithmic time lookup the binary tree has to be kept balanced. Several algorithms are available for balancing binary trees; ideally we would like the balancing technique to keep addresses that were referenced recently near the top of the tree to exploit locality characteristics of traces. A splay tree [10] is a binary tree that has this property. In a splay tree, the referenced node is moved to the top of the stack by a series of operations (left and right rotations), which are collectively called a *splay*. The splay procedure achieves two objectives: first, it brings the referenced node to the top of the tree, and since recently referenced nodes are more likely to be accessed in the future this makes subsequent searches faster. Second, it reduces the distance to the root of other nodes in the path traversed, and as a result has a logarithmic search time in the worst case also. The tendency of a splay tree to keep recently accessed nodes close to the root makes it well suited for stack simulation. In contrast, in an AVL tree [1] (another commonly used balanced binary tree), the referenced nodes tends to get added to the bottom of the tree. In addition, the splay tree is a robust structure in that we can take any binary tree, and apply splays to it to obtain the desired properties. This robustness permits skipping the splay procedure for a fraction of trace references to reduce the cost of restructuring operations.

Techniques for doing a lookup, insertion or deletion on a splay tree are given in [10]. In this application the node that is looked up is always deleted and inserted back at the top. Owing to this specific pattern of lookup, delete and insert, a combination operation that does all three with just one splay step may be used. The referenced node is looked up and deleted as in an ordinary binary tree. The node that replaces the referenced node in deletion is then splayed to the top. A new node is created for the line referenced and the entire tree is made the left subtree of the new node.

An example illustrating the operation of the tree algorithm is shown in Fig 1. The most recent arrival time of the addresses are stored in the nodes. The number in the parenthesis is the number of nodes in the right subtree. Note that the referenced node goes to the top of the tree, with its arrival time set to the current time.

2.2 M-ary Tree Algorithm

The m-ary tree algorithm exploits the property that under LRU replacement the minimum cache size that is hit (i.e. the depth of reference in the LRU stack) is the number of distinct lines referenced since the last reference to the line. Here a bit vector containing a bit for every reference in the trace is maintained. A bit is set to one if the trace reference corresponding to it is the last reference to a line, and is set to zero otherwise. This bit vector constitutes the zeroth level array. At the first level array, sums of the number of ones in m-entry blocks of the zeroth level array are maintained; the zeroth level array thus has m bits for each entry in the first level array. Similarly, at the second level array, sums of m-entry blocks of the first level array are maintained, and higher

Search Structure   Stack

Address	Arr. Time
10	808
07	812
28	787
19	803
15	825
33	835
25	799
31	847
35	793
14	840
23	850
21	831

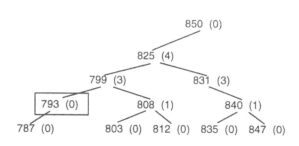

Stack Depth = (0+1)+(4+1)+(3+1)+1
= 11

Search Structure   Stack

Address	Arr. Time
10	808
07	812
28	787
19	803
15	825
33	835
25	799
31	847
35	851
14	840
23	850
21	831

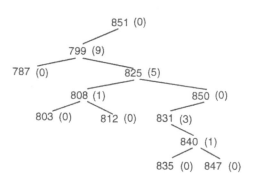

Figure 1 Example illustrating operation of the splay tree algorithm.

level arrays are similarly maintained until the number of entries at a level is less than m. For each reference read in during simulation, the bit in the zeroth level array corresponding to the previous reference to the same address is located (using a hash table). This bit is then set to zero since a later reference to this address has now occurred, and the location in the array corresponding to the current reference is set to one. The number of ones separating the current location and the previous location of the address is then determined efficiently by traversing the m-ary tree structure. The m-ary tree structure is updated during this traversal.

The memory required for the m-ary tree algorithm is proportional to the number of trace references. For long traces, therefore, a periodic packing step is needed to keep memory requirements within limits.

2.3 Few Cache Sizes Algorithm

As the name indicates this algorithm is oriented towards situations where miss-ratios are required for only a few fully associative cache sizes. Quite often miss-ratios are desired only for some types of cache sizes (e.g. power-of-two), and this simple algorithm is effective in such situations. Here the stack is maintained as a doubly linked list, and each entry of the stack is annotated with the smallest cache size of interest that contains this entry. An array of pointers to stack entries that are at cache boundaries (i.e. the entries with the least priority in each of the caches of interest) is also maintained. For each trace reference the stack element that the address maps to is determined through a hash lookup and from the stack element the smallest cache containing it is determined. Stack update is accomplished by first moving the entry that is hit to the top of the stack. Entries that are of lowest priority in their caches and that are between the top of the stack and the location of hit drop out of their caches. Such entries are located using the array of boundary pointers and their cache residency status is updated. Along with this step the boundary pointers are also moved up the stack by one entry.

2.4 Complexity

The complexity of basic stack simulation, binary tree simulation with splay trees and AVL trees, and the m-ary tree algorithm are given in Table 1. These expressions are derived assuming the fractal model of trace characteristics [16]. N_d is the number of distinct entries and C_c is the working set size (loosely,

Stack form	Lines examined	
	Hit depth = x	Mean
List	x	$O(C_c^{\beta+1} + N_d^{2-\theta})$
Splay	$O(\log x)$	$O(C_c^{\beta} \log C_c)$
AVL	$O(\log N_d)$	$O(\log N_d)$
m-ary	$O(\log x)$	$O(C_c^{\beta} \log C_c)$

Table 1   Search complexity

the point where a knee occurs in the cache size versus miss-ratio curve). θ is a measure of the locality of the trace (loosely, the slope of the cache size versus miss-ratio curve) and β is another model parameter. The first column is of greatest interest. We see that complexity is proportional to log of the stack depth of hit for splay tree and m-ary tree. For AVL trees it is proportional to log of the number of entries in the stack, i.e., AVL trees do not exploit trace locality. The few cache sizes algorithm does not fit in this table since it obtains the miss ratio for only a few cache sizes. Its complexity is proportional to the number of cache sizes simulated.

Empirical performance evaluations support these analytical complexities. Splay tree and m-ary tree algorithms perform best with the m-ary tree algorithm (without the compression step) running faster than the splay tree algorithm by about 15% on the average. The m-ary tree algorithm is easier to implement, and for doing LRU simulations it is probably the best choice. Binary tree methods may be used for some other replacement policies and for simulating multiple line sizes also; so if this wider range of capabilities is of interest the splay tree algorithm would be a good choice.

2.5   Literature Review

The m-ary tree algorithm was proposed by Bennett and Kruskal [2]. That paper is also the first to publish the idea of using a hash table to locate previous references to an address. Such lookup helps basic list-based stack simulation too, since it avoids the stack lookup on the first reference to an address. The binary tree algorithm was first proposed by Olken [8] who proposed storing the stack as an in-order AVL tree. Thompson [17] proposed an improvement to the AVL tree algorithm which uses a list for references that hit close to to the top of the stack and an AVL tree for references that hit further down. Sugumar and Abraham [11] investigated the use of splay trees. They also generalized binary tree algorithms to work with other replacement policies (OPT [12] and PCOR[1]), and extended the binary tree algorithms to simulate multiple line sizes along the lines of Slutz and Traiger [18]. Sugumar and Abraham also present analytical and empirical comparisons of the list algorithm, the AVL tree algorithm, the splay tree algorithm and the m-ary tree algorithm, and empirical evaluations of a tree based algorithm for OPT replacement.

3 BINOMIAL FOREST SIMULATION

In this section, we describe cache simulation algorithms for the single-pass simulation of a group of set-associative caches with fixed line size, least recently used (LRU) replacement, bit-selection[2], but varying associativities and varying number of sets. As before the input is a trace of addresses generated by the CPU, and the simulation algorithm outputs the miss-ratio of each cache configuration.

Three algorithms have been proposed to simulate this group of caches — All-associativity simulation [7, 5] (called AA in the following), a generalization of forest simulation [5] (called FS+ in the following), and an algorithm using generalized binomial trees [14] (called GBF_LS in the following). AA is a stack-based simulation algorithm that has been described in an earlier chapter. In this chapter we will describe FS+ and GBF_LS.

In order to develop an intuitive understanding for the algorithms, consider the simulation of caches with one and two sets, and of maximum associativity n. The data structures maintained by AA, FS+ and GBF_LS are shown in Fig. 2 ($n = 4$ in the figure). AA maintains one list of length at least $2n$, and searches the list till the referenced line is found or the end of the list is reached. FS+ maintains three lists of length n, one representing the caches with one set, and two more representing each of the two sets in the caches with two sets. For each trace reference, FS+ first searches the list of the one-set caches. If the referenced line is not found at the top of the list, one of the lists of the two-set caches is searched. GBF_LS maintains the first list of n entries representing the one-set caches similar to AA; after that, however, GBF_LS maintains two separate lists, one of some length n_1 ($< n$) consisting of lines in set-0 of the

---
[1] Priority Change on Reference
[2] A bit-field of the address determines the set

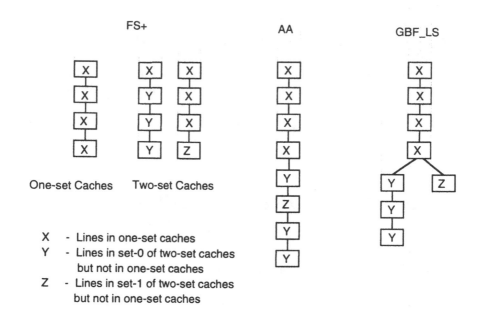

Figure 2   Data structures used in FS+, AA and GBF_LS

two-set caches but not in the one-set caches ($n_1 = 3$ in the figure), and the other of length $(n - n_1)$ consisting of the lines in set-1 but not in the one-set caches. On a reference the first list is searched; if the referenced line is not found, the set that the line maps to is determined and the corresponding list is searched.

AA is a stack algorithm, and maintains all lines in a single list. This causes lines that belong to the "wrong set" to be examined; e.g. lines that are only in set-1 of the two-set caches while searching for a line that maps to set-0. FS+, on the other hand, splits the lists and avoids unnecessary examination of lines in wrong sets. However, in FS+ the n entries in the list for one-set caches are repeated in the lists for two-set caches, and so the same line may be examined twice — once in the list for the one-set caches, and then again in one of the lists for the two-set caches. GBF_LS splits the lists similar to FS+, but keeps just entries that are not in the one-set cache list in the new lists.

In the next two subsections we describe FS+ and GBF_LS in greater detail, and in the subsection following that we discuss the complexity of the algorithms and some implementation issues. The following notation is used: a set-associative cache with 2^S sets, line size 2^L and associativity n is denoted as $C_S^L(n)$ (S is the width of the set field and L is the width of the line field). $[X]_{lines}$ denotes the lines contained in X where X may be a set, a group of sets or a cache. The input to the simulation is a trace $x_1, x_2, \ldots, x_{TL}$ of addresses. For any address, set number or line number y, $y[i : j]$ denotes the bit field between bits i and j (inclusive) in the binary representation of y. The least significant bit is numbered 0. The number of bits in an address is denoted by W.

3.1 FS+

FS+ is based on the inclusion property stated in the following lemma.

Lemma 1 *For each set p in $C_S^L(n)$ there are exactly 2^k ($k \geq 0$) sets, P, in $C_{S+k}^L(n)$ such that $[p]_{lines} \subseteq [P]_{lines}$ and $([P]_{lines} - [p]_{lines}) \cap [C_S^L(n)]_{lines} = \phi$.*

Proof :
k extra bits are used for selecting a set in $C_{S+k}^L(n)$ than in $C_S^L(n)$. So lines mapping to a single set, p, in $C_S^L(n)$ map to one of 2^k sets in $C_{S+k}^L(n)$, given by $P = \{s \text{ s.t. } s[S - 1 : 0] = p\}$. Only n of the $n2^k$ lines of P are present in $C_S^L(n)$ and those are the n lines that arrived most recently. That is, $[p]_{lines}$ consists of the n lines that arrived most recently in P.

Conversely, lines mapping to one of the sets in P in $C_{S+k}^L(n)$ can only map to p in $C_S^L(n)$. So $C_S^L(n)$ does not have any of the contents of P apart from $[p]_{lines}$.
□

The following two corollaries follow from the lemma and the proof.

Corollary 1
The least significant S bits of the set numbers of the sets in P are identical, and give the set number of p.

Corollary 2
$[C_{S_1}^L(n_1)]_{lines} \subseteq [C_{S_2}^L(n_2)]_{lines}$, if $S_1 \leq S_2$ and $n_1 \leq n_2$.

Let the caches to be simulated be $C_{S+i}^L(j)$, $i = 0, \ldots M$, $j = 1, \ldots, n$. A separate two-dimensional array is maintained for each of the caches $C_{S+i}^L(n)$,

$i = 0, \ldots, M$, with sets along one dimension and the n lines mapping to the set in LRU order along the other. From the inclusion property the contents of $C^L_{S+i}(j)$ for $j < n$ is the first j lines in each set in $C^L_{S+i}(n)$. For each incoming line, the appropriate set in each array is searched, starting at the array with the minimum number of sets. If the reference hits at depth m in cache $C^L_{S+k}(n)$, the reference hits in caches $C^L_{S+k}(j)$, $j = m, \ldots, n$ by the inclusion property. Hit information for these caches is updated, and the referenced line is moved to the top of its set. Also when $m = 1$ the line is known to hit in all the remaining caches by the inclusion property, and the simulation moves on to the next trace reference.

Fig. 3 shows an example illustrating FS+ and AA. Here the number of sets ranges from one to four and the associativities are one and two. The state of the data structures after line 1011 is processed are shown. If the next reference is to line 0101, it is found at the top only in $C^L_2(2)$ and FS+ requires five comparisons, whereas it is at the second position in the AA stack and AA requires just two comparisons. FS+ requires more comparisons in this case, because it reexamines lines that it has seen in earlier caches. However, if the next reference is to line 0011, AA requires eight comparisons, whereas FS+ requires only six comparisons. FS+ is better in this case because the LRU stack for $C^L_0(2)$ contains lines that are not in the set 0011 maps to in any of the caches, $C^L_0(2)$, $C^L_1(2)$ or $C^L_2(2)$.

3.2 GBF_LS

Understanding GBF_LS requires some knowledge of the generalized binomial tree (gbt) data structure which we describe in the following subsection. The algorithm itself is described in the next subsection.

Generalized Binomial Trees

A gbt is a combination of binomial trees and lists; the binomial tree structure captures the subsetting relationship between caches with varying number of sets, and the list structure captures the relationship between caches of varying associativities.

Definition 1 *The following is a definition by construction of a gbt of order n (gbt(n)). (Fig. 4). A gbt(n) of degree zero, $B_0(n)$, is a list of length n.*

Trace: 0011, 1010, 0100, 0001, 0110, 1000, 0101, 1011

Conventional representation (for FS+)			Stack representation (for AA)

Cache	Tag	Set No.	
$C_0^L(2)$	1011, 0101	-	1011
			0101
			1000
$C_1^L(2)$	100, 011	0	0110
	101, 010	1	0001
			0100
$C_2^L(2)$	10, 01	00	1010
	01, 00	01	0011
	01, 10	10	
	10, 00	11	

Incoming Address	Method	No. of Comparisons
0101	FS+	5
	AA	2
0011	FS+	6
	AA	8

Figure 3 FS+ and AA — Example

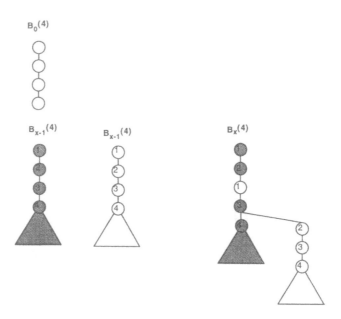

Figure 4   Definition of the generalized binomial tree

A gbt(n) of degree x, $B_x(n)$, is constructed by putting together two gbt(n)s of degree $x - 1$, $B_{x-1}(n)$ and $B'_{x-1}(n)$, as follows:

1. *Two segments of lengths n_1 and n_2 beginning at the roots of $B_{x-1}(n)$ and $B'_{x-1}(n)$ are removed so that $n_1 + n_2 = n$.*

2. *These two segments are merged in an order, determined by the application, to form the root-list of $B_x(n)$.*

3. *The remaining parts of $B_{x-1}(n)$ and $B'_{x-1}(n)$ are attached to the end of this root-list.*

Here are some definitions and one lemma relating to a gbt that are necessary for understanding the algorithm. The *rank* of a node in a gbt is defined to be[3]

$$\log(\lceil \frac{\text{Number of descendants (inclusive)}}{n} \rceil).$$

The *tree* rooted at a node in a gbt consists of the node and all its descendants. The *degree* of a tree is the rank of the root of the tree. The *list-child* of a node

---

[3] All logarithms are to base two.

in a gbt is that child which at some stage in the combining process was a child of that node in the root-list. A *tree-child* of a node in a gbt is any child that is not the list-child.

Lemma 2 *(i) A node of rank 0 in a gbt either has no children (leaf node) or has one list-child. (ii) A node of rank k, $k > 0$, (a) has exactly k tree-children of ranks 0 through $k - 1$, if it does not have a list-child, or (b) has exactly r, $r \leq k$, tree-children of ranks $k - r$ through $k - 1$, if it has a list-child of rank $k - r$.*

A *subtree* of a gbt is now defined as follows. A node of rank k has a subtree of degree r, $r < k$, *iff* it has a tree child of rank r, and this subtree is the tree left after pruning tree-children of rank r and greater from the tree rooted at the node. A node of rank k always has a subtree of degree k which is the tree rooted at the node.

Two operations are defined on this data structure: SWAP and EXCHANGE. SWAP(v) is permitted only when v is a tree-child and causes the tree of degree k rooted at v to be swapped with the subtree of degree k rooted at its parent. EXCHANGE(v) is permitted only when v is a list-child and causes v to be exchanged with its parent node. The children of v become the children of its parent and vice versa. SWAP and EXCHANGE are used to move lines up the tree when their priorities change.

3.3 Simulation Algorithm

Lemma 1 leads to the generalized binomial tree representation of caches used in GBF_LS. Consider the sets in cache $C^L_{S+2}(n)$, where each set contains a list of n lines. Group sets in $C^L_{S+2}(n)$ mapping to the same set in $C^L_{S+1}(n)$ into pairs. Combine the line lists in the two sets in each pair by forming a list of the n most recently referenced lines in either set. Use this list as the root-list, leaving the remaining n lines in two separate branches, each branch containing lines from distinct sets in $C^L_{S+2}(n)$. Clearly, we now have a forest of gbt(n)s of degree one. The lines in the root-list are in $C^L_{S+1}(n)$, while the other lines are only in $C^L_{S+2}(n)$. The structures formed can be further grouped into pairs and combined resulting in a gbt(n) of degree two with the line in the root-list being in $C^L_S(n)$. Further combining may similarly be done obtaining gbt(n)s of higher degrees. Fig. 5 illustrates the construction of the gbt representation for the example of Fig. 3. Here $S = 0$; the tag-field for $C^L_{S+2}(n)$ is shown

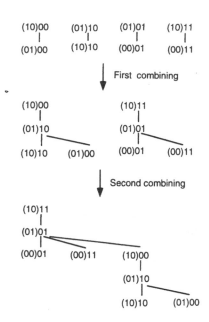

Figure 5   Construction of a gbt representation — Example

within parentheses; the line field is not shown. To simulate caches $C_{S+i}^{L}(j)$, $i = 0, \dots M$, $j = 1, \dots, n$, the sets in $C_{S+M}^{L}(n)$ are combined until there are 2^{S} distinct gbt(n)s of degree M. In the following, set number and tag are with respect to $C_{S+M}^{L}(n)$ unless stated otherwise.

The algorithm is presented in page 125. For each address x, the tree that will contain the corresponding line is first identified using the set field in the smallest cache $x[S+L-1:L]$. The tree is then searched for the line as follows:
1. On a right-match of k at a node, the tree-child of rank $S + M - k - 1$ is searched next if the tree-child is present. If the node does not have a tree-child of rank $S+M-k-1$ the list-child is of rank greater than or equal to $S+M-k-1$ (Lemma 2) and is searched next.
2. When there is a complete set match and tag match at a node, the line is found and the search is successful. If the line is of rank k then the reference hits in caches $C_{S+i}^{L}(n)$, $i = M - k, \dots, M$. The number of right-matches of $S + i$ or greater is calculated for $i = 0, \dots, M$ from the right-match counts obtained during the search. When the number of right-matches of $S + i$ or greater is t, the reference hits in $C_{S+i}^{L}(j), j = t + 1, \dots, n$.
3. When there is a complete set match at a node and the node does not have a list-child the search has failed. The line at the node examined last is replaced

Algorithm GBF_LS

```
sim_gbf_ls()
    Initialize()
    for every reference x in trace
        set_no_C0 ← Set number in C₀ (x[S + L − 1 : L])
        set_no_CM ← Set number in C_M (x[S + M + L − 1 : L])
        tag ← Tag in C_M (x[W − 1 : S + M + L])
        cur_node ← Root_Map[set_no_C0]
        found ← 0; end_of_tree ← 0
        for i ← 0 to M
            RM_Count[i] ← 0
        end for
        while (NOT found AND NOT end_of_tree)
            if ((cur_node→set_no = set_no_CM) AND (cur_node→tag = tag))
                /* Search successful */
                found ← 1
                for i ← M to 0
                    sum ← sum + RM_Count[i]
                    Hit_Array[i][sum] ← Hit_Array[i][sum] + 1
                end for
            else
                k ← Right_Match(cur_node→set_no, set_no_CM)
                next_node ← Child(cur_node, S+M-k-1)
                if (next_node == NULL)
                    /* Search failed */
                    cur_node→tag ← tag
                    end_of_tree ← 1
                else
                    /* Increment Right Match count and continue search */
                    RM_Count[k] ← RM_Count[k] + 1
                    if (next_node is a tree-child of cur_node)
                        SWAP(next_node)
                    cur_node ← next_node
            end while
            Move_to_Top(cur_node)
    end for
    for m ← 1 to n:
        Hits in cache C^L_{S+k}(m) = ∑^m_{i=0} Hit_Array[k][i]
    end for
Move_to_Top(node)
    while (node not at root of tree)
        EXCHANGE(node)
    end while
    Root_Map[set_no_C0] ← node
Child(node, d)
    if (d < 0)
        /* Complete match at node */
        if (node has no list-child)
            return(NULL)
        else
            return(list-child)
    else if (node has tree-child of rank d)
        return(tree-child of rank d)
    else
        return(list-child)
Initialize()
    Build 2^S gbt's from 2^{S+M} line lists (Using the combining procedure, assuming arbitrary ordering)
    Set all tags to invalid
```

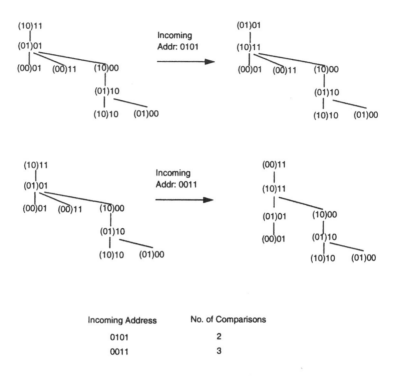

Figure 6   Examples illustrating Algorithm GBF_LS

with the incoming line, which is now the most recently referenced line, and is moved to the root by a series of SWAPs and EXCHANGEs.[4]

In Fig. 6, the examples of Fig. 3 are shown processed by Algorithm GBF_LS.

1. For the incoming line 0101, the first line checked is 1011. The set field of the referenced line does not match the set field of 1011; the right match of one is noted and the search moves to the only child 0101. Here the set field and the tag field match. One right-match of one is seen along the path and so the reference hits in $C_0^L(2)$, $C_1^L(1)$, $C_2^L(1)$ and $C_2^L(2)$. 0101 is now moved to the top of the tree, which in this case is accomplished through an EXCHANGE.

2. For the incoming line 0011, the tag does not match at the root; the right-match of two is noted and the search goes to 0101. Here the set field does not match. The right-match of the set fields of 0011 and 0101 is one; so

---

[4] In the algorithm the SWAPs are done during the search which is equivalent.

$(S + M - k - 1) = (0 + 2 - 1 - 1) = 0$. Since 0011 is a tree-child of rank zero, the subtree rooted at 0011, {0011}, is swapped with the subtree {0101, 0001} and searched. Both the set and tag fields match at 0011. The search is successful. Since right-matches of one and two were seen along the search path, the reference hits only in $C_2^L(2)$. 0011 is moved to the root through an EXCHANGE.

The search takes two comparisons for 0101 and three comparisons for 0011.

3.4 Complexity

$O((M+1)n)$ comparisons are required in the worst case in GBF_LS and in FS+. In FS+ this worst case occurs when the reference misses in all the caches, and in GBF_LS it occurs when all combinings occur with $(n_1, n_2) = (n, 0)$ or $(0, n)$ and the search is along the longest path from the root to a leaf. $O(n2^M)$ comparisons are required in the worst case in AA simulation (assuming that there are no additional nodes in the stack), where the worst case occurs when the reference misses in all the caches. In practice, AA does not perform as badly as the worst-case numbers indicate owing to locality characteristics of traces. Empirical comparisons show GBF_LS running about a factor of 1.5 times faster than FS+ and about a factor of 2.5 times faster than AA. (This comparison was done using the authors' implementations of the three algorithms. Our implementation of AA is a factor of about 8 times faster than the implementation of AA in Tycho [4], another cache simulation package that is publicly available.)

Clever implementation is critical to the performance of all three of the algorithms (in fact any cache simulation algorithm). In particular, a large percentage of the references normally hit in the smallest cache simulated. Making the first check a special case and coding it carefully leads to significant performance improvements. Another aspect to watch out for is the time spent in trace processing. When creating trace formats there is an impulse to add in a lot of information and to make the trace easily readable. This helps in debugging trace-generation, but it often results in a large fraction of the simulation time being spent in extracting addresses out of traces. Other good rules of thumb are:

1. Implement tree structures with arrays whenever possible (please see [14] for details of implementing GBF_LS with arrays).

2. Minimize processing in the simulation loop which iterates over all trace references. It pays to speed up maintenance of output metrics during simulation, and use a post-processing step at the end of the simulation to extract output information.

3.5 Literature Review

The inclusion property on which both FS+ and GBF_LS are based was first stated by Puzak [9] for reduced trace generation. FS+ as a single-pass algorithm was suggested by Hill and Smith [5]. GBF_LS was introduced by Sugumar and Abraham [14]. In this paper, they also introduce an algorithm for simulating direct mapped caches of varying line sizes but of a fixed size using binomial trees. Analytical and empirical comparisons of the various algorithms are also presented.

4 WRITE-BUFFER SIMULATION

In this section, we describe multi-configuration simulation algorithms for write-buffers. Write-buffers are small queues interposed between the CPU and main memory. On a store, the CPU enters the address and data into the write-buffer. Subsequently, the data is written to main memory when free cycles are available on the bus and main memory. The main advantage of a write-buffer is that the CPU does not stall on stores unless the write-buffer is full and so the latency of stores is hidden by the write-buffer usually. Additionally, some write-buffer designs (coalescing write-buffers) can merge closely spaced writes to a single cache line into a single write of the entire cache line. Therefore, another significant advantage of such coalescing write-buffers is that they reduce write traffic to the second-level cache.

An important parameter in write-buffer design is its size. Larger buffers reduce the likelihood of write-buffer stalls and also merge more writes. However they take up more space on-chip, and increase the cost of maintaining program consistency. In this chapter we describe an algorithm for the single-pass simulation of write-buffers of a range of sizes. The input to the simulation is a trace of store addresses and their inter-arrival times[5]. The output of the simulation consists of the number of CPU stall cycles and write traffic to second-level cache for a range of write-buffer sizes.

---

[5] Inter-arrival time is the time interval in CPU clock cycles between two successive stores

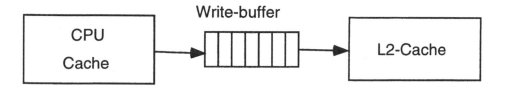

Figure 7 Write-buffer Simulation Model

We consider both *coalescing* and *non-coalescing* write-buffers. A non-coalescing write-buffer creates a separate entry in the write-buffer for each store. A coalescing write-buffer checks if it already has an entry that maps to the same cache line as the incoming store and merges (coalesces) the incoming store with such an entry, if the entry is not one that is being written out. In a non-coalescing buffer, entries are written out when bus cycles are available; however, with a coalescing write-buffer delaying writes is advantageous since subsequent writes might merge into the line reducing write-traffic. Lines may be written out whenever free cycles to memory are available (*greedy* policy), or they may be written out when the number of entries in the write-buffer exceeds a certain limit (*minimum occupancy* policy).

We focus mostly on non-coalescing write-buffer simulation — the algorithm for coalescing write-buffer simulation is based on the former.

4.1 Preliminaries

Simulation Model

As shown in Fig. 7, the write-buffer is modeled as a queue between the CPU-cache subsystem which functions as the requestor and the second-level cache subsystem which functions as a server. Each store from the CPU-cache subsystem is a request and the inter-arrival time between requests is varying because the time interval between stores is varying. Assuming that the second-level cache always hits, the service time is the time to write an L1 cache line into the second-level cache and we assume that this service time is constant.

The input to the model is a trace of store addresses from the CPU-cache subsystem, along with the separation, in CPU clock cycles, between successive stores. The goal of write-buffer design is to minimize both stall cycles, which directly degrade the CPI performance measure, and bus-traffic which increases contention at the second-level cache. Therefore, the desired output of the simulation are the number of stall cycles that occur because of a full write-buffer, and the write-traffic to second-level cache. Here we consider algorithms that simulate write-buffers of multiple lengths, and report stall cycles and write-traffic.

A few simplifying assumptions are made in this model. First, there is the assumption that the trace of inter-arrival times and the addresses of the lines are independent of the write-buffer size and the service discipline. This assumption may not be strictly true; for instance, on a buffer stall other functions in the CPU could continue, and the inter-arrival time might be shorter than when the buffer does not stall. However, such effects are usually not significant and are normally ignored in memory hierarchy simulation to maintain tractability. Second, the contention effects of write-traffic with read miss traffic from the L1 data cache or instruction fetch traffic from the L1 instruction cache are ignored.

Definitions and Notation

The *miss-penalty*, S, is the constant service time required to write an entry into the second-level cache. This is often also the penalty of a read miss in the L1 cache.

A *merge* occurs in a coalescing write-buffer if the incoming store maps to a cache line already in the buffer, and is not the line that is currently being written out.

A *stall* occurs if the buffer is full on the arrival of a store. The number of *stall cycles* is the number of cycles it takes for the entry currently being written out, to leave the buffer and create an empty space.

A *clear out* occurs if the buffer empties out completely between two successive arrivals to the buffer. The *cycles to clear out* at any instant is the number of cycles it would take for the buffer to clear out; that is, it is the number of entries in the write-buffer (excluding the entry being written out) times the miss-penalty plus the time to complete the write of the entry being written out. The cycles to clear out is a measure of the occupancy of the write-buffer. The number of *empty cycles* between two successive arrivals is the number of cycles for which the buffer is empty and the server sits idle.

We denote a buffer with a maximum capacity of i entries as B_i. We denote the number of stall cycles of B_i on an arrival k as $St(i, k)$. We denote the cycles to clear out of B_i just before the kth arrival as $CC(i, k-)$ and just after the kth arrival as $CC(i, k+)$. The $k\pm$ is omitted if it is clear from the context. Finally, we denote the number of empty cycles between arrivals k_1 and k_2 as $Em(i, k_1, k_2)$.

4.2   Non-Coalescing Write-Buffer Simulation

This section develops a multi-configuration simulation algorithm for a range of non-coalescing write-buffers of varying sizes. Simple write-buffer implementations often use non-coalescing write-buffers. Also, the simulation algorithm for coalescing write-buffers is an extension of the algorithm developed in this section.

We use Fig. 8 to illustrate various relations between write buffers. Fig. 8 shows the cycles-to-clearout, CC, of three non-coalescing write-buffers with one to three entries as a trace of ten stores is processed. The miss-penalty is 10 cycles. The state of a non-coalescing write-buffer is determined completely by its cycles to clear out. The vertical bars in the figure indicate arrivals, and the cycles to clear out of the three buffers just before the arrival is shown to the left of the bar. The cycles between successive arrivals is shown between the corresponding bars. The stall cycles (on the following arrival) and the empty cycles (between the arrivals) is shown below each buffer. In this example, ten arrivals are shown. The one-entry buffer stalls for a total of 34 cycles, the two-entry buffer for 21 cycles and the three-entry buffer for 11 cycles.

In our development of the theory behind the simulation algorithm, we first state a basic result which says that the difference in state between two buffers of different sizes is affected only when either of the buffers stalls or experiences a clear out (Lemma 3). We then bound the difference in states between two buffers, B_i and B_{i+1} (Lemma 4), and use this bound to show that a buffer stalls only when all smaller buffers stall. Finally, we derive an expression for the state of a buffer in terms of its previous state and the state of smaller buffers between stalls (Lemma 6 and Lemma 7). These results allow us to simulate a small buffer in detail, and examine larger buffers only when smaller buffers stall. Since stalls are usually infrequent, this approach leads to significant reductions in simulation time. omit proofs of many lemmas here; for proofs and more detail please refer to [13, 11]. The algorithm itself with a brief explanation of how it works appears in pages 135 and 136. Readers might prefer going to

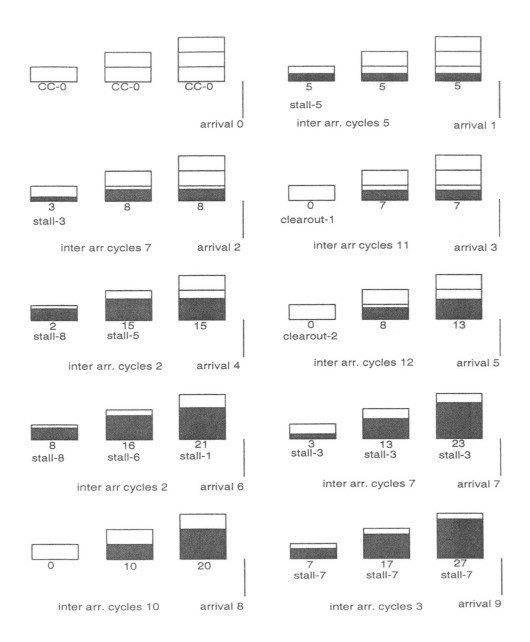

Figure 8   State change in write-buffers — Examples

the algorithm directly, and coming back to the lemmas later for justification as required.

Lemma 3 *Consider two buffers B_i and B_{i+1}. If neither buffer stalls nor experiences a clear out from Arrival k_1 to Arrival k_2 (exclusive),*

$$CC(i+1, k_2-) - CC(i, k_2-) = CC(i+1, k_x-) - CC(i, k_x) \blacksquare$$
$$CC(i+1, k_x+) - CC(i, k_x+) = CC(i+1, k_1+) - CC(i, k_1+)$$

where k_x is any arrival between k_1 and k_2.

In Fig. 8, consider buffers B_2 and B_3 between Arrival 0 and Arrival 4. Both buffers do not stall or clear out in this interval, and we see that the difference between their cycles to clear out stays constant at zero in the interval.

Lemma 4 *On any arrival, k,*

$$0 \leq CC(i+1, k\pm) - CC(i, k\pm) \leq S$$

Proof :
$0 \leq CC(i+1, k\pm) - CC(i, k\pm)$:
$CC(i+1)$ can decrease relative to $CC(i)$ under two circumstances.

1. B_i clears-out and B_{i+1} clears-out for fewer cycles or not at all between arrivals.

2. B_{i+1} stalls and B_i stalls for fewer cycles or not at all on an arrival.

In the first case, $CC(i+1)$ cannot go below $CC(i)$, since $CC(i)$ is already at zero. In the second case, B_{i+1} has $i+1$ entries since it is stalling. B_i can at most have i entries, and so $CC(i)$ remains below $CC(i+1)$.

$CC(i+1, k\pm) - CC(i, k\pm) \leq S$:
$CC(i+1)$ increases relative to $CC(i)$ under two circumstances.

1. B_{i+1} clears-out and B_i clears out for fewer cycles or not at all.

2. B_i stalls on an arrival and B_{i+1} stalls for fewer cycles or not at all.

In the first case $CC(i+1)$ is at zero and cannot go above $CC(i)$. In the second case, when B_i stalls on an arrival, k, $CC(i, k+) = i * S$. But $CC(i + 1, k+) \leq (i + 1) * S$; therefore, $CC(i + 1) - CC(i)$ is less than or equal to S. □

The following corollaries to the lemma state that *stall inclusion* and *clear out inclusion* hold between the queues. As a consequence we can simulate the smallest queue in detail and progressively update the state of bigger queues as the smaller queues stall.

Corollary 1
B_{i+1} stalls only if B_i stalls.

Corollary 2
If there is a clear out of B_{i+1} between two successive arrivals k and $k+1$, there is a clear out of B_i for at least as many cycles in the same interval.

Lemmas 6 and 7 give us a means for determining the cycles to clear out of one buffer from the cycles to clear out of the other, provided the cycles to clear out of both buffers is known at some earlier arrival, and both buffers have not stalled after that arrival. Lemma 6 gives an expression for the number of empty cycles of B_{i+1} between two arrivals k_1 and k_2 in terms of the cycles to clear out of B_{i+1} and B_i at k_1+, the cycles to clear out of B_i at k_2-, and the number of empty cycles of B_i in the interval k_1 to k_2. Lemma 7 gives an expression for determining the state of B_{i+1} from the number of empty cycles. We first state Lemma 5 needed for the proof of Lemma 6.

Lemma 5 *If B_i and B_{i+1} clear out between arrivals k_1 and $k_1 + 1$, and if the next stall after Arrival k_1 for either of them occurs at Arrival k_2 then*

$$CC(i, k_x-) = CC(i + 1, k_x-),$$

$$CC(i, k_x+) = CC(i + 1, k_x+)$$

and

$$CC(i, k_2-) = CC(i + 1, k_2-),$$

where k_x is any arrival between k_1 and k_2.

Lemma 6 *If neither B_i nor B_{i+1} stalls between writes k_1 and k_2 (exclusive), then $Em(i+1, k_1, k_2)$ is given as*

$$Em(i+1, k_1, k_2) = \begin{cases} CC(i, k_2-) - CC'(i+1, k_2-), & CC(i, k_2-) > CC'(i+1, k_2-) \\ 0, & otherwise \end{cases}$$

where $CC'(i+1, k_2-) = CC(i+1, k_1+) - CC(i, k_1+) - Em(i, k_1, k_2) + CC(i, k_2-)$

Proof :
There are two cases.

Case 1: $CC(i, k_2-) > CC'(i+1, k_2-)$
In the following, we prove by contradiction that $Em(i+1, k_1, k_2) \neq 0$. By Lemma 7, $CC(i+1, k_2-) = CC'(i+1, k_2-) + Em(i+1, k_1, k_2)$. Assume $Em(i+1, k_1, k_2) = 0$. Then $CC(i+1, k_2-) = CC'(i+1, k_2-)$. But, $CC(i+1, k_2-) \geq CC(i, k_2-)$(Lemma 4) $> CC'(i+1, k_2-)$, a contradiction. Therefore if $CC(i, k_2-) > CC'(i+1, k_2-)$, $Em(i+1, k_1, k_2) \neq 0)$.

Since $Em(i+1, k_1, k_2) \neq 0$, B_{i+1} experiences a clear out at some point in the interval k_1 to k_2. By Lemma 5 B_i also experiences a clear out before B_{i+1}. By Lemma 7, $CC(i, k_2-) = CC(i+1, k_2-)$. Since from Lemma 7, $CC(i+1, k_2-) = CC'(i+1, k_2-) + Em(i+1, k_1, k_2)$, it follows that $Em(i+1, k_1, k_2) = CC(i, k_2-) - CC'(i+1, k_2-)$.

Case 2: $CC(i, k_2-) \leq CC'(i+1, k_2-)$
We prove by contradiction that $Em(i+1, k_1, k_2) = 0$. Assume $Em(i+1, k_1, k_2) \neq 0$ Then since both buffers clear out in the interval k_1 to k_2, $CC(i, k_2-) = CC(i+1, k_2-)$. From Lemma 5, $CC(i+1, k_2-) = CC'(i+1, k_2-) + Em(i+1, k_1, k_2) > CC'(i+1, k_2-)$ i.e., $CC(i, k_2-) > CC'(i+1, k_2-)$, a contradiction. Therefore, $Em(i+1, k_1, k_2) = 0$. □

Lemma 7 *If neither buffer stalls between arrivals k_1 and k_2 (exclusive),*

$$CC(i+1, k_2-) - CC(i, k_2-) = CC(i+1, k_1+) - CC(i, k_1+) - (Em(i, k_1, k_2) - Em(i+1, k_1, k_2))$$

The simulation technique can now be developed as follows. The smallest buffer is simulated for each store in the trace. The cycles to clear out and the empty cycles of this buffer since the last stall are maintained. As long as it does not stall, we know that a bigger buffer also does not stall. If the smallest buffer

Algorithm NC_WBUF:

```
sim_nc_wbuf()
for each store (or dirty-miss):
          sep ← Inter-arrival cycles CC[0] ← CC[0] - sep;
          if (CC[0] < 0)
                    /* Clear Out in smallest buffer */
                    Em[0] ← Em[0] - CC[0]; /* Add —CC— */
                    CC[0] ← S;
          else if (MIN_BUF_SZ ≥ (CC[0] + S))
                    /* Neither Clear Out nor Stall in smallest buffer */
                    CC[0] ← CC[0] + S;
          else
                    /* Stall in smallest buffer */
                    St[0] ← St[0] + CC[0] + S - MIN_BUF_SZ;
                    for i=1 to Q_RANGE
                              if (first stall in buffer i-1)
                                        CC[i] ← CC[i-1] + S;
                                        Em[i-1] ← 0;
                                        break;
                              else
                                        change ← (MIN_BUF_SZ + S * (i-1)) - CC[i-1];
                                        CC[i] ← CC[i] - (change + Em[i-1]);
                                        Em[i-1] ← 0;
                                        if (CC[i] < CC[i-1])
                                                  /* buffers "i" and "i-1" are clear out synchronized */
                                                  Em[i] ← Em[i] + CC[i-1] - CC[i];
                                                  CC[i] ← CC[i-1] + S;
                                                  CC[i-1] ← MIN_BUF_SZ + S * (i-1);
                                                  break;
                                        else if ((MIN_BUF_SZ + S*i) ≥ (CC[i] + S))
                                                  /* No Stall in buffer "i". No clear out sync with "i-1" either *
                                                  CC[i-1] ← MIN_BUF_SZ + S * (i-1);
                                                  CC[i] ← CC[i] + S;
                                                  break;
                                        else
                                                  /* Stalls in both buffer "i-1" and "i" */
                                                  St[i] ← St[i] + CC[i] + S - (MIN_BUF_SZ + S*i);
                                                  CC[i-1] ← MIN_BUF_SZ + S * (i-1);
                                        end if
                              end if
                    end for
          end if
end for
```

Figure 9   Non-coalescing write-buffer simulation — Algorithm

stalls on an arrival we can determine the state of the next larger buffer using Lemmas 6 and 7. From that state we can determine if the buffer stalls and if so for how many cycles. Lemma 6 also lets us determine the number of empty cycles of the larger buffer. If the larger buffer stalls we can go to the next larger buffer and continue as before. The detailed algorithm is given in Fig 9.

4.3 Coalescing Write-Buffer Simulation

In this section we consider the simulation of coalescing write-buffers. The main new result is that a limited form of inclusion holds; that is, under certain conditions, we can show that when a merge occurs for a smaller buffer, one occurs for a larger buffer as well. Additionally, the property proved in the previous section that a buffer stalls only when all smaller buffers stall continues to hold. The lemmas proved in the previous section also hold with some modifications to account for merges. In the description below we first demonstrate that data inclusion holds between the buffers. We then discuss the changes that need to be made in the simulation algorithm to account for merging.

The state of a coalescing write-buffer, is a combination of the cycles to clear out and the addresses of the lines in the buffer. The key observation we use is that the W lines in a write-buffer, excluding the line being written out, are the top W lines in an LRU stack of write-lines. This observation follows from the policy of retiring the least recently written line from the write-buffer to the second-level cache. The write-buffer is thus similar to a fully-associative cache, except that it is not always full. We maintain the number of lines in each write-buffer using the techniques similar to those of the previous section, and as much of the LRU stack as needed. From these two data structures we can determine the addresses of the lines in each write-buffer.

When there are merges the techniques of Section 4.2 have to be modified appropriately. The most significant change is to Lemma 4, and we restate it below as Lemma 8. We see that now $CC(i)$ may be greater than $CC(i-1)$, and as a result, Corollary 2 of Lemma 4 does not hold. Lemma 6 is true provided $CC(i, k_1+) \leq CC(i+1, k_1+)$ with the additional condition that a merge does not occur only in B_{i+1} in the interval k_1 to k_2. Lemma 7 is also true if a merge does not occur in only one of B_i and B_{i+1}. Lemma 9 is for the case where $CC(i, k_1+) > CC(i+1, k_1+)$.

Lemma 8 *On any arrival, k,*

$$-S \leq CC(i+1, k\pm) - CC(i, k\pm) \leq S$$

In addition

$$-S \leq CC(i+n, k\pm) - CC(i, k\pm) \forall n > 0$$

Proof :
  In addition to the cases we considered in the proof of Lemma 4, we need to consider the case when differences in state occur as a result of merges.

That is, apart from the two cases mentioned earlier, $CC(i+1)$ can increase above $CC(i)$ when a line merges in B_i, and not in B_{i+1}. But this occurs only when B_i has an additional entry. The increase when this happens is a maximum of S, and so $CC(i+1)$ cannot go more than S above $CC(i)$. Similarly $CC(i)$ can increase above $CC(i+1)$ when a line merges in B_{i+1} but not in B_i, and for similar reasons $CC(i)$ cannot increase to more than S above $CC(i+1)$ when this happens. Further, note that $CC(i)$ can increase above $CC(i+n)$, $n > 0$, only when a merge occurs in B_{i+n} and not in B_i, and so $CC(i)$ can never increase more than S above $CC(i+n)$ by the earlier argument. □

Lemma 9 *If neither B_i nor B_{i+1} stall between writes k_1 and k_2 (exclusive), and*
if $CC(i, k_1+) > CC(i+1, k_1+)$ and there is no merge in B_i alone, then

$$CC(i+1, k_2) = \begin{cases} CC(i+1, k_1+) + (CC(i, k_2-) - CC(i, k_1+)), \\ \qquad\qquad Min(CC(i, k_1+, k_2-)) \geq \\ \qquad\qquad\qquad\qquad (CC(i, k_1+) - CC(i+1, k_1+)) \\ CC(i, k_2-) + Min(CC(i, k_1+, k_2-)), \qquad otherwise \end{cases}$$

where $Min(CC(i, k_1+, k_2-))$ is the minimum value of CC(i) in the interval k_1+ to k_2-.

By the inclusion property of LRU fully-associative caches, when a merge occurs in a buffer, a merge will occur in other buffers with as many or more entries. Also, by Lemma 8 a buffer can have at most one more entry than larger buffers. In the simulation, we first determine if there is a merge in any of the buffers. If there is, we start at the smallest buffer size and examine larger buffer sizes till a merge occurs somewhere other than the last entry examined. Then we know that a merge would occur for all larger buffer sizes as well, and we do not examine larger buffer sizes. If we know that there is no merge in any of the buffers we start at the smallest buffer size and examine buffers till there is no stall at some buffer. We maintain counts of empty cycles and minimums, and use them to derive the state of buffers.

4.4   Performance

Empirical performance evaluations of implementations of these algorithms show that for the non-coalescing case the single-pass simulation algorithm is on the average about five times faster than the naive algorithm which examines all buffer sizes each time. The number of buffer sizes that need to be examined is about three on the average where the total number of buffer sizes is 32. For the coalescing case the single-pass algorithm is about three times faster on the average. The number of buffers examined is about 15 on the average where the total number of buffer sizes is 32. These evaluations were done on traces of some of the SPEC benchmarks, with write-through caching.

4.5 Literature Review

The write-buffer simulation algorithms were introduced by Sugumar and Abraham [13, 11]. Related work has also been published in work on perturbation analysis in the context of manufacturing systems. In Ho, et al. [6] the simulation of two buffer sizes simultaneously in an assembly line is described. Also when assumptions are made about the stochastic behavior of the inter-arrival times, methods like augmented systems analysis [3] are available for evaluating the effect of varying buffer sizes. The stochastic nature of write inter-arrival times is a topic for future research. For a good overview of the perturbation analysis perspective see [15].

5 DIRECTIONS FOR FUTURE WORK

In this chapter single-pass simulation algorithms have been described for three architectural subsystems. All the algorithms presented in this and the previous chapter belong to the class of single-pass algorithms, that accept a common trace to a range of configurations as an input and generate performance metrics for each configuration. We believe opportunities exist for developing single-pass simulation algorithms that are not necessarily based on a trace input but can simulate multiple configurations of interest simultaneously. We propose the less restrictive term *multi-configuration simulation* for this type of simulation.

The work presented here may be extended in a couple of directions. First, multi-configuration simulation algorithms need to be developed for other types of architectural simulators such as CPU simulators, multiprocessor simulators and interconnection network simulators to name a few. Such work will lead to the development of efficient simulation algorithms for these components. Further, as more work on multi-configuration simulators is done, unifying aspects of multi-configuration simulation development might emerge. Second, most work

on multi-configuration simulation algorithms has been on isolated architectural
features, such as, caches or write-buffers. Multi-configuration simulation algorithms are likely to be even more important in complete system simulators,
since in such systems the time spent simulating any one part of the architecture
is probably small compared to the total system simulation time, and rerunning
the entire system simulation for each small architectural change is inefficient.
In such systems, changes made to one architectural feature might propagate to
other parts of the system, and handling such effects efficiently is a challenging
problem that needs to be addressed.

Exercises

5.1 Construct a simple cache simulator for simulating a single set-associative cache. Determine the percentage of time spent in (1) Reading in addresses from the trace and (2) Actually simulating the cache.

5.2 Define Ran(k) as an infinitely long trace of random addresses chosen from integers $1 \ldots k$. Define $S(i)$ as the fraction of hits at depth i of the stack in a fully associative stack simulation. For a Ran(k) trace derive an expression for $S(i)$ under the following replacement schemes

   (a) Least recently used (LRU)

   (b) Least frequently used (LFU)

  Is $S(i)$ defined for FIFO. Why or why not?

5.3 Construct a stack simulator for OPT using complete lookahead to obtain priority information. Use the simulator to determine $S(i)$, $i = 1, \ldots, k$ for Ran(k) for $k = 4, 8, 16$.

  Derive an expression for $S(i)$ for Ran(k) under OPT replacement from first principles.

5.4 The OPT stack can be broken up into groups within which addresses are in priority order [e.g if stack is 2 3 7 4 5 9 8 6 , where numbers represent priorities of addresses at those positions and lower numbers indicate higher priorities, it may be broken up into groups as follows (2 3 7) (4 5 9) (8) (6)].

   (a) Use the simulator constructed for Exercise 5.3 to determine the number of groups in a stack on average for the Ran(k) trace for different values of k. How can groups be used to avoid a sequential search of the OPT stack (Hint: Use the fact that hits always occur at the leading entry of a group) How can groups be used for a tree simulation of OPT?

   (b) Derive an expression for the average number of groups in a stack for Ran(k) from first principles.

5.5 Develop a tree simulation algorithm for fully associative caches under LFU replacement. The number of operations per trace reference should be O(log of number of stack entries). (Hint: Consider maintaining a list of lines that are not in their correct priority position and performing update operations only for members of that list.)

5.6 Prove that the SWAP operation defined in page 123 is always possible.

5.7 Describe an implementation of the multiprogramming (context switching) technique of the previous chapter with the gbt algorithm.

5.8 Enumerate all distinct gbt(2)s of degree 4. Which of these do you think would be most common in a cache simulation? Construct a gbt simulator or modify the gbt simulator available as a part of the Cheetah package to output statistics on gbt structure frequencies. Run a trace of a real applications through the simulator and check if your intuition is correct.

5.9 The non-coalescing write-buffer simulation algorithm described in Section 4.2 examines buffer sizes until there is no stall at some buffer size, which is efficient when stalls are infrequent – the common case. However, programs go through periods of excessive write activity during which even large buffers fill up and cause stalls. Think of an optimization to avoid examining all buffer sizes on each write under such situations.

5.10 Take a public domain timing simulator of a CPU (such as DLX or SPIM) and evaluate the effect of altering the depth of the add pipeline on the course of a simulation. Implement a single pass simulator of multiple pipeline depths by duplicating necessary state variables. Compare the simulation speed of your single pass implementation against simulating each pipeline depth separately. Think of ways to improve the efficiency of your single pass simulator.

REFERENCES

[1] G. M. Adeĺson-Veĺskii and E. M. Landis. An algorithm for the organization of information. *Soviet Math. Doklady*, 3:1259–1263, 1962.

[2] B. T. Bennett and V. J. Kruskal. LRU stack processing. *IBM J. of Research and Development*, pages 353–357, July 1975.

[3] C. G. Cassandras and S. G. Strickland. On-line sensitivity analysis of Markov chains. *IEEE Trans. on Automatic Control*, 34(1):76–86, jan 1989.

[4] M. D. Hill. *Man page of* tycho.

[5] M. D. Hill and A. J. Smith. Evaluating associativity in CPU caches. *IEEE Trans. on Computers*, 38(12):1612–1630, December 1989.

[6] Y. C. Ho, M. A. Eyler, and T. T. Chien. A gradient technique for general buffer storage design in a production line. *Int. J. Prod. Research*, 17(6):557–580, 1979.

[7] R. L. Mattson, J. Gecsei, D. R. Slutz, and I. L. Traiger. Evaluation techniques for storage hierarchies. *IBM Systems Journal*, 9(2):78–117, 1970.

[8] F. Olken. Efficient methods for calculating the success function of fixed space replacement policies. Technical Report LBL-12370, Lawrence Berkeley Laboratory, 1981.

[9] T. R. Puzak. *Analysis of Cache Replacement Algorithms*. PhD thesis, University of Massachusetts, Amherst, 1985.

[10] D. D. Sleator and R. E. Tarjan. Self adjusting binary search trees. *J. of the ACM*, 32(3):652–686, 1985.

[11] R. A. Sugumar. *Multi-Configuration Simulation Algorithms for the Evaluation of Computer Architecture Designs*. PhD thesis, University of Michigan, 1993. Also available as Tech. Report CSE-TR-173-93, CSE Division, University of Michigan.

[12] R. A. Sugumar and S. G. Abraham. Efficient simulation of caches under optimal replacement with applications to miss characterization. In *Proc. ACM SIGMETRICS Conf.*, pages 24–35, 1993.

[13] R. A. Sugumar and S. G. Abraham. Fast efficient simulation of write-buffer configurations. In *Hawaii Intl. Conf. on Systems Sciences — Architecture Track*, 1994.

[14] R. A. Sugumar and S. G. Abraham. Set-associative cache simulation using generalized binomial trees. *ACM Trans. on Computer Systems*, 1995 ? Conditionally accepted pending minor revisions.

[15] R. Suri. Perturbation analysis: The state of the art and research issues explained via the GI/G/1 queue. *Proceedings of the IEEE*, 77(1), jan 1989.

[16] D. Thiebaut. On the fractal dimension of computer programs and its application to the prediction of the cache miss ratio. *IEEE Trans. on Computers*, 38(7):1012–1026, July 1989.

[17] J. G. Thompson. *Efficient analysis of Caching Systems*. PhD thesis, University of California, Berkeley, 1987.

[18] I. L. Traiger and D. R. Slutz. One pass techniques for the evaluation of memory hierarchies. Technical Report RJ 892, IBM, 1971.

6

EXECUTION DRIVEN SIMULATION OF SHARED MEMORY MULTIPROCESSORS

Bob Boothe

University of Southern Maine, Portland, Maine

1   INTRODUCTION

Execution driven simulation[7] is a technique for building fast instruction level computer simulators. It is applicable when the instruction set of the simulation host machine is the same as, or very similar to, that of the machine being simulated. In this chapter we examine three execution driven simulators designed to study shared memory multiprocessors using a uniprocessor as the simulation host machine.

In building a simulator one can take advantage of the fact that some events are of greater interest than others. For instance a simulator of shared memory multiprocessors is primarily concerned with the load and store instructions which access memory. For other instructions, such as arithmetic and control, the only concern is that they get performed and that their execution time is properly accounted for. The key idea of execution driven simulation is that rather than simulate each individual instruction, the bulk of the instructions can be directly executed by the host computer. Only those instructions requiring special treatment need to be simulated.

The simulation involves two stages: first a preprocessing of the application and then the actual simulation. In the preprocessing stage, the application program is modified by inserting extra instructions that will perform simple operations needed by the simulator and by inserting calls to simulator routines at important events. Figure 1 shows a simple example. Here the register Rtime is used to accumulate the execution time (in processor cycles) as the program is executed. Each application instruction is followed by an extra instruction that increments this time register. The load word instruction (lw) in this

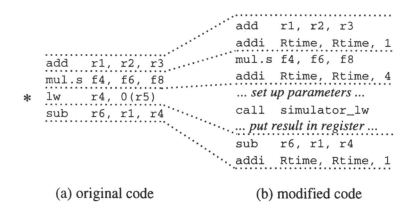

(a) original code   (b) modified code

Figure 1 A simple example of code augmentation. The lw instruction (marked with the asterisk) causes an event of interest to the simulator, and thus in the modified code it is replaced with a call to the simulator. All examples in this chapter use the MIPS instruction set.

example causes an event of interest to the simulator; it is replaced by a call to a simulator routine. When the modified application is executed, these inserted calls will feed events to the simulator. This general technique is called *execution driven simulation* because it is the execution of the modified application and the inserted calls that drives the simulation process.

The preprocessing stage of modifying the application code is called *augmentation*. It is generally done at the machine language level on either object files or the executable file. In general it is more sophisticated than in the example. For instance, a simple improvement can eliminate most of the time counting instructions. Instead of inserting a time counting instruction after every original instruction, one time counting instruction can be used for an entire basic block. (A basic block is a group of contiguous instructions that is always executed in sequence. The only jumps into the block are to the first instruction. The only jumps out are from the last instruction.) The single time counting instruction for a basic block would update the time counter by the sum of the times of its component instructions.

The two augmentations seen so far, time counting and event call-outs, form the basic mechanism used by an execution driven simulator. Later we will see several other useful augmentations.

Code augmentation is currently an important technique for building other tools besides simulators. Profilers such as **pixie**[12] augment the application code to increment counters each time a basic block is entered. After execution is completed, these basic block counts are then used to calculate the amount of execution time spent throughout the application. Address trace generation tools[10] have been built by augmenting the code to record the sequence of basic blocks that are executed. This sequence is then used later to reconstruct the full reference stream.

The advantage of execution driven simulation is speed. By directly executing most instructions at the machine's execution rate, the simulator can operate one to two orders of magnitude faster than cycle by cycle simulators[13] that decipher and emulate each individual instruction. Since the scope of simulation studies often seems to be limited by the speed of the simulator, execution driven simulation is a valuable technique.

The remainder of this chapter is organized as follows: Section 2 discusses the four main implementation decision involved in designing an execution driven simulator. Section 3 compares the different choices made by three different execution driven simulators to these implementation decisions. Sections 4 and 5 then look more closely at one of these simulators. Section 6 presents performance measurements, and Section 7 summarizes and concludes the chapter.

2 IMPLEMENTATION DECISIONS

In this section we discuss the major implementation decisions that must be made in designing an execution driven simulator. Some of these decisions apply to any execution driven tool, while others arise when trying to simulate multiple processors or when simulating shared memory.

2.1 Decision 1: Where do extra registers come from?

Extra registers are needed for many code augmentations. For example, in Figure 1 the extra register (Rtime) was used to count the execution time. A good compiler, however, generally tries to use all available registers, and thus extra registers are not available.

Some possible solutions are:

Modify the compiler: An easy solution, if you can control the compiler, is to reserve a few registers and not allow the compiler to use them when generating code. One problems is that a restricted register set will cause the compiler to generate more register to memory spills. Timings generated from this code will not match exactly timings that would have been produced if the entire register set were available. A second problem modifying the compiler is that library routines, whose source code is usually not available, would need to be recompiled before they could be simulated.

Memory to memory instructions: Another potentially easy solution avoids the problem altogether by using only memory to memory instructions. This can't be done directly, however, since memory to memory operations are not provided by RISC processors. The next two implementations are mechanisms for freeing up a few temporary registers long enough for a RISC processor to update a memory resident value.

Save registers to stack: By convention, the compiler uses one register to hold a stack pointer. This provides a base address for pushing the contents of a few registers onto the stack. These registers can then be used to perform the memory update, and then the registers' values can be restored from the stack.

Save to global pointer area: Another convention is that of having a certain register that holds a pointer to the base of a memory block containing global variables. If a few locations in this block are reserved, they can be used like the stack was to temporarily stash the contents of a few registers.

Commandeer and remap: A more efficient technique than obtaining new temporary register for each augmentation is to commandeer three unfrequently used registers for use by the code augmenter. The original values of these registers are stashed in memory. One of these registers is now used to hold a memory base address, and the other two are used in loading operands and storing the result. In the rare cases when any of these commandeered registers are used in the original code, additional code is inserted to remap the instruction and to load and store the registers' real values. An example of this is shown in Figure 2. This technique was used in the pixie profiler.

Virtualize the register file: The most sophisticated solution is to virtualize the register file. The virtual register set consists of the registers used in the original code as well as the additional registers used in the augmented code. These virtual register are assigned home locations in memory and then mapped into whatever physical registers are available at the points

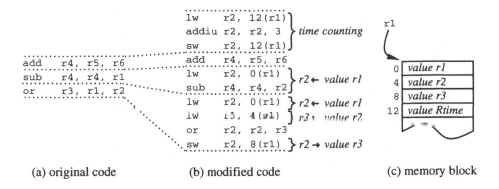

(a) original code   (b) modified code   (c) memory block

Figure 2 Commandeering three registers to provide memory to memory operations. In this example, the three commandeered registers are r1, r2, and r3. Part (a) shows the original code. This is then transformed into the modified code in part (b). The original values from the registers are stashed in the memory block shown in part (c). In the modified code, the first piece increments the time value to account for all 3 instructions. It uses the commandeered registers to load, increment, and store the time value in the memory block. The second piece, the **add** instruction, is unchanged. The third piece, the expansion of the **sub** instruction, uses the commandeered register r1, and thus it is preceded by an extra instruction to load the value that would have been in r1. This value is loaded into r2, and then the **sub** instruction is remapped to use r2 instead. The last piece shows how an instruction that uses all three commandeered registers is remapped.

in the program where they are used. An efficient implementation of this will be described in Section 4.

2.2 Decision 2: How do you get the original instruction addresses?

The object code will be expanded by all of the extra augmenting instructions inserted into it. If we wish to accurately simulate the instruction caches, we need to obtain the original addresses of the application's instructions. Below are a few approaches to obtaining the original addresses:

Fixed expansion factor: In a simulator designed by Jeff Rothman[15] all instructions are expanded by a fixed factor into 8 instructions. Usually all of these aren't needed, so **nops** are used for padding. This is an easy solution that makes calculating the original addresses simple.

Complete address map: At the other extreme, one might choose to provide a complete map of new instruction addresses back to their original addresses.

Partial address map: A more compact mapping takes advantage of sequential portions known as basic blocks. In this mapping a basic block number maps into a starting address and an instruction count. This technique has been used for compact storage of address traces[10].

Don't care: Tradeoffs must be made in any simulator, and in most multiprocessor simulators the tradeoff is made to ignore instruction accesses. Instruction caches generally have very high hit rates, and thus ignoring instruction misses should have only minor affects on timing accuracy. If, however, instruction caches are simulated, they will dominate the simulation time since instruction accesses occur every cycle where as other events occur much less frequently.

2.3 Decision 3: How do you create multiple processes?

To simulate multiprocessors we need multiple processes, each with their own set of registers, stack, and local variables. The simulator running on a single processors will then cycle amongst these processes. Our implementation options are:

Unix processes Use the mechanisms available in UNIX for creating and communicating among processes. This may be simple, but there is a very large overhead in using operating system level context switching and scheduling. A typical simulation will have events occurring every 10 to 100 instructions, and thus a 10,000 cycle UNIX context switch would dominate the execution time.

Lightweight threads A much better choice is to use lightweight threads. An example of this implementation is the Proteus[9] simulator. It performs a context switch in just 135 instructions. Most of this being used to save and restore the 64 registers on the MIPS R3000.

In-line context switching An even faster approach named *in-line context switching* is used in the FAST[2] simulator. It takes advantage of the fact that usually only a small fraction of the registers are used between simulation events. It augments the application with code that loads just those registers that are used and stores just those registers that are changed between simulation events.

2.4 Decision 4: How do you specify and identify shared memory references?

Real shared memory machines such as the Sequent[14] support an extended C language that allows the declaration of static shared global variables as well the dynamic allocation of shared memory. A shared integer is declared: "`shared int i;`", and shared memory is allocated with "`ptr = shmalloc(size);`". Since shared memory accesses are events of interest to the simulator, a mechanism is needed for identifying these accesses within the application program.

Compiler tagging The cleanest solution would be to modify the compiler to recognize the shared memory language extension and then to tag accesses to shared memory variables in the assembly language code. The compiler could easily tag direct accesses to shared variables, but indirect accesses through pointers would be difficult if not impossible to determine.

Source code manipulation The approach taken in Proteus[9] was to modify the source code to use a new operator `@>` for indirect accesses to shared memory instead of the usual `->` operator. They then run a preprocessor on the source code to transform these new operators into procedure calls to the simulator. The main drawback of this method is that the inserted procedure calls will substantially change the way an optimizing compiler produces code, and the timings derived from such code will be inaccurate.

Dynamic address testing If all shared memory is allocated from a single block of memory, shared memory references can be identified by comparison to an address range. This comparison can be done either within the simulator or more efficiently as an additional code augmentation. A good place for this shared memory block is at the top of user memory space, since then only a single address comparison will be needed to identify a shared reference.

Variable naming While dynamic address testing can catch indirect accesses to shared memory, a mechanism is still needed for declaring shared global variables. The approach used in the FAST[2] simulator is to require shared variable names to begin with the prefix "`shared_`". These names

Simulator	Extra Registers	Instruction Addresses	Multiple Processes	Shared Variables
Tango	save to stack	don't care	Unix processes	dynamic address testing
Proteus	save in globals	don't care	lightweight threads	source code manipulation
FAST	virtual registers	don't care	in-line context switching	dynamic address testing and variable naming

Table 1   Design decisions in three example simulators.

are available to the code augmenter because all global variable names are stored by the compiler in an object file's symbol table for later use during linking. The advantages of this approach are that the original compiler can be used, and there are no semantic changes made to the application programs being studied. Since the application is semantically unchanged, the object code produced is unperturbed.

3   EXAMPLE SIMULATORS

In this section we look at three execution driven simulators that were all designed for basically the same purpose: simulating a variety of large shared memory multiprocessors at the instruction level. Table 1 shows the design choices made in these simulators.

3.1   Tango

The Tango simulator[8] was developed at Stanford. It is based on Unix shared memory, and it uses Unix context switches in order to switch from executing one process to another. These heavy weight context switches require thousands of cycles, and thus dominate the execution time of their simulator.   They report slowdown factors ranging from 500 to 6000. This slowdown factor is a measure of a simulator's speed. The slowdown is equal to the average number of machine cycles taken to simulate one cycle of one processor.

Because of the large cost of Unix context switches, they provide an option to tradeoff accuracy for faster execution by letting the individual processor clocks get out of sync. This allows them to accumulate a number of global events before context switching and thus reduces the context switch frequency. These faster simulations, however, no longer accurately interleave the shared memory references.

Recently they have rewritten their simulator to use a light weight thread package. This should significantly reduce the magnitude of their context switch overhead problem.

Tango requires all shared memory to be dynamically allocated. The drawback of this is that all accesses to shared global variables require two memory accesses instead of just one. In the extreme case this could double the reference rate of an application.

3.2   Proteus

The Proteus simulator was developed at MIT[5, 9]. It uses a light weight thread package and is substantially faster than Tango. They report typical slowdown factors ranging from 35 to 100.

As mentioned in Section 2.4, they identify shared variables by modifying the application's source code. They replace shared memory references in the C source code with calls to the simulation routines (and optionally also insert statistics gathering calls.) They then compile this modified code and apply code augmentation for timing on the assembly language. Because each shared reference (which should be just a single instruction) is replaced with a procedure call, the compiler optimizations that can be applied and the object code produced are substantially changed from that which would have been produced if the original code were compiled directly.

In fact, their good performance is partially due to the fact that their insertion of procedure calls causes the compiler to save away important registers. This allows them to "exploit 'partial' context switches" in which they only save a limited amount of the register file. This is good for performance, but bad for timing accuracy.

3.3 FAST

The FAST simulator was developed by this chapter's author at Berkeley[2]. It uses sophisticated code augmentation techniques in order to provide both high speed and high accuracy. Its slowdown has been measured as ranging from 10 to 100.

The remaining section of this chapter explore the FAST simulator in greater detail. Section 4 explains the complete set of code augmentations used in FAST. Section 5 describes the rest of the simulator, and Section 6 presents detailed performance statistics.

4 CODE AUGMENTATIONS

As described earlier, code augmentation is the process of taking an original piece of code and adding to it and modifying it so that it can perform additional functions. In this section we describe all of the code augmentation used in the FAST simulator. We then show a detailed example that includes some of the more complex augmentations.

Time Counting: The code augmenter breaks the code into basic blocks and then adds an instruction that increments a time counter by an amount equal to the number of cycles that would be required to execute the original basic block.

Accurately determining timing is more complicated than just counting instructions; the processor pipeline must be modeled. Usually looking just within a basic block is adequate, but sometimes long latency floating point operations continue executing past the end of a basic block and affect the timing of subsequent blocks. If these subsequent blocks are selected by conditional branches, the exact timing will depend upon the branch paths taken at execution time. These cases are rare, and for FAST we used timings based on static prediction of branch paths. Accurate timing would be further complicated if modeling a superscaler processor.

Event Call-Outs: At special events, such as shared memory references, code is inserted to call out to the simulator in order to let the simulator regain control and process the events.

For FAST these events are load and store instructions. There are several variants of these instructions: byte, half-word, long, and double. Each is replaced with a small template that sets up the parameters for the procedure call and later upon return from the simulator moves the result into the destination register specified by the original instruction.

Reference Indirection: For a single process program, for which the compiler thinks it is compiling, static local variables are assigned to fixed memory addresses. However, we are simulating multiple processes within a single address space. Each thread needs its own copy of the local variables, and all references to local variables must therefore be transformed into references that are relative to the currently executing thread.

In FAST, one register is used as a context pointer. This points to the current thread's context block which contains the thread's local state (register values, local variables, and stack). All local variables are reassigned new addresses in this context block, and all instructions accessing local variables are then modified to be relative to the context pointer.

Reallocation of Shared Variables: Since a uniprocessor's compiler does not distinguish references to shared variables, shared memory references must be identified by the code augmenter.

In FAST shared variables are identified by the prefix "shared_" that is used on all shared variable names. These variables are then reallocated to locations within the shared memory block.

Dynamic Reference Discrimination: The code augmenter can not determine by looking at the code whether an indirect reference is to a local or to a shared location. It therefore adds code that tests at execution time if the referenced address falls within the shared memory region. Based on this test the code then either directly executes the local access or calls out to the simulator to simulate the shared memory reference.

In our research into parallel machines[3, 4], we proposed language extensions that *would* allow a compiler to classify indirect references as directed either to local or to shared memory. Current compilers can not perform this classification, but we needed this classification for our studies of code reorganization techniques. (We were studying grouping of shared memory references to help hide remote memory latency.) We used code augmentation to collect a trace file that recorded for each memory referencing instruction whether it was used to access local or shared variables. This trace file was gathered on the first simulation run of the application and then fed back into a second pass of the code augmenter to provide complete classification.

Re-Optimization: Having obtained a trace classifying each access as either local or shared, we now wanted to study how an optimizing compiler might reorganize the code to group independent shared memory references. We implemented this as just another code augmentation within the code augmenter. This augmentation operated on basic blocks and moved shared memory load instructions upwards until their movement was blocked by a data dependency. During this process there were sometimes false dependencies caused by the allocation of temporary registers in the original code. To bypass these we added a few temporary registers using the augmentation technique of virtual registers, which will be discussed shortly.

Extended Instruction Sets: For the most part we accepted the instruction set of the processor on which simulations were being executed: the MIPS R3000[11]. However we wanted to add a number of new instructions such as: double word load and stores, local and shared memory versions of all loads and stores, an explicit thread switch instruction, fetch-and-add, and other special synchronization instructions. These were all added by having the code augmenter convert these new instructions into calls to special simulator routines.

In-line Context Switching: The augmented code typically runs for a small number of instructions before reaching an event and returning control to the simulator. During this short execution, only a small subset of the register file is ever accessed, and it would therefore be wasteful to load and store the entire register set. We avoid this waste by inserting customized context loading and storing code into the application at basic block boundaries.

Between basic blocks all register values reside in memory in a thread's context block. At the start of a basic block we insert code to load just those registers that are going to be used, and at the end of the basic block we insert code to save any registers whose values may have changed. When only a few registers are used between context switches, this in-line context switching provides a large savings in context switch overhead compared to a routine that loads and stores all 64 registers. Performance statistics are presented in Section 6.

Virtual Registers: When performing code augmentation, extra registers are needed for a variety of purposes, such as for holding the time counter. We call our technique for making these extra registers available *virtual registers*. By *virtual registers* we mean extra registers that can be used in an assembly language program but that do not exist in the actual processor. For example, the register Rtime (used in the Figure 1) could be provided as a virtual register.

The idea of virtual registers was motivated by the technique of in-line context switching. It usually leaves most register values residing in the context block, *not* in the actual register file. The key to providing virtual registers is that when a register is loaded and later used, it can be loaded into any physical register as long as the later use of that register is changed to match. Thus the *virtual* registers used in the original code need not be the same as the *physical* registers used in a modified basic block. Over the course of the program, different basic blocks might use different physical registers to hold a particular virtual register.

The benefit is that we can now have more virtual registers than there are physical registers. For FAST, the virtual register `Rtime` and two other virtual registers (`Rsbp` and `Rcp` to be discussed in the next example) are used so frequently that we chose to let them permanently reside in physical registers. Any uses of the original registers were remapped to other physical registers.

The mapping between virtual and physical registers is possible as long as each individual basic block does not use more virtual registers than there are physical registers. Mapping problems are rare and occur only for large basic blocks; they are easily handled by splitting these large blocks into multiple smaller blocks.

Virtual registers simplify the implementation of complex code augmentations because additional virtual registers can be added without concern for the details of how those extra registers are to be provided. For example, in the re-optimization augmentation a few extra temporary registers were needed. These extra registers were made available as virtual registers.

4.1   An example

Figure 3 uses a small C code fragment to demonstrate several of the code augmentations described above. The original assembly language instructions are shown in part (a); the modified code is shown in part (b).[1] These instructions were generated by the compilation of the expression $A = B + C + X$, where the variables B and C will be loaded from local memory, the variable X is already in register `r8`, and the result A will be stored to shared memory. Assume for this example that this expression by itself forms a basic block. Basic blocks are the granularity at which we perform analysis and code augmentation, and thus this small basic block can serve as a complete example.

---

[1] The instruction set is approximately that of the MIPS R3000[11], but it has been simplified slightly to make the example clearer.

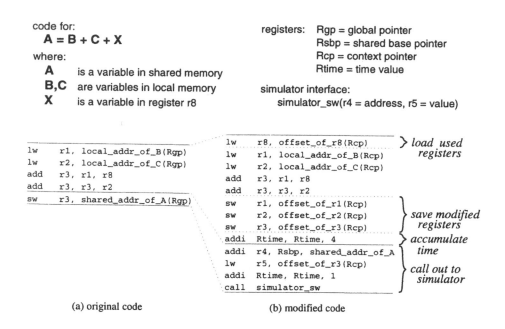

code for:

A = B + C + X

where:

A   is a variable in shared memory

B,C are variables in local memory

X   is a variable in register r8

registers: Rgp = global pointer

   Rsbp = shared base pointer

   Rcp = context pointer

   Rtime = time value

simulator interface:

   simulator_sw(r4 = address, r5 = value)

```
lw    r1, local_addr_of_B(Rgp)
lw    r2, local_addr_of_C(Rgp)
add   r3, r1, r8
add   r3, r3, r2
sw    r3, shared_addr_of_A(Rgp)
```

```
lw    r8, offset_of_r8(Rcp)        ⎫ load used
lw    r1, local_addr_of_B(Rcp)     ⎭   registers
lw    r2, local_addr_of_C(Rcp)
add   r3, r1, r8
add   r3, r3, r2
sw    r1, offset_of_r1(Rcp)        ⎫
sw    r2, offset_of_r2(Rcp)        ⎬ save modified
sw    r3, offset_of_r3(Rcp)        ⎭   registers
addi  Rtime, Rtime, 4              ⎱ accumulate
addi  r4, Rsbp, shared_addr_of_A   ⎰   time
lw    r5, offset_of_r3(Rcp)        ⎫
addi  Rtime, Rtime, 1              ⎬ call out to
call  simulator_sw                 ⎭   simulator
```

(a) original code   (b) modified code

Figure 3   Example of code augmentation

The first step is to identify which instructions can be directly executed by the host processor and which instructions will require a call out of the application to a simulator routine. In this example the last instruction references shared memory and thus will be replaced with a call to the simulator function "simulator_sw" that simulates a shared memory store word instruction. The other four instructions are local to the processor and can be directly executed. For ease of manipulation, the call-out instruction is isolated into its own basic block, as indicated by the horizontal lines separating the instructions.

The second step is to calculate the timing of the basic blocks. The first block has four instructions and takes four cycles. The second block has one instruction and takes one cycle. The timing of each basic block is computed statically and is used in the inserted instructions which accumulate the running execution time in register **Rtime**.

The third step is reference indirection. The loads of local variables B and C are originally relative to the global pointer (register Rgp). These are changed to be thread relative by indexing off of the thread context pointer (register Rcp).[2]

Step four involves adding code for in-line context switching. In our implementation, we maintain the invariant condition that between basic blocks all register values should be correctly stored in the context block of the executing thread. This context block is pointed to by the Rcp register, and thus register load and stores are relative to this pointer.

At the start of each basic block we insert code to load the registers whose values will be used. In the example, only the value in register r8 is used. The registers r1, r2 and r3 also appear, but they do not need to be loaded since their original values are not used. At the end of each basic block we append code to store any registers who's values have been redefined. In the example these are r1, r2 and r3.

We do not show any remapping of registers in this example, but suppose r8 had already been used to hold the virtual registers Rtime. The lw instruction could be changed to load the value of r8 into the physical register r9 instead. The later use of r8 in the add instruction would then also be changed to r9. After these changes, the application program would operate the same even though the assembly language code uses a different register.

This completes the code augmentation for the first basic block. The second basic block is the save word instruction (sw) that originally saved the value in register r3 to an address in shared memory. It is replaced by a sequence of instructions which load parameters and then call out to a simulation routine to perform the shared memory operation. The address and data values are loaded into the argument registers (r4 and r5), and the time counter (Rtime) is incremented by 1 (the time taken by the original instruction). If the simulator finds that more time would be needed by this instruction, for instance if the memory network is clogged or there is a cache miss, the simulator would add the extra time.

This completes code augmentation. The code has now been converted so that it is context block relative. The simulator can now switch threads by changing the context pointer and time counter and then jumping into the new thread to be executed.

---

[2] Here reference indirection is simply changing from Rgp to Rcp and possibly changing the offset. It is more involved when the original reference is not relative to Rgp.

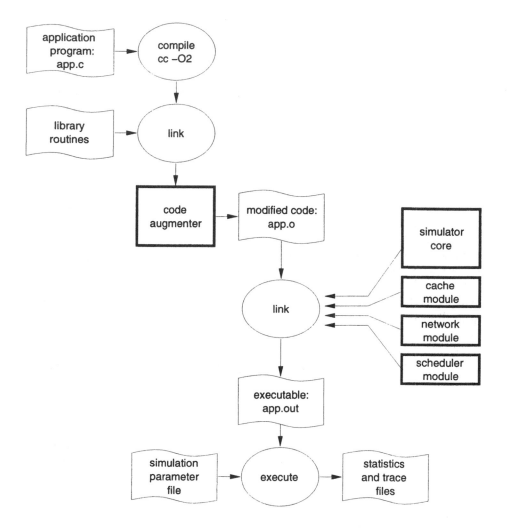

Figure 4 This diagram shows the process of using FAST to simulate an application program.

5   THE SIMULATOR HALF

Code augmentation is the unique aspect of an execution driven simulator, but it is only half of the simulator. The other half is the actual simulation code. This is a discrete event simulator, and we describe it in much less detail. Figure 4 shows a diagram of the complete FAST simulator and the process of using it. The *code augmenter* part and the *simulator* part are shown in heavy boxes.

The simulator part consists of the core of the simulator as well as additional configurable modules for the cache, network, and thread scheduling. Other simulators have similar modular and configurable design.

To use the simulator, the application program to be simulated is first compiled with full optimization, just as it would be for a real machine. It is then linked with any libraries that is uses, such as math routines. The linked object code is then fed into the code augmenter which performs the various code augmentations. It is important that augmentation also be done on library functions since some applications use these extensively.

One limitation of our system is that system calls, such as I/O, execute outside of the simulation. Their timing and memory access patterns are therefore not simulated or properly accounted for. Fortunately, the parallel applications that we studied did not use system calls during their parallel computations phases, which were the phases from which we needed accurate timing and access results.

After code augmentation, the modified code is then linked with the simulator core and selected modules that simulate the caches, network, and scheduler. A large number of these modules have been written, and they can be selected based on what is of interest to the user. For caching there are modules for various cache configurations and protocols, or for no caching at all. For networks the simulator is usually used with a simple constant time network approximation, but it has also been used with a detailed simulator of packet switched networks. The scheduler module is used for multithreading studies and implements simple scheduling policies such as FIFO, or more complex policies like priority scheduling or timeouts.

The single executable file produced includes the simulator core, the various modules, and the modified application code. When it is run, the simulator core starts first. It reads in a simulation parameter file that specifies the number of processors, level of multithreading, network latency, and other parameters. It then calls initialization routines for the various modules, and starts up and manages the execution driven simulation of the application program.

The simulator core is a time wheel scheduler. This is just a linear array with one slot per time step (modulo the array size), where each slot points to a linked list of events that will occur at that time step. The simulator operates by removing an event at the current time step, simulating it (using execution driven simulation), and then placing the resulting event into the proper slot to be executed in the future. This data structure is very efficient since there is no polling to test for ready events. For simulations of large parallel machines,

App.	Description	Context switch cost		Average interval between switches	Average cost per instr.
		switch in	switch out	between switches	cost per instr.
sieve	finds primes	9.8	7.9	7.0	2.5
blkmat	blocked matrix multiply	47.7	50.3	48.0	2.0
sor	solves Laplace's equation	8.5	5.5	4.2	3.3
ugray	ray tracing renderer	11.8	9.1	10.1	2.1
water	system of water molecules	27.7	22.2	33.1	1.5
locus	standard cell router	8.0	5.2	4.0	3.3
mp3d	rarefied hypersonic flow	8.1	6.3	4.7	3.1

Table 2   Context Switch Costs

there are so many events that typically every slot has one or more events in it, and thus the amortized cost of scheduling an event is constant.

6   PERFORMANCE CHARACTERISTICS

In this section we discuss three aspects of the performance of the FAST simulator: the cost of in-line context switching, the slowdown factors of basic simulations, and the affects on slowdown when simulating multithreading or caching.

6.1   Cost of in-line context switching

Table 2 shows the effectiveness of in-line context switching. It gives the context switch frequency and the average context switch costs for the applications that we have used in our simulation studies. **Sieve**, **blkmat**, and **sor** are toy applications developed by the author. **Ugray** is from Berkeley[1]. **Water**, **locus**, and **mp3d** are from the Stanford SPLASH[16] benchmark set.

The *switch in* cost listed in the table is the average number of registers loaded per context switch into the application from the simulator. The *switch out* cost is the average number of registers saved per context switch from the application out to the simulator. Recall that these register loads and stores do not all occur at the points of context switching between the simulator and threads, but are spread among the prefixes and suffixes of the sequence of basic blocks executed between context switches. Also included in these context switch costs are the overheads incurred by the simulator in saving and restoring reserved registers such as the program counter, time counter, stack pointer and context pointer.

The column labeled *average interval between switches* shows the average number of simulated cycles between context switches. For those applications that context switch most frequently, the context switch cost is less than 10 cycles. The locus program, for example, accesses shared memory very frequently and thus context switches at an average rate of once every four cycles. The average cost of these context switches is 8.0 cycles to switch in and 5.2 cycles to switch out. In all cases, the context switch cost is less than the size of the register set[3]. In comparison, the light-weight thread package used in Proteus[9] loads and stores the entire register set and takes 135 cycles per context switch.

In our system, the cost of context switching is roughly proportional to the period between switches. The longer an application executes, the more registers it is likely to use. The blkmat and water applications, for example, context switch less frequently than the other applications, and their average context switch costs are higher. However since they do not context switch as frequently, the higher context switch costs are amortized over a longer period. Overall, the total context switch overhead ranges from 2 to 3 cycles per simulated cycle.

6.2 Slowdown factors for basic simulations

Figure 5 shows the performance of the FAST simulator on the set of benchmark applications. Results are shown with the number of processors varied from 1 to 1024. The slowdown factors shown in this graph are the number of cycles taken to simulate a single cycle of a single processor. Since most instructions are directly executed and the context switching cost has been reduced to just 2 to 3 cycles per simulated cycle, one might expect slowdown factors of 3 or 4. The slowdowns are larger because of the remaining overhead which comes from the scheduling mechanism within the simulator, the simulation of shared references, the memory simulator, and statistics gathering. For this graph the memory model is a simple ideal memory that has 0 latency and no contention.

Two interesting trends can be observed from this graph. First, the slowdowns vary for different programs. Programs such as blkmat and water have typical

---

[3] On a Mips processor there are 29 integer, 32 floating point and 3 special purpose registers in the usable register set.

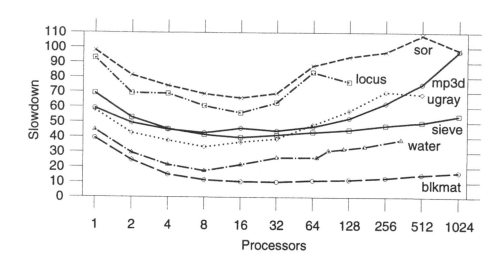

Figure 5   Simulation Slowdown Factors

slowdowns from 10 to 30, while programs such as locus and sor have typical slowdowns from 60 to 100. The difference comes from the different frequencies at which the applications interact with the simulator. Sor and locus had context switches every 4 cycles compared to blkmat and water which have context switches only every 30 to 50 cycles and thus require much less scheduling by the simulator. The cost of simulated events is amortized over a larger number of instructions, and thus the overall slowdown factors for blkmat and water are lower than those for the other applications.

The second interesting trend is that as the number of processors is increased, the slowdown factor initially drops and then slowly rises. The initial decrease in slowdown is due to the time wheel algorithm used to schedule threads and events. It works best when there are many processors and thus there are many events per cycle. The later increase in the slowdown factor occurs because the applications use more synchronization operations as the number of processors is increased. Synchronization operations, especially spinning on locks or barriers, involve many shared accesses and thus increase the work of the simulator.

6.3   Multithreading and caching

FAST was designed in a modular fashion and can be configured to perform a wide variety of different simulations depending upon what is of interest to the

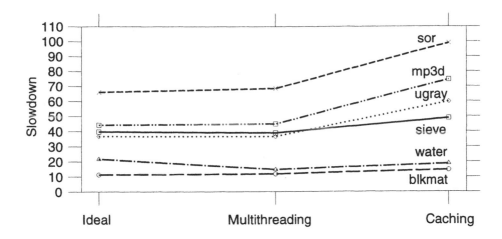

Figure 6 Comparison of slowdowns when simulating machines with different configurations. (16 processors were simulated for these tests.)

researcher conducting the simulation studies. The main uses of the simulator have been for studies of multithreading under long memory latencies and for performance studies of cache coherency protocols[4].

Figure 6 shows the performance of the simulator under three configurations: the *ideal* case which has 0 latency, the *multithreading* case which has 200 cycle latency and several threads per processor, and the *caching* case which uses a cache simulator of the Censier and Feautrier[6] directory based cache coherence protocol. The ideal case and the multithreading case have roughly the same performance. This occurs because studying multithreading was one of the primary intended uses of FAST, and thus multithreading support was built in from the start. Single threaded execution is simply a special case of multithreading in which there is just one thread per processor. The cache simulator typically takes hundreds of cycles per reference to check and manipulate the caches' states, and this extra overhead slows the simulations. The change in performance is moderated by the fact that the cache simulation cost is amortized over the total number of simulated cycles.

7 SUMMARY

In this chapter we have shown the importance of execution driven simulation techniques for building fast computer simulators. We discussed the major design choices in building such a simulator and explained the collection of code augmentations that have been used in our execution driven simulator FAST as well as the design choices made in two other execution driven simulators.

The performance of a simulator can be quantified as its *slowdown* factor. For FAST we measured slowdown factors ranging from 10 to 100 depending on the application and configuration being simulated. A comparable simulator using cycle by cycle emulation written by O'Krafka[13] exhibited slowdown factors of 2000. The speed advantage of execution driven simulation comes from the fact that most instructions are directly executed in a single cycle. The analysis of the code's timing and the identification of important events are performed once during the preprocessing stage rather than repeatedly during the simulation.

Since the scope of simulation studies often seems to be limited by the speed of the simulator, execution driven simulation is a valuable technique.

FAST is available by anonymous ftp from: `ftp.usmcs.maine.edu` .

Exercises

6.1 Assume we have a cycle by cycle simulator that takes on average 1000 cycles to decipher and emulate each instruction. Compare its performance to that of an execution driven simulator in which only 1 in 10 instructions is emulated and the rest are directly executed at an average of 5 cycles each (including overhead). What is the preformance difference if only 1 in 20 instructions needs to be emulated?

6.2 In Figure 1 the original lw instruction is meant to load the value from the address in register r5 and put that value into register r4. Work out the code that needs to be inerted before and after the call instruction to set up the parameters and put the result into the destination register. (Hint: Figure 3 shows the code for sw.)

6.3 For this exercise assume that the four instructions in the original code block from Figure 1 form one basic block. Also assume that the lw instruction is a local load and thus can be directly executed. If in-line context switching were performed on this block, what registers would need to be loaded at the start, and which would need to be stored at the end. Add the necessary code to the basic block.

6.4 In the previous exercise, what if the register r1 had already been used to hold the value of Rtime. Remap the r1 register in the code block and in the register loading and storing code to use an unused register.

6.5 In the original code block in Figure 1, consider what could be done if it were not known by the code augmenter whether the lw instruction referenced a local memory address or a shared memory address. A reference to a local address can be directly executed, but a reference to a shared address requires a call to the simulator. Add code to perform dynamic reference discrimination by comparing the referenced address to the base address of shared memory held in the register Rsbp.

6.6 Delayed branch instructions cause a difficulty when augmenting code. If the instruction in the branch delay slot is to be replaced by more than one instruction, they won't all fit in the delay slot. The easy case can be solved by moving the delay slot instruction before the branch instruction and putting a nop in the branch delay slot. Work out the hard case where there is a register dependency between the branch instruction and the delay slot instruction. For example BGEZ r1, label followed by ADD r1, r2, r3.

6.7 Some optimizing compilers will generate a branch into the delay slot of another branch instruction. The unfortunate effect of this from the perspective of the code augmenter is that the delay slot instruction belongs to two basic blocks. Work out how to rearrange the instructions to eliminate this overlap. (Hint: you may need to duplicate the delay slot instruction as well as add other instructions.) Add time counting instructions so that the correct timings from the original code are preserved in all cases.

6.8 Estimate how much memory will be needed to store the context block for a thread (this contains its registers, stack, and local variables). How much memory would it take to support a simulation with 1000 parallel threads? Estimate how much memory it would take to store the state of a simulated processor's cache. How much memory would be required to simulate a parallel machine with 1000 caches?

6.9 Estimate how long it would take an execution driven simulator with a slowdown factor of 20 to overflow a 32 bit time counter. What would be the best way solve this problem?

6.10 What can you do to verify that a simulator is working correctly?

REFERENCES

[1] Bob Boothe. Multiprocessor Strategies for Ray-Tracing. Master's thesis, U.C. Berkeley, September 1989. Report No. UCB/CSD 89/534.

[2] Bob Boothe. Fast Accurate Simulation of Large Shared Memory Multiprocessors. In *Proc. 27th Annual Hawaii International Conf. on System Sciences*, pages 251–260, January 1994.

[3] Bob Boothe and Abhiram Ranade. Improved Multithreading Techniques for Hiding Communication Latency in Multiprocessors. In *The 19th Annual Int. Symp. on Computer Architecture*, pages 214–223, May 1992.

[4] Robert Francis Boothe. *Evaluation of Multithreading and Caching in Large Shared Memory Parallel Computers*. PhD thesis, University of California at Berkeley, July 1993. published as Technical Report No. UCB/CSD 93/766.

[5] E. A. Brewer, C. N. Dellarocas, A. Colbrook, and W. E. Weihl. PROTEUS: A High-Performance Parallel-Architecture Simulator. Technical Report MIT/LCS/TR-516, Massachusetts Institute of Technology, September 1991.

[6] L. M. Censier and P. Feautrier. A New Solution to Coherence Problems in Multicache Systems. *IEEE Transactions on Computers*, C-27(12):1112–1118, December 1978.

[7] R. C. Covington et al. The Rice Parallel Processing Testbed. In *Proc. 1988 ACM SIGMETRICS*, pages 4–11, 1988.

[8] Helen Davis, Stephan R. Goldschmidt, and John Hennessy. Multiprocessor Simulation and Tracing using Tango. In *Proc. 1991 Int. Conf. on Parallel Processing*, pages II 99–107, 1991.

[9] Chrysanthos N. Dellarocas. A High-Performance Retargetable Simulator for Parallel Architectures. Technical Report MIT/LCS/TR-505, Massachusetts Institute of Technology, June 1991.

[10] Susan J. Eggers et al. Techniques for Efficient Inline Tracing on a Shared-Memory Multiprocessor. Technical report, University of Washington, 1989. Technical Report 89-09-18.

[11] Gerry Kane. *MIPS RISC Architecture*. Prentice Hall, 1989.

[12] MIPS Computer Systems. *MIPS language programmer's guide*, 1986.

[13] Brian W. O'Krafka. An Empirical Study of Three Hardware Cache Consistency Schemes for Large Shared Memory Multiprocessors. Technical report, Electronics Research Laboratory, University of California, Berkeley, May 1989. Tech Report UCB/ERL M89/62.

[14] Anita Osterhaug, editor. *Guide to Parallel Programming on Sequent Computer Systems*. Prentice Hall, 1989.

[15] Jeff Rothman, 1992. personal communication.

[16] Jaswinder Pal Singh, Wolf-Dietrich Weber, and Anoop Gupta. SPLASH: Stanford Parallel Applications for Shared-Memory. Technical report, Computer Systems Laboratory, Stanford, 1991. Tech. Rpt. #CSL-TR-91-469.

7

SAMPLING FOR CACHE AND PROCESSOR SIMULATION

Kishore N. Menezes

Department of Electrical and Computer Engineering
University of South Carolina, Columbia, South Carolina

1 INTRODUCTION

There are a wealth of technological alternatives that can be incorporated into a cache or processor design. The memory configuration and the cache size, associativity and block size for each of the components in the heirarchy are some of these applicable to memory subsystems. For processors, these include branch handling strategies, functional unit duplication, and instruction fetch, issue, completion and retirement policies. The deciding factor between the various choices available is a function of the performance each adds, versus the cost each incurs. The large amount of available design choices inflates the design space. The profitability of a given design is measured through the excution of application programs and other workloads. *Trace-driven simulation* is used to simplify this process.

Workloads or *benchmarks* may be instrumented to generate traces that contain enough information to test the performance of the processor subsystem under test. The SPEC92 suite [1] is one such set of benchmarks that has been widely used to measure performance. These benchmarks execute for billions of instructions. An exhaustive search of the design space using these workloads is time-consuming. Given the stringent time to market for these designs, a more efficient method is required. The large amounts of information in a trace also makes storage a problem. Statistical sampling [2],[3],[4],[5]., has been used successfully to alleviate these problems in cache simulations. In recent years it has also been extended to the simulation of processors [6],[7],[8].

Statistical sampling techniques involve the drawing of inferences from a sample rather than the whole, using statistical rules. The primary goal is to make the results obtained from the sample representative of the entire workload. The method used to collect the sample is therefore critical. Sampling for caches has received a lot of attention in the past. This chapter discusses some of these methods. An accurate method for statistical trace-sampling for processor simulation is then developed. The method can be used to design a sampling regimen without the need for full-trace simulations. Instead, statistical metrics are used to derive the sampling regimen and predict the accuracy of the results. When the method is tested on members of the SPEC92 benchmarks, the maximum relative error in the predicted parallelism is less than 3%, with an average error of 0.74% overall.

In the past, studies which have employed sampling to speed up simulation have not established error bounds around the results obtained or have used full–trace simulations to do so. It is necessary that confidence intervals be mentioned in such work as an indication of the error that might be expected in the results. Error bounds can be obtained from the sampled simulations alone without the need for full–trace simulations. An example of validation of sampling methods for processors and the establishment of confidence intervals is included in this chapter.

2   STATISTICAL SAMPLING

Sampling has been defined as the process of drawing inferences about the whole by examining a part [9]. It is a technique frequently used by statisticians in estimating characteristics of large populations to economize on time and resources. Sampling may be broadly classified into two types, *probability sampling* and *non-probability sampling*. Probability samples contrast with non-probability samples in that they are chosen by a randomized mechanism. This assures selection of samples independent of subjective judgements. *Simple random sampling* is known to be one of the most accurate methods for sampling large populations. It involves a random selection of single elements from the population. However, the cost associated with this technique makes its application infeasible in some cases. Another less accurate, but cost-effective technique is *cluster sampling*. This technique collects contiguous groups of elements at random intervals from the population.

An element on which information is required is known as a *sampling unit*. Where the sampling unit for cache simulation is a memory reference, the sampling unit for a processor is a single execution cycle of the processor pipeline.

The total number of sampling units from which the performance metric is drawn is called a *sample*[1]. The larger the size of the sample, the more accurate the results are. Since larger samples also mean a greater cost in time and resources, the choice of an efficient sample size is critical. A parameter is a numerical property of the population under test. The primary parameter for cache simulations is the *miss ratio*, whereas that for processors is the *mean instructions per cycle*(IPC).

Consider a processor running a benchmark which executes in n time cycles, $t, t+1, t+2, \ldots, t+n$, where $t+i$ is a single execution cycle. For a processor, these execution cycles constitute a complete list of the sampling units or what may be termed as the *total population*. The corresponding population in cache simulations is the total set of memory references in the address trace. Simple random sampling involves random selection of sampling units from this list for inclusion in the sample. The gap between two sampling units is randomized and calculated so that the majority of the benchmark is traversed. The sampling unit immediately following each gap is included in the sample. To be able to extract single execution cycles with such precision requires simulation of the full trace. This does not yield any savings in simulation cost. An alternative method is to extract subsets of the trace at random gaps and execute these. The execution cycles that result are then included in the sample. The random gap is calculated in the same manner as mentioned above. This method of sampling is essentially cluster sampling. Cluster sampling when implemented in caches has been referred to as *time sampling* [2],[4],[6],[10].

Another technique called *stratified sampling* [11] requires some prior knowledge about the elements of the population to be sampled. The elements are ordered into groups based on this information. Elements are then chosen from each of the groups for inclusion in the sample. This method is known as *set sampling* when applied to caches [5],[12].

2.1 Sample design

Sample design involves the choice of a robust (*i*) *sample size*, (*ii*) *cluster size* and, (*iii*) *number of clusters*. The accuracy of estimates for a particular sample design is primarily affected by two kinds of bias [11]:

---

[1] Several cache trace-sampling studies refer to a cluster as a "sample," in contrast to common statistical terminology. We will retain the statistical conventions and reserve the term *sample* for the entire set of sampling units.

Nonsampling bias arises when the population being sampled (*the study population*) is different from the *actual target* population. In a full-trace cache simulation the address references at the beginning of the trace encounter an empty cache. This leads to excessive misses at the start of the simulation and can adversely affect the performance estimates. This phenomenon is known as the *cold-start effect*. When sampling is employed clusters are extracted from different locations in the full trace. The cache state seen by each of these clusters is not the same as in a full trace simulation. Therefore, the *cold-start effect* appears at the start of every cluster. This leads to bias in the estimation of the parameter being measured. Recovering an approximately correct state to reduce the effect of this bias is largely an empirical sample design consideration.

The bias due to the *cold-start effect* also affects processors. The processor maintains state in the reservation stations, functional unit pipelines, etc. Contemporary processors have branch handling hardware which also maintains considerable state.

Sampling bias is measured as the difference between the mean of the sampling distribution and the sample mean. It is a result of the sampling technique employed and the sample design. Since clusters from different locations may be selected from sample to sample, the estimates may vary across repeated samples (i.e., across repeated sampled simulations). Repeated samples yield values of means that form a distribution. This distribution is known as the *sampling distribution*. Statistical theory states that, for a well designed sample, the mean of the sampling distribution is representative of the true mean. Sampling techniques and the estimates derived from them may be prone to excessive error if the sample is not properly designed. Increasing *sample size* typically reduces sampling bias. In case of cluster sampling, *sample size* is the product of the *number of clusters* and *cluster size*. Of these two, the *number of clusters* should be increased to reduce sampling bias, since it constitutes the randomness in the sample design.

An additional consequence of the selection of clusters at random is *sampling variability*. The standard deviation of the sampling distribution is a measure of the variation in estimates that might be expected across samples. Sampling bias and variability can be reduced by making the clusters internally heterogeneous, (i.e., large standard deviation of the parameter within the cluster), making the cluster means homogeneous, and by increasing the number of clusters [11],[9]. This is demonstrated for processors in Section 3.3.

The reduction of bias requires that the design of the sample be robust and all factors that could increase error be taken into consideration. Some of the methods that have been used to overcome or reduce the total bias are discussed in the following subsections.

2.2 Sampling for caches

Trace sampling has been used frequently for cache simulation studies. Two different types of sampling are possible for caches: time sampling [2],[4],[6],[10] and set sampling [12],[5]. Time sampling involves the extraction of time-contiguous memory references from different locations in a very long address trace. In contrast to time sampling where a contiguous subset of references forms a member of the sample, a single set in the cache forms a member of the sample in set sampling.

Time Sampling

□ Laha, *et al.* [2]: This is one of the foremost studies in time sampling for caches. For small caches, Laha, *et al.* [2] obtained reliable results using as little as 35 clusters of contiguous references. Their method takes advantage of the fact that under normal circumstances a small cache would be completely purged on a context switch. Thus references after a context switch would encounter an empty cache. If clusters were made up of these references, their behavior would be the same in a sampled simulation as in a continuous trace simulation. This reduces the non-sampling bias as a consequence of the elimination of the *cold-start effect*.

The sampling method is as follows: The average sampling interval is calculated as the ratio of the length of the total trace to the number of clusters required. Clusters of a few thousand references are collected after each sampling interval. These clusters are selected immediately following a context switch.

The above assumption that a cache is flushed on a context switch does not hold for large caches. In large caches (larger than 16KB) [2], some information is almost always retained across a context switch. Since the clusters of memory references are selected from different places in a continuous trace, the cache state needs to be reconstructed before each cluster. Laha, *et al.* achieved this by using some address references from each cluster to warm up the cache state. Statistics were calculated only for the sets that had been filled by previous references in the sample, in a method similar to that of Stone [3]. Such sets were referred to as *primed sets*. Any references to unprimed sets were recorded as *fill references* or *unknown references* since their behavior in full trace simulations could not be known. When a set was primed, a number of continuous hits were observed to the just filled block in the set. Laha *et al.* found that dependable estimates were possible if these references were also neglected in addition to the fill references. In other words, statistics collected from the first miss in a primed set were found to be more accurate.

□ Wood *et al.*: Wood, Hill and Kessler [4] discussed methods to estimate the miss ratio for the *unknown (fill) references* used to warm-up the cache. Whereas the fill method assumes that these references had a miss ratio equal to the overall miss ratio, Wood, Hill and Kessler showed that the miss ratio of such references is in fact higher than the overall miss ratio.

This study models each block frame in the cache in terms of generations. A block frame is a part of the cache set capable of holding a single block. Each generation is composed of a live time and a dead time. A block frame is said to be live if the next reference to that frame is a hit, and dead if the next reference to it is a miss. A generation therefore starts after a miss occurs and ends when the next miss occurs. The miss that ends the generation is included in the generation, whereas the miss that starts it is not. The miss ratio at any instant in time during a simulation is the fraction of block frames that are dead at that instant.

The probability that a block frame is dead at any instant in time is the fraction of the generation time during which the block is dead. Assuming that the live and dead times for the block frames are identically distributed for all the block frames in the cache, the miss ratio is given by:

$$\mu_{long} \quad = \quad \frac{E[D_j]}{E[G_j]}, \tag{7.1}$$

where, $E[D_j]$ = Expected dead time in generation j, and $E[G_j]$ = Expected generation time for generation j.

Since the distributions of the live and dead times are not known, the two times can be calculated as means of the respective times computed throughout the trace. When sampling is employed, these are computed using only the sampled references. The live and dead times for each block frame are counted in terms of the number of references to that block frame. Equation 7.1 holds true only when every block in the cache is referenced at least once. This is true only when large clusters are used. Thus, the miss ratio for the *unknown references* computed in this manner is called μ_{long}.

For short traces it may not be possible to have every block frame addressed at least once. This makes the above method inaccurate. Wood *et al.* suggest estimates for the miss ratio of *unknown references* for short traces. μ_{last} is based on the assumption that any block frame that is not referenced by any of the address references in the cluster is dead. For a cache with S sets and associativity of A, the total number of block frames is SA. If U is the number of unknown references then, $(SA - U)$ is the number of block frames that are never referenced by the cluster. Therefore,

$$\mu_{last} = \frac{max\left(0, SA \times \frac{E[D_j]}{E[G_j]} - (SA - U)\right)}{U}. \tag{7.2}$$

It is possible that not all live block frames are referenced by a small cluster. Thus, the maximum with 0 in Equation 7.2. Another metric, μ_{split} is the arithmetic mean of μ_{long} and μ_{last}. μ_{tepid} simply assumes that exactly half of the block frames are dead i.e. 50% of the unknown references are misses. μ_{tepid} is therefore defined as 0.5. Empirical results show μ_{split} and μ_{tepid} to be the best estimators. μ_{tepid} may be preferred over μ_{split} since it requires no computation.

□ Fu and Patel: This study recommends a metric other than the miss ratio. The metric is similar to the generation time used by Wood *et al.* and is called the *miss-distance*. The miss-distance is computed as the distance between misses for the complete cache rather than for each block frame. The results are validated by comparing the distributions of the miss-distance for the sampled and continuous traces. Each cluster of address references in the sample consists of a priming interval and an evaluation interval. The priming interval is used to warm up the cache, effectively reducing the number of *unknown* or *fill references*. The algorithm is as follows: In the priming interval, if a miss occurs, compute and store the miss distance in an history table. If a fill reference occurs, ignore it. In the evaluation interval, if a fill occurs and the history table is empty, predict it as a hit. If not, the history table is checked to see if the miss distance is within the range of those in the history table, in which case a hit is predicted. If the miss distance is not within the range of the miss distances in the history table, but the sets adjacent to the set being referenced contain addresses of adjacent memory blocks, a hit is predicted, else a miss is predicted. If all the above conditions fail, a miss is predicted. The history table need have only the last three computations of the miss distance. Greater than three history table entries are not seen to provide any additional performance gain. This study also includes an analysis for multiprocessor caches.

Set Sampling

A cache that can hold C blocks, and has associativity A can be divided into C/A sets i.e. each set contains A block frames. The set sampling method varies from the time-based techniques above, since in this approach the sets in the cache are sampled rather than the workload. The sets for inclusion in the sample may either be selected at random, or by using information about the parameters of the caches. The method employed in [12] consists of two phases. The first phase uses a partial run of the workload on the whole cache to obtain information about the behavior of each set in the cache. Based on this information, certain sets are selected for inclusion in the sample. The actual simulation is done in the second phase using only the sets in the sample. Another interesting method is that suggested by Kessler *et al.* [5]. Referred to as the *constant-bits* method, it can be used to simulate a heirarchy of multi-megabyte caches. It can also be used to simulate multiple caches in a single simulation. Both of these methods are explained below.

□ Liu and Peir: The authors characterize each set by a metric called *weighted miss*. The sampling procedure is initiated with a preliminary run using a subset of the workload. Liu and Peir used 15 million address references for this purpose. Let μ_{prel} be the miss ratio of the cache under study for this phase of the sampling procedure. Let μ_i be the miss ratio of the ith set in the cache due to the references r_i to the set. The *weighted miss*, W_i, for set i is given by:

$$W_i = (\mu_i - \mu_{prel}) \times r_i. \tag{7.3}$$

In words, the *weighted miss* of a set is the number of misses that may be attributed to the references to that set. After the preliminary run, the weighted miss metric is computed for every set in the cache. The sets are arranged in ascending order of W_i. The list of sets is then divided into equal sized groups. One set is chosen from each group for inclusion in the sample. This set is chosen according to some heuristic. One heuristic is to choose the pth set from each group. Other heuristics that were seen to perform well were the *median* and *best-fit*. In the former, the set with the median weighted miss value in the group is chosen. The latter is used to select the set whose weighted miss value is the closest to the average weighted miss of the group.

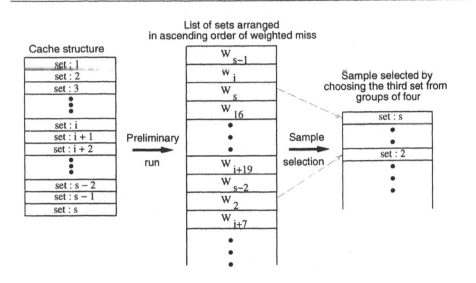

Figure 1 Set sampling by weighted misses

The second phase of the procedure simulates the sets in the selected sample. The complete workload is simulated on these sets. The miss ratio is then computed as the ratio of misses to the references to the sets in the sample.

This method of sampling does not suffer from non-sampling bias as much as the time-based techniques. However, the bias due to the empty cache at the start of simulation still exists. This is overcome by Liu and Peir by warming up the sets in the sample with around 500K instructions. The sampling bias, due to the design of the sample, can be reduced by using better heuristics such as the *best-fit* method, mentioned above, for the selection of the sample. The sets to be included in the sample may be selected on criteria other than the *weighted miss*. These include number of references, number of misses and miss ratios of each set. The *weighted miss* was, however, found to be the best.

☐ Kessler *et al.*: By far the most comprehensive and statistically sound study of cache trace sampling is by Kessler, Hill and Wood [5]. It is a comparison between set sampling and time sampling for caches [5]. The authors suggest a method for set sampling whereby a single trace may be used to simulate multiple caches or cache heirarchies. The method is called the *constant-bits* method and will be explained below. The metric used to measure cache performance in this study is *misses per instruction*(MPI). An instruction includes the instruction fetch as well as the data references for an instruction. Therefore, if the sample selected contains n from a total of s sets, the MPI becomes,

$$MPI = \frac{\sum_{i=1}^{n} m_i}{\sum_{i=1}^{n} inst_i}, \qquad (7.4)$$

where, m_i is a miss recorded in set i, and $inst_i$ is an instruction fetch from set i.

A further refinement is applied to obtain a more accurate metric. The number of misses is normalized by the fraction of the sets included in the sample times all of the instruction fetches. The MPI is then given by,

$$MPI = \frac{\sum_{i=1}^{n} m_i}{\frac{n}{s} \sum_{i=1}^{s} inst_i}. \qquad (7.5)$$

The *constant-bits method* uses a filter which selects address references with the same value in the portion of the address used to select the set. The filtered trace is then applied to the cache. The sets referenced by the filtered trace constitute the sample. The sets are thus chosen as a consequence of the selection of references. This method can be used to simulate more than one cache at a time. The method is illustrated in Figure 2. It depends on the knowledge of the value of the address rather than that of the sets in the cache as in the method in [12]. If p bits in the set selection portion of the address are used to filter the address references, $(1/2^p)^{th}$ of the cache sets in each cache are included in the sample. The disadvantage of this method is that the sample is chosen systematically rather than in a random manner and could possibly provide flawed estimates when a workload exhibits a regular pattern.

The trace of address references to a secondary cache consists of the references that miss in the primary cache. When sets are selected at random it is difficult to simulate a hierarchy of caches. The misses generated from a randomly sampled primary cache when applied to a randomly sampled secondary cache do not provide reliable estimates. The *constant-bits method* does not encounter this problem and may be conveniently used to simulate an heirarchy of caches.

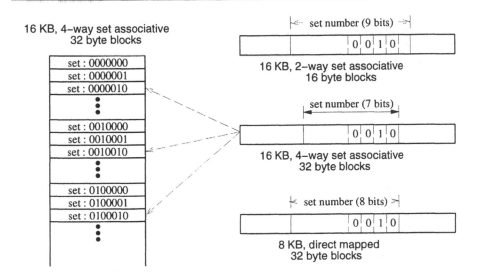

Figure 2   The *constant-bits method* used to simulate multiple caches ($p = 4$)

To summarize, there are two widely accepted sampling methods in caches. Set sampling chooses sets from the cache and considers these to be representative of the entire cache. The choice of sets may be random or based on some information about the sets in the cache (e.g. sampling by weighted misses). The choice of sets may also be a consequence of information available in the trace as in the *constant-bits method*. Set sampling has been found to provide accurate estimates at low simulation cost [5]. However, it fails to capture time-dependent behavior (such as the effects of prefetching). Though set sampling reduces the time required for simulation it does not solve the trace storage problem. If many different caches are to be simulated the full trace needs to be stored. Time sampling, on the other hand, requires the storage of only the sampled portion of the trace. It can also capture time-dependent behavior. The drawback of time sampling is the bias due to the   *cold-start effect*. Many different techniques have been employed to overcome this bias. Most of these methods require additional references in each cluster thus lengthening simulation. The decision as to which method to use depends on the resources available and the desired nature of the simulation.

2.3   Trace sampling for processors

The sampled unit of information for processor simulations is not the instructions in the trace, rather it is the execution cycles during a processor simulation. The metric that may be measured from each execution cycle is the *instructions/cycle* (IPC). Since IPC varies between benchmarks, the *relative error*, RE(IPC) may be used to validate results. The relative error is given,

$$\text{RE(IPC)} \quad = \quad \frac{\mu_{IPC}^{true} - \mu_{IPC}^{sample}}{\mu_{IPC}^{true}}. \tag{7.6}$$

where μ_{IPC}^{true} is the true population mean IPC, and μ_{IPC}^{sample} is the sample mean IPC. RE(IPC) relies on μ_{IPC}^{true} from a full-trace simulations of each test benchmark. (Reduction in sampling bias, sampling variability and determination of error bounds do not require μ_{IPC}^{true}.)

Table 1   Relative error for a 10 million instruction single-cluster sampling technique.

Benchmark	μ_{IPC}^{true}	μ_{IPC}^{sample}	RE(IPC)
compress	2.786	3.207	-15.11
eqntott	2.523	3.072	-21.76
espresso	2.440	2.879	-17.99
gcc	2.574	2.336	9.25
li	2.481	2.510	-1.17
sc	2.214	3.358	-51.67
doduc	3.425	3.465	-1.17
mdljsp2	2.545	1.902	25.27
ora	2.932	2.932	0.0
tomcatv	4.964	5.949	-19.84
		average:	16.32%

Many published studies of instruction-level parallelism use a convenience sampling regimen based on a single cluster from the beginning of a benchmark's execution. Table 1 presents the results of simulations using the first 10 million instructions from the trace of each benchmark. These results were obtained using the processor model described in a later section. The results presented here and throughout this chapter use 10 of the shorter-running SPEC92 benchmarks. These include all SPECint92 benchmarks (*compress, espresso, eqntott, gcc, li,* and *sc*) and four of the SPECfp92 benchmarks (*doduc, mdljsp2, ora,* and *tomcatv*). SPEC92 benchmarks are described in [1]. Several benchmarks achieve relatively accurate results with this technique, but this is by no means a universal conclusion. The μ_{IPC}^{sample} of one benchmark is over-estimated in excess of 50% (*sc*), with the majority of benchmarks experiencing in excess of 15% error. The majority of the μ_{IPC}^{sample} values are over-estimates, which should be expected since initialization often involves setup for code sequences much later in execution.

□ Conte: One of the earliest studies of trace-sampled processor simulation used a systematic sampling method [6]. For state repair, a strategy similar to that used for caches by Laha, *et al.* was used. The method used 40 contiguous clusters of sizes either 10,000 or 20,000 instructions each at regular intervals. Results for a highly-parallel microarchitecture with unlimited functional units showed a maximum relative error of 13% between the sampled parallelism and the actual value.

□ Poursepanj: In a similar study [7], performance modeling of the PowerPC 603 microprocessor employed a method using one million instructions in 200 clusters of 5,000 instructions each. The geometric mean of the parallelism for the SPECint92 benchmarks was within 2% of the actual value. However, the error for individual benchmarks varied as much as 13%. As with [6], the error was described using a comparison between the sampled and the full-trace simulations.

□ Lauterbach: This study discussed an iterative sampling-verification-resampling method in [8]. The sampling method used consists of extracting 100 clusters of 100,000 instructions each, at random intervals. Quick checks involving instruction frequencies, basic-block densities and cache statistics are done to investigate the validity of the sample. The checks are done against the full trace for the benchmark. In the case that the sampled trace is not representative of the full trace, additional clusters are collected. This is done till the required criterion is reached. Final validation of the sampled trace consists of the comparison of the execution performance of the sampled trace with that of the full trace. This study simulates the cache along with the processor. The state of the cache at a new cluster is stored along with the instructions of the cluster.

This state is loaded in before the beginning of the cluster during the sampled trace simulation. This is done in order to reduce the influence of the *cold-start effect* in the cache subsystem on the processor simulation. The need to collect cache statistics makes a full trace simulation necessary. The process of collecting the trace can therefore be time-consuming. The full-trace simulation is also required to validate the sampled trace and determine error bounds.

3   AN EXAMPLE

A solid body of work exists for the application of trace-sampling for cache simulations. This is, however, not true for processor simulations. The remainder of this chapter demonstrates how sampling techniques can be applied to processors. The problems unique to trace-sampling in processor simulations are discussed. An accurate method to alleviate non-sampling and sampling bias using empirical results is presented. Also, shown is a method to calculate error bounds for results obtained using sampling techniques. These bounds can be obtained without full simulations using the sampling results alone.

Where previous studies have tried to reduce all bias as a whole and make a prescription for *all* trace-sampled processor simulation, this study separates bias into its nonsampling and sampling components. It develops techniques for reducing nonsampling bias. Reduction in sampling bias is achieved using well-known techniques of sampling design [9],[11].

As the first step in the sampling process, clusters of instructions are obtained at random intervals and written to a disk file. The choice of clusters at random satisfies the conditions of probability sampling. The clusters of instructions are then simulated to obtain clusters of execution cycles. The fixed number of instructions in a cluster yields a variable number of execution cycles. Statistics are ultimately calculated from these execution cycles. The number of execution cycles that would be obtained on the execution of a sampled instruction trace, N_E^{sample}, is given by,

$$N_E^{sample} = \frac{N_I^{cluster} \times N_{cluster}}{\mu_{IPC}} \tag{7.7}$$

where, $N_I^{cluster}$ is the number of instructions in a cluster, $N_{cluster}$ is the number of clusters, and μ_{IPC} is the mean IPC. The term *cluster* is used interchangeably for the group of instructions that yield a set of contiguous execution cycles, and for the set of execution cycles themselves.

3.1 The Processor Model

A highly-parallel processor model is used in this study to develop a robust nonsampling bias reduction technique and to test the method for sample design.

The processor model considered is a full-Tomasulo, *out-of-order* execution engine. The model is based on a RISC design methodology. It assumes a perfect cache and has 7 different types of functional units. (The processor model is summarized in Table 2.) The model issues instructions at an aggressive rate of eight instructions/cycle. In addition, there are multiple copies of key functional units, and each functional unit has access to an unlimited supply of reservation stations. The performance of this model may also be considered as a projection of the performance of future processor designs.

Table 2   Processor model design parameters.

Issue rate: 8 *instructions/cycle*			
Scheduling: *Full-Tomasulo, out-of-order*			
Branch handling: *Two-level adaptive training* ("PAs")			
Branch speculation degree: 3 *branches ahead*			
Functional unit	Description	Number	Latency
Alu	Arithmetic logic unit	4	1
Load	Load	8	2
Store	Store	64	1
FPAdd	FP add	3	2
FPMul	FP multiply	3	3
FPDiv	FP divide, remainder	1	13*
Branch	Branch	3	1

* FPDiv is unpipelined.

Highly-accurate branch prediction and speculative execution are generally accepted as essential for high superscalar performance. In the spirit of the other high-performance design parameters, a hardware predictor with high prediction accuracy is incorporated. The specific predictor used here is the *two-level adaptive training branch predictor* (specifically, the "PAs" scheme from [13])[2]. This scheme consists of a 1024-entry table known as the *History Register Table*

---

[2] Our simulation is based on the textual descriptions in [13]. Although every effort has been made to faithfully duplicate the design described there, some inconsistencies in our simulation may exist.

(HRT), which maintains a history of the last eight executions of a branch. The entries in the HRT point to locations in another 1024-entry table called the *Pattern Table* (PT). The prediction is made using a 2-bit counter predictor in the PT. (The entire branch prediction hardware including the HRT/PT tables will be referred to as the *branch history buffer* (BHB) for the remainder of the chapter.) In addition, the processor is able to use the results of the predictor to speculatively execute beyond three branches (for comparison, the PowerPC 604 can speculate beyond two branches [14]).

The standard performance metric for superscalar processors is the *IPC*, measured as the number of instructions retired per execution cycle. IPC is ultimately limited by the issue rate of the processor, since flow out of the processor cannot exceed the flow in. For the SPECint92 benchmarks, the processor model achieves an IPC with a harmonic mean of 2.5 (lowest IPC = 2.214 (*sc*), highest IPC = 2.786 (*compress*)), demonstrating it is indeed highly parallel.

3.2 Reduction of nonsampling bias

Nonsampling bias is due to any state information contained in the simulation. State in a processor is kept in the reservation stations (scheduling window), the functional unit pipelines, and in the branch handling hardware (the BHB). Analysis showed that the largest amount of state is contained in the BHB for the processor model considered here.

A study of the nonsampling bias for the processor model is shown in Figure 3. This data shows RE(IPC) between a complete run of the benchmark and a sampled run. For these runs, the number of clusters is made large enough so that it does not contribute considerably to the error (2,000 clusters are used). The size of each cluster is then varied from 1,000 to 10,000. Two different approaches to sampling the processor were tried. In *fresh-BHB*, the BHB was flushed between the simulation of each cluster i.e. each cluster starts with an empty BHB. The relative error is high when *fresh-BHB* is used. For example, it can be as high as 24.71% for integer benchmarks (*gcc*) and 27.33% for the floating-point benchmarks (*doduc*), for a cluster size of 1,000 instructions. As cluster size increases, the error reduces, since the BHB warms up using the initial part of each cluster.

The characteristics of the branch instructions in the benchmarks explain much of the behavior seen in Figure 3. Table 3 presents these characteristics. The data in the table represents the distribution of unique branch instructions during execution. The "E-x" column presents the number of branches that occupy x percent of the benchmark's execution. For example, of the 1323 branches in eqntott, only 502 (E-100) are actually executed. Of these, only one branch accounts for 25% (E-25) of the execution, and one more branch for a total of two branches account for 50% of the execution (E-50). This table shows that most of the benchmarks exercise only a very small number of dynamic branches for the majority of their execution (E-50). The E-100 column reveals three groups of benchmarks. Benchmarks that execute unique branches numbering in the hundreds include *eqntott* and *compress*. These benchmarks have a very small pool of branches and should therefore be relatively easy to sample. The *fresh-BHB* results agree with this observation. Benchmarks that have an intermediately-sized pool of executed branches include *espresso, li* and *sc*. These benchmarks are consequently moderately hard to sample. The *gcc* benchmark has a high number of active branches across all categories (e.g., 14382 for E-100, 348 for E-50, 72 for E-25). This benchmark is the hardest of the integer benchmarks to sample (see Figure 3). A similar trend can be seen for the floating-point benchmarks, where *doduc* has the highest relative

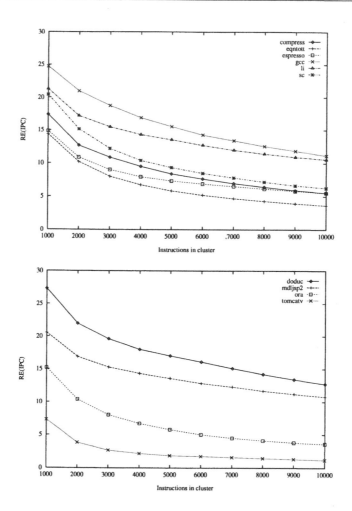

Figure 3   Relative error vs. Cluster size (*fresh-BHB*)

error. The relative error for the other benchmarks follow the ordering given in the E-100 column. Particularly interesting is *mdljsp2*, which in spite of the lowest number of static branches of the four floating-point benchmarks (848), executes 96.8% (821) of them. *Mdljsp2* has the second-highest relative error in Figure 3.

Table 3 Dynamic branch distributions.

The *E-x* columns present the number of branches that occupy *x* percent of the benchmark's execution. E-100 is the total number of branches that are dynamically executed. *Static branches in program* is the total number of static branches in the program text.

Benchmark	Branch instructions					Static branches in program
	E-25	E-50	E-90	E-99	E-100	
compress	2	5	17	21	135	432
eqntott	1	2	6	34	502	1323
espresso	15	49	225	842	2838	7582
gcc	72	348	2610	6535	14382	34347
li	10	34	119	264	1058	3138
sc	2	7	52	135	1529	4634
doduc	1	7	283	468	1596	3643
mdljsp2	2	5	15	35	821	848
ora	3	6	13	24	396	1791
tomcatv	3	6	12	14	372	1318

Since the branch distributions of Table 3 predict the difficulty of sampling the benchmarks (Figure 3), it is clear that the major component of nonsampling bias is due to the BHB. The effect of flushing the BHB in *fresh-BHB* is similar to a context switch during actual program execution. For the latter, one method to reduce the impact of context switching is to save and restore the contents of the BHB around every context switch (see [13], among others). A similar approach was tested here, called the *stale-BHB* approach. *Stale-BHB* preserves the contents of the BHB between the simulation of each cluster. The two approaches differ because, in the case of sampling, parts of the benchmark are missing between each cluster.

The results for *stale-BHB* are presented in Figure 4. Here the relative error is much lower than *fresh-BHB*, and in many cases reduced to half its value. Specifically, floating-point benchmarks experience dramatic reductions between Figures 3 and 4. One theory for why this occurs is based on the difference between the dynamic lifetimes of branch instructions. Based on the data in Table 3, branches can be divided into two categories: *short-lifetime* branches (e.g., those accounted for solely in categories E-50 through E-100), and *long-*

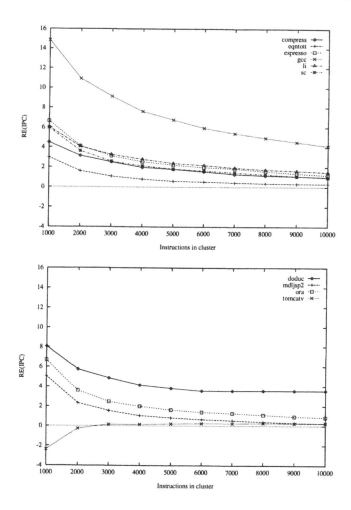

Figure 4   Relative error vs. Cluster size (*stale-BHB*)

lifetime branches (e.g., those in category E-25). Short-lifetime branches are accurately captured by either *fresh-BHB* or *stale-BHB* as cluster size increases. Either a large cluster size captures the entire lifetime of these branches, or the effect these branches have on the IPC is relatively minor.

Few branches are long-lifetime branches in the benchmarks (E-25 category). *Fresh-BHB* must restore the state of these branches for each cluster. The *stale-BHB* approach succeeds because it preserves these branches in the BHB between clusters. Overall, the results of Figure 4 suggest that a large portion of nonsampling bias can be reduced using large cluster sizes coupled with the *stale-BHB* policy.

Although large clusters reduce nonsampling bias, increasing cluster size directly increases the amount of simulation work required for accurate results. One reason that RE(IPC) reduces for the data of Figures 3 and 4 may be that the instructions at the beginning of the clusters repair the state for the remainder of the cluster. Nonsampling bias is then introduced by recording the IPC for this repair region. Overcoming this bias in turn requires additional instructions in the cluster. This suggests that not recording IPC for the repair or *warm-up* region of a cluster has the potential to reduce the overall number of instructions required. To study this, the effects of warm-up were considered using two approaches, *partition* and *fixed*. These are depicted in Figure 5. *Partition* uses a movable boundary between warm-up and sampled instructions for each cluster. The boundary is static for a given sample. The overall cluster size is kept as a constant of 5,000 instructions. The location of the partition is measured in terms of the warm-up portion. The second method, *fixed*, uses a fixed size for the cluster and prepends variable numbers of warm-up instructions to each cluster.

The results for *partition* are presented in Figure 6. The results show that warm-up works towards greater accuracy of the sample design. The errors are lower than those for the *stale-BHB* case (Figure 4). The left edge of the plot shows areas of high relative error due to lack of warm-up. The major portion of the groups of instructions in this area is made up of the actual cluster, with very little dedicated to warm-up. A better balance between the two yields lower relative errors. This is indicated by the dip in RE(IPC) between 40%–80% warm-up. However, RE(IPC) begins to increase again towards the right when the sizes of the actual clusters begin to reduce (warm-up > 80%). Several benchmarks (e.g., *espresso* and *li*) show reductions in RE(IPC) when the warm-up constitutes about 98% of the group of 5,000 instructions, suggesting these benchmarks have a large amount of state information. In general, for the majority of benchmarks the relative error is lowest in the 40% to 80% warm-up region.

The results for *fixed* were generated using the cluster size recommendations of 1,000 and 2,000 from *partition*. Figure 7 (1,000 cluster size) and Figure 8 (2,000 cluster size) present the *fixed* results. The warm-up is varied within the range of 1,000–10,000 instructions. The overall relative error decreases as the amount of warm-up increases. For the same amount of warm-up, the errors for a cluster size of 2,000 are generally lower than those for a cluster size of 1,000. The data indicates that a cluster size of 2,000 requires a warm-up greater than 7,000 instructions.

In summary, reduction in nonsampling bias can be achieved using three parameters: *stale-BHB*, cluster size and warm-up. Results indicate an appropriate cluster size is 2,000 or more instructions, in conjunction with a warm-up in excess of 7,000 instructions. It is important to underscore that this empirical evidence is for a highly-parallel processor model that includes a large branch predictor (1024-entry HRT, 1024-entry PT). Current processor designs have much less state information. Sample designs based on our recommendations for these and other less-parallel processors will be robust, and should not suffer significantly from nonsampling bias. Full-trace simulations were used in this section to demonstrate the reduction in non-sampling bias. It is also possible to achieve the same from the mean IPC statistics available from the sampled simulations using the different cluster sizes.

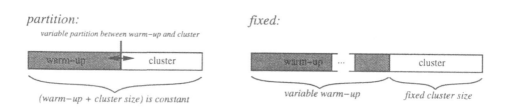

Figure 5   The two approaches to measuring the effects of warm-up.
The *partition* approach moves a partition between warm-up and the cluster for a fixed cluster size. The *fixed* approach fixes the cluster size and varies the warm-up.

3.3   Reduction in sampling bias and variability

It is accepted in sampling theory that bias exists in every sample due to the random nature of the sample. It is possible to predict the extent of the error caused by this bias. The *standard error* of the statistic under consideration is used to measure the precision of the sample results (i.e., the error bounds) [9]. Standard error is a measure of the expected variation between repeated sampled

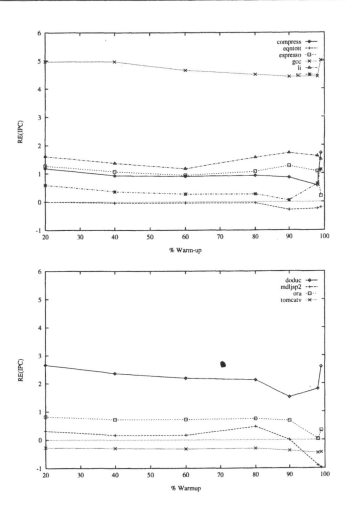

Figure 6 Relative error vs. %Warm-up (*partition*).

simulations using a particular regimen. These repeated simulations yield mean results that form a distribution. The standard error is defined as the standard deviation of this distribution. It's use is based on the principle that mean results of all simulations for a particular regimen are normally distributed, regardless of whether or not the parameter is normally distributed within the population.

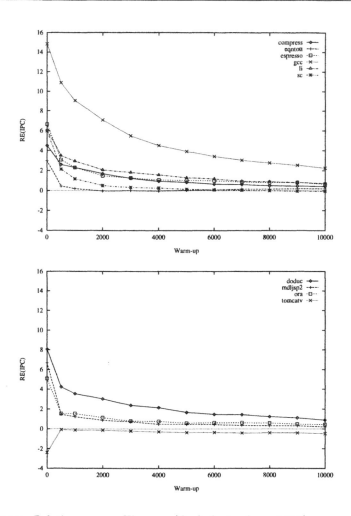

Figure 7   Relative error vs. Warm-up (*fixed*, cluster size = 1,000).

Based on this principle, the properties of the normal distribution can be used to derive the error bounds for the estimate obtained from a simulation.

It is not cost-effective to perform repeated sampled simulations to measure the standard error. Sampling theory allows the estimation of the standard error from a single simulation. This is termed as the *estimated standard error* and

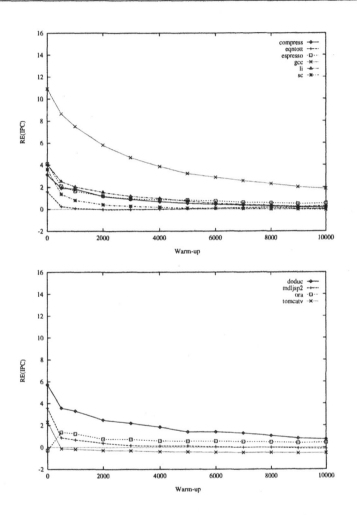

Figure 8 Relative error vs. Warm-up (*fixed*, cluster size = 2,000).

is denoted by $S_{\overline{IPC}}$. This method of measurement and the results obtained from it are used in the rest of this section. The standard deviation for a cluster sampling design is given by,

$$s_{IPC} = \sqrt{\frac{\sum_{i=1}^{N_{cluster}}(\mu_{IPC}^i - \mu_{IPC}^{sample})^2}{(N_{cluster}-1)}}, \tag{7.8}$$

where μ^i_{IPC} is the mean IPC for the i_{th} cluster in the sample. The estimated standard error can then be calculated from the standard deviation for the sample as,

$$S_{\overline{IPC}} = \frac{s_{IPC}}{\sqrt{N_{cluster}}}. \tag{7.9}$$

The estimated standard error can be used to calculate the *error bounds* and *confidence interval*. Using the properties of the normal distribution, the 95% confidence interval is given by $\mu^{sample}_{IPC} \pm$ *1.96* $S_{\overline{IPC}}$, where the error bound is $\pm 1.96 S_{\overline{IPC}}$. A confidence interval of 95% implies that 95 out of 100 sample estimates may be expected to fit into this interval. Moreover, for a well designed sample, where nonsampling bias is negligible, the true mean of the population may also be expected to fall within this range. Low standard errors imply little variation in repeated estimates and consequently result in higher precision.

Figure 9 shows the manner in which standard error reduces with increasing sample size, measured by the number of clusters. Using the recommendations of the previous section, the sample designs use a 2,000-instruction cluster size with an 8,000-instruction warm-up and the *stale-BHB* policy. All benchmarks exhibit standard errors that decrease rapidly as the number of clusters is increased. Although low standard errors are seen for small samples (using 25 clusters) for *gcc* and *li*, such observations are a matter of chance and the search for a better standard error should be continued. With the exception of *ora*, the floating-point benchmarks are not as easy to sample as the integer benchmarks. These benchmarks have very large $S_{\overline{IPC}}$ when the sample consists of around 25 clusters. All benchmarks reach the target precision when 1,000 clusters are used to make up the sample.

Table 4 shows the values of $S_{\overline{IPC}}$ for a sample made up of 1,000 clusters. The 95% error bounds are also shown. *Doduc* has the maximum standard error and therefore larger error bounds. It's confidence interval indicates that the mean IPC for repeated samples should be between 3.293–3.489 ($\mu^{sample}_{IPC} \pm$ CI). Whether or not the precision provided by this range is acceptable depends on the tolerable error decided upon. The values of the true mean (μ^{true}_{IPC}) are included in the table to show that the confidence interval also contains μ^{true}_{IPC}. This is true for all the benchmarks except *ora*. The true mean IPC for *ora* lies just outside the range specified by the confidence interval. This is because the standard error presented in Table 4 is only an estimate. Since *ora* has a very small $S_{\overline{IPC}}$, the range provided by the confidence interval becomes very tight.

Figure 10 provides insights into why some benchmarks are more difficult to sample than others. It shows the distribution of the mean IPCs of the clusters

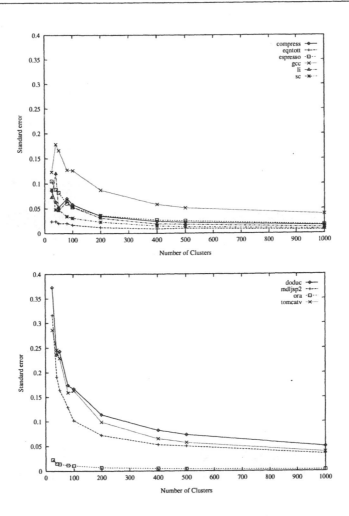

Figure 9   Standard Error vs. Number of Clusters

in the 1,000-cluster sample. Note that benchmarks with small variations among cluster means, such as *eqntott* and *ora*, are conducive to accurate sampling. Benchmarks such as *gcc*, *doduc*, *mdljsp2* and *tomcatv* exhibit high variation in the cluster means and are therefore difficult to sample. It is clear that the precision of a sampling regimen depends upon the homogeneity of the cluster

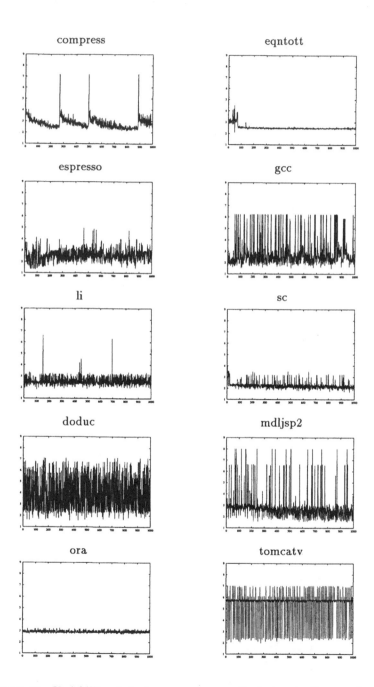

Figure 10 Variability of cluster means across all clusters in the samples. X-axis is the cluster number and y-axis is the mean IPC for the cluster.

Table 4 Confidence interval measurements from estimates obtained from single samples ($N_{cluster} = 1,000$).

Benchmark	True mean (μ_{IPC}^{true})	Estimated mean (μ_{IPC}^{sample})	Standard Error $(S_{\overline{IPC}})$	95% Error Bound	Relative Error (RE(IPC))
compress	2.786	2.768	0.016	± 0.031	0.65
eqntott	2.523	2.521	0.007	± 0.014	0.08
espresso	2.440	2.414	0.017	± 0.033	1.07
gcc	2.574	2.498	0.039	± 0.076	2.95
li	2.481	2.488	0.012	± 0.024	-0.28
sc	2.214	2.220	0.009	± 0.018	-0.27
doduc	3.425	3.391	0.050	± 0.098	0.99
mdljsp2	2.545	2.551	0.035	± 0.069	-0.24
ora	2.932	2.919	0.003	± 0.006	0.44
tomcatv	4.964	4.983	0.039	± 0.076	-0.38

means. For these benchmarks, the number of clusters need to be large enough to offset the effects of the highly-heterogeneous cluster means.

Since the full-trace simulations are available in this study, it is possible to test whether sample design using standard error achieves accurate results. The estimates of μ_{IPC}^{sample} when compared to μ_{IPC}^{true} show relative errors of less than 3% for all benchmarks (Table 4). The conclusion is that a robust sampling regimen can be designed without the need for full-trace simulations. When nonsampling bias is negligible, the sampling regimen can be designed from the data obtained solely from a single sampled run.

4 CONCLUDING REMARKS

This chapter has described techniques that have been used in sampling for caches. Though the survey of techniques may not be exhaustive, an attempt has been made to describe some of the more efficient methods in use today. Since techniques for processor simulation have not developed as rapidly, techniques have been developed for accurate processor simulation via systematic reduction in bias. A highly-parallel processor model with considerable state information is used for the purpose. The techniques were verified with empirical results using members of the SPEC92 benchmarks.

The use of the nonsampling bias reduction techniques were demonstrated by sample design for the test benchmarks. To reduce sampling bias, statistical sampling design techniques were employed. The results demonstrate that a regimen for sampling a processor simulation can be developed without the need for full-trace simulations. It is unlikely that all nonsampling bias was eliminated using the techniques. However, since the error bounds calculated using estimated standard error bracketed the true mean IPC, it can be concluded that the nonsampling bias reduction technique is highly effective.

The recommended steps for processor sampling design are:

7.1 **Reduce nonsampling bias:** This requires a state repair mechanism. Empirical evidence from a highly-parallel processor with a robust branch predictor suggests selection of a cluster size of 2,000 instructions or more, with a warm-up greater than 7,000 instructions per cluster, and the *stale-BHB* policy for branch predictor state repair.

7.2 **Determine the sample design:**

   (a) **Select a number of clusters:** Simulate using a particular number of clusters. From Figure 9, suggested test numbers are between 200 to 1,000 clusters.

   (b) **Determine error bounds:** Estimate standard error (Equations 7.8 and 7.9) to determine error bounds/precision of the results. If the error is acceptable, the experiments are completed. Otherwise, increase the sample size by increasing the number of clusters, and resimulate until the desired precision is achieved.

The results of this study demonstrate the power of statistical theory adapted for discrete-event simulation.

Exercises

7.1 Cluster sampling (*time sampling* in cache simulations) is found to be less accurate when compared to other types of probability sampling methods such as simple random and stratified (*e.g. sampling by weighted misses*) sampling. Why?

7.2 What are the causes of non-sampling bias in cache simulations (full and sampled)? List some of these for processors. What effect does non-sampling bias have on the estimated mean from a sampled simulation?

7.3 How do the distribution of a metric within a cluster, the cluster means and the number of clusters affect sampling bias and variability?

7.4 Laha,*et al.* suggested the extraction of a cluster soon after a context switch for inclusion in the sample. Why? They also suggested that statistics be collected from the first miss to a primed set rather than as soon as the set is primed. Why?

7.5 By intuition, which of the four metrics μ_{long}, μ_{last}, μ_{split} and μ_{tepid} suggested by Wood *et al.* for *unknown references* in short traces can be expected to provide the best estimates. Give reasons.

7.6 State the advantages and disadvantages of set sampling in contrast to time sampling in cache simulations.

7.7 The requisite reduction of non-sampling bias in the processor simulations in this chapter is detected by plotting relative error. This requires full-trace simulations. However, it is possible to achieve the same with the means obtained from the sampled simulations alone (i.e., without full-trace simulations). Explain how.

7.8 Statistics may be collected throughout the simulation of a cluster. Alternatively, they may be collected after a certain *warm-up* period. Why is the latter method better?

7.9 Describe the procedure to be followed in setting error bounds around an IPC measurement obtained from a sampled simulation. How is this bound interpreted?

7.10 The processor simulations in this chapter have assumed a perfect cache. For a processor simulation with a cache included, it becomes necessary to be able to predict an *unknown* or *fill reference* as a hit or miss immediately, rather than at the end of the simulation. The processor can then take the appropriate action. Which of the methods to predict an *unknown reference* described in this chapter is suitable for this purpose? Would the addition of a cache require an adjustment in the warm-up period?

REFERENCES

[1] K. M. Dixit, "CINT92 and CFP92 benchmark descriptions," *SPEC Newsletter*, vol. 3, no. 4, 1991. SPEC, Fairfax, VA.

[2] S. Laha, J. A. Patel, and R. K. Iyer, "Accurate low-cost methods for performance evaluation of cache memory systems," *IEEE Trans. Comput.*, vol. C-37, pp. 1325–1336, Feb. 1988.

[3] H. S. Stone, *High-performance computer architecture*. New York, NY: Addison-Wesley, 1990.

[4] D. A. Wood, M. D. Hill, and R. E. Kessler, "A model for estimating trace-sample miss ratios," in *Proc. ACM SIGMETRICS '91 Conf. on Measurement and Modeling of Comput. Sys.*, pp. 79–89, May 1991.

[5] R. E. Kessler, M. D. Hill, and D. A. Wood, "A comparison of trace-sampling techniques for multi-megabyte caches," *IEEE Trans. Comput.*, vol. C-43, pp. 664–675, June 1994.

[6] T. M. Conte, *Systematic computer architecture prototyping*. PhD thesis, Department of Electrical and Computer Engineering, University of Illinois, Urbana, Illinois, 1992.

[7] A. Poursepanj, "The PowerPC performance modeling methodology," *Communications ACM*, vol. 37, pp. 47–55, June 1994.

[8] G. Lauterbach, "Accelerating architectural simulation by parallel execution," in *Proc. 27th Hawaii Int'l. Conf. on System Sciences*, (Maui, HI), Jan. 1994.

[9] J. C. H. McCall, *Sampling and statistics handbook for research*. Ames, Iowa: Iowa State University Press, 1982.

[10] J. W. C. Fu and J. H. Patel, "Trace driven simulation using sampled traces," in *Proc. 27th Hawaii Int'l. Conf. on System Sciences*, (Maui, HI), Jan. 1994.

[11] G. T. Henry, *Practical sampling*. Newbury Park, CA: Sage Publications, 1990.

[12] L. Liu and J. Peir, "Cache sampling by sets," *IEEE Trans. VLSI Systems*, vol. 1, pp. 98–105, June 1993.

[13] T. Yeh, *Two-level adaptive branch prediction and instruction fetch mechanisms for high performance superscalar processors*. PhD thesis, Department of Electrical Engineering and Computer Science, University of Michigan, Ann Arbor, MI, 1993.

[14] S. P. Song and M. Denman, "The PowerPC 604 RISC microprocessor," tech. rep., Somerset Design Center, Austin, TX, Apr. 1994.

PERFORMANCE BOUNDS FOR RAPID COMPUTER SYSTEM EVALUATION

Bill Mangione-Smith

Department of Electrical Engineering
University of California at Los Angeles

1   INTRODUCTION

Simulation is generally used to model program execution characteristics under some set of conditions, for example the execution of a finite element application on a high speed workstation. The simulation output may include several performance metrics, such as the expected runtime, memory utilization, register usage, or processor cache performance.

This chapter will summarize a body of work that provides an effective performance evaluation tool that can either complement simulation or serve as an alternative analysis tool. A group of researchers, primarily at the University of Michigan, have been refining a set of techniques for finding useful upper bounds on performance for scientific codes. These techniques have been applied to a wide range of computer architectures, including vector (Cray-1, Cray X-MP, Cray-2, Convex C-240), Decoupled Access Execute (Astronautics ZS-1), superscalar (IBM RS/6000), and traditional commodity RISC (Mips R2000). While the specific studies considered here focused on one or more machines in detail, they form a consistent history of refining the overall techniques by broadening their applicability, formalizing each step in the process, and tightening the resulting bound.

1.1   Rationale For Performance Bounds

The performance bounds discussed here were originally applied to scientific workloads, and this chapter will focus on this class of applications. The classic model of a scientific application is a set of Fortran DO-loops executing floating-point intensive operations on dense matrices. While this characterization does not cover the full range of scientific applications, it does contain an important subset, in particular those that can be executed efficiently on vector or massively-parallel supercomputers. The scientists and engineers who develop and use these applications generally are committed to achieving extremely high performance, and have been known to exert massive effort in order to optimize their codes. Additionally, many scientific applications have scalable algorithms which allow increased compute bandwidth to be directly translated into finer detail (e.g. finer meshes for fine-element codes) or more complete models (e.g. more components in an n-body problem). For these problems, the performance requirements are essentially unbounded.

Historically, developers of scientific applications generally are not interested in expected performance as much as achievable performance. Good performance bounds serve this purpose. A bound that is significantly above delivered performance indicates an opportunity for optimization. This is in contrast to an accurate simulation or performance model that is close to the delivered performance, but fails to reveal existing opportunities for improvement. Performance bounds also identify the complimentary case, where the achieved performance is poor but no significant opportunity exists for improvement. These results help focus optimization efforts on the best targets.

Performance bounds have also been beneficially applied to a number of Real-Time applications, particularly those involving communications. Real-Time systems generally have a number of statically known tasks that have well defined workloads. For example, MPEG codes must typically produce 30 frames of video a second and a V.32bis modem must move data at 14.4 kbps. Once these tasks achieve high enough performance to meet their required data rates, no further performance increases can be beneficially used. Performance bounds may serve to quickly identify those cases where a physical computer system can never provide enough performance for a given Real-Time workload, and thus help in redesigning or partitioning the system in a new manner.

While a number of scientists have focused on capacity (or bandwidth) to understand and frame performance issues, this specific line of research began with Tang and Davidson [20, 21, 22]. They considered performance on the Cray-1 [17, 4], Cray-XMP, and Cray-2 [5] processors, and developed the simple workload and processor models that are central to this chapter. The original workload was restricted to vectorizable kernels. They used an ad-hoc approach to identifying and resolving performance inhibitors when achieved performance significantly lagged the performance bound.

Mangione-Smith, Abraham and Davidson [8, 9, 10, 11] expanded on this work by extending both the workload and processor models. They included some application codes that are not vectorizable. The new workload was executed on machines that are not nearly as deeply pipelined as the Cray computers, and where instruction issue capabilities could impact performance.

The next improvement was by Boyd and Davidson [1], who focused on explaining the gap between achieved and bounded performance. They developed a hierarchy of performance inhibitors, which proved effective for understanding common features among multiple factors. This hierarchy also serves to structure the efforts to explain the performance gap.

2 OUTLINE OF APPROACH

The performance bounds presented here focus on two concepts: the workload presented by an scientific program and the available processor bandwidth. A workload is composed of fundamental operations that are essential to executing a particular program and generally are realized as atomic operations in the processor's instruction set. Examples include floating-point additions, multiplications, and memory operations. The workload also includes enough information to account for the performance impact of some well understood data dependencies.

Each processor is modeled by a set of hardware units that service this workload, e.g. floating-point pipelines, instruction issue units, and memory ports. These hardware units are represented by mathematical expressions that calculate a minimal number of processor clock cycles required by each unit for a given workload.

The processor necessarily requires at least as many clock cycles as each of its function units. Thus, by taking the maximum value for all of the function unit expressions, a lower bound on the number of clock cycles for the whole processor can be determined. This number can be translated into a megaflop rate (the more common performance number for scientific computers) by combining it with the number of floating-point operations (flops) in the workload and the processor clock period.

2.1   Problems With Performance Bounds

Unfortunately, three factors have combined to thus far limit the applicability of performance bounds: automatic program transformations, conditional operations, and library routines.

Consider the question of what constitutes a scientific application. The following code fragment implements a matrix multiplication using a straight forward approach that is frequently used for an initial implementation:

```
DO I = 1 TO ILIMIT BY 1
    DO J = 1 TO JLIMIT BY 1
        DO K = 1 TO KLIMIT BY 1
            C[J,I] = C[J,I] + A[I,K]*B[K,J]
```

Figure 1   Naive matrix multiplication algorithm

Unfortunately, this algorithm contains a data dependence between successive iteration of the inner loop, which is carried through the `C[J,I]` cell. This dependence will drastically limit performance on any machine with deep function unit pipelines, as is typically the case with high speed computers. One well known technique for achieving higher performance for this task on such machines is to swap the second and third loop construct. This algorithm transformation, called loop interchange, produces the same numerical result as the original algorithm. Fortunately, a number of modern compilers will identify the unnecessary dependence in the original code and automatically execute the loop interchange. However, an abstract performance bounding technique can not know a priori whether or not such a transform will be conducted.

The resolution to this problem has been to specify that the performance bounds are only applicable to the actual algorithms that are executed. Thus, the workload and dependencies under consideration are only those that exist after all optimizations (either explicit or automatic) have been fully applied. This rule does not really reduce the range of applications to which the performance bounds can be applied, but rather limits *when* the techniques should be used.

Conditional statements, such as Fortran **IF/THEN/ELSE** structures, increase the complexity of any program analysis. Consider the example in Figure 2. If **E** is true 50% of the time, a workload could model half of the requirements of **A** and half of those for **B**. This approach would be inappropriate if **E** is highly skewed, for example when **B** handles a rarely occurring exception. Profiling statistics may help in these cases, but programs do not always have accurate profiles due to data set variations and sensitivities. Because to these reasons, none of the programs considered in this chapter have conditional statements.

```
DO
    IF (E)
        THEN
            A
        ELSE
            B
ENDDO
```

Figure 2 Problematic conditional program fragment

Library functions (or subroutines in general) are difficult to model, because the actual workloads can vary significantly over multiple executions. For example, consider a square-root function that has a short-circuit return path for values of 1, 0, and -1. If a majority of the actual parameters fell into the short-circuit category any conservative performance bound (i.e. one that assumed worst case performance) would be too loose to be useful.

Though some functions do lend themselves to inline expansion and analysis, the general case is difficult to model with satisfactory results. None of the benchmarks discussed below invoke library functions.

2.2 Benchmark Programs

Each of the projects considered in this chapter used the Livermore Fortran Kernels [13] (LFK), also known as the Livermore Loops, for their workload. The Livermore Fortran Kernels are 24 small subroutines that were extracted from key production codes in use by the Livermore Labs community. Each LFK is structured as nested Fortran DO-loop (though some are composed of only a single DO-loop) with predominantly double precision floating-point operations. The suite was originally comprised of only 14 LFKs, and most studies either use that subset or all 24. Of the original 14 LFKs only number 13 and 14 contain subroutine calls (to library mathematical functions) in the inner most loop.

The 12 remaining LFKs can be characterized in one of three ways. Some of the LFKs can be vectorized with modern compiler technology, and execute with relatively high performance. For arbitrary long vector lengths, these kernels have essentially infinite available parallelism, and should saturate some system resource during steady state execution. These kernels will be referred to as Vector kernels (marked with with a V in Table 1).

LFK 1 will be used as an example for the vector kernels and is shown in Figure 3. Clearly, each iteration of the inner-loop is independent of all other iterations, and thus they can be executed concurrently to achieve high performance.

```
DO 1 K = 1, N
   X[K] = Q+Y[K]*(R*ZX[K+10]+T*ZX[K+11])
```

Figure 3   Livermore Fortran Kernel 1

LFKs 5 and 11 are called recurrence kernels (and are marked with an R in Table 1) because they contain strong data dependencies between iterations. Figure 4 shows the code for LFK 5. It is apparent that the result from one iteration (X[K]) is needed in the immediately succeeding iteration (as X[K-1]). These kernels present little opportunity for concurrent execution[1], and generally execute slowly on high speed processors due to deep function-unit pipelines. However, the performance impacts of such data recurrences are very easy to model, and thus these kernels generally result in very tight performance bounds.

```
DO 1 K = 1, N
   X[K] = Z[K] + (Y[K] - X[K-1])
```

Figure 4   Livermore Fortran Kernel 5

The third class of kernels exists between vector and recurrent and are termed Vector Reductions. Vector reductions operate in a bimodal fashion: first a function is applied to the data in a vector-like manner, and then an evaluation tree is used to reduce the dimension of the result. LFKs 3, 4 and 6 are vector reduction kernels (and are marked VR in Table 1). Because of this bimodal operation, neither of the previous simpler characterizations is successful at bounding the execution of reduction loops. These loops show the highest average disagreement between the performance bound and actual performance.

---

[1] Program transformations do exist that can loosen the constraints of some recurrences, though at the expense of more total floating-point and memory operations. The bounds developed in this chapter can be effectively applied in these situations after such transformations have been applied.

3 SIMPLE BOUNDS MODEL

This section focuses on the work of Tang and Davidson, who were interested in understanding performance issues for the Cray-1, Cray X-MP, and Cray-2 vector supercomputers. The Cray-1 will be considered in detail to frame and evaluate their work.

3.1 Cray-1 Processor Architecture

The Cray-1 is a uniprocessor vector supercomputer. The CPU is composed of a scalar and integer execution unit and a vector execution unit. In general, scalar instructions do not have a significant impact on performance for the Cray-1, though achieving this goal requires the compiler to apply very specific and nontrivial instruction scheduling techniques. Furthermore, since the workload is dominated by floating-point operations, the execution of scalar unit instructions should have negligible impact on performance. Therefore, the scalar execution unit was not modeled in the performance bounds.

The memory system services requests from a single processor port. It is interleaved and provides reasonably high bandwidth (one operation per processor clock). However, the bandwidth can be degraded by non-unit stride vector memory operations. The achieved memory latency is also relatively high.

The vector unit contains eight vector registers, each composed of 64 elements which are 64 bits wide. The vector registers source all memory store operations and sink all loads. Because of this, the Cray-1 is generally referred to as a load-store (or register based) vector processor.

The Cray-1 introduced the concept of vector register chaining, which is used to mask the latency of deep floating-point pipelines and memory. Floating-point add operations require 6 clock cycles to complete, while multiplications require 7. Depending on memory bank access conflicts caused by non-unit stride reference requests, memory load latency can vary dramatically. However, typical memory access startup latencies tend to be around 15 clock cycles. Vector operation chaining can often mask the impact of these latencies for a series of dependent instructions. For example, consider the case where a floating-point addition uses the result of a preceding multiplication. The Cray-1 can forward the results from the multiplier directly to the adder, while each element of the result is on the register write-back bus. Thus the adder need not read its input out of the vector register file. As Russel points out [17],

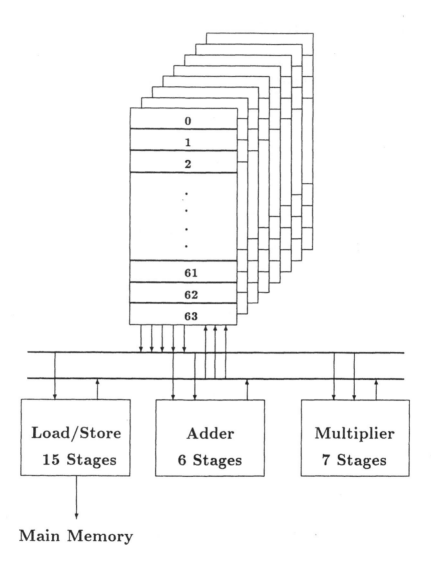

Figure 5   Architecture of the Cray-1 processor

this approach is similar to the technique of data forwarding used in the IBM 360/195 [14], though the 195 can only forward scalar values.

It is important to understand how the vector registers are actually implemented on the Cray-1. Each register has a control bit that marks whether it is being read or written, a count register for the number of elements left to be used for the current operation, and an access pointer that addresses the next element to use. Since there is only a single pointer, only one access can be active for each vector register. Thus, continuing with the example, if the first element in the multiplication has already been written into the result register and is no longer present on the result bus when the addition is ready to begin operation, the addition will be stalled until the entire vector multiplication has completed. At that time a new access can begin on the register which stores the multiplication result. The maximum time between when the multiplication begins execution, and when the addition must be ready to begin execution in order to use chaining, is termed the chain slot time. If the chain slot time is met the two coupled instructions require 7 clocks for the multiplication, 6 for the addition, and 64 to write each result, for a total of 77 clocks. If the chain slot time is not met, the addition will be stalled for 64 clock cycles before it can begin execution, resulting in a completion time of 141 clocks.

It is worth pointing out that Cray computers have used a number of different approaches to chaining. The immediate successor to the Cray-1 was the X-MP, which provided flexible chaining. On this machine a second access is supported into each vector register, which effectively removed the constraint of the chain slot time. However, the succeeding Cray-2 dropped chaining from the architecture.

3.2   Workload Model

Tang and Davidson did not consider the vector reduction and data recurrence kernels, since these cannot be vectorized effectively on the Cray-1. Their approach to modeling the remaining workload was to focus on fundamental operations that are supported by the hardware, in this case floating-point additions and multiplications as well as memory loads and stores. Table 1 shows the break down for these operations in the inner loops of the LFKs under consideration. Additions are noted as A, multiplications as M, loads as L, and stores as S. These counts were derived by simple inspection of the inner-loops as written in Fortran, and for the floating-point operations do not necessarily reflect the actual operation counts that occur in the compiled code.

The bounds model developed by Tang and Davidson is very straight forward. Even though the Cray-1 has a number of deeply pipelined function units, it is

LFK	Type	Adds	Mults	Memory Operations		
		A	M	L	S	L+S
1	V	2	3	2 (3)	1	3 (4)
2	V	2	2	2 (4)	1	3 (5)
3	VR	1	1	2	0	2
4	VR	1	1	2	0	2
5	R	1	1	2	1	3
6	VR	1	1	2	0	2
7	V	8	8	4 (9)	1	5 (10)
8	V	21	12	15	6	21
9	V	9	8	10	1	11
10	V	9	0	10	10	20
11	R	1	0	1 (2)	1	2 (3)
12	V	1	0	1 (2)	1	2 (3)

Table 1   Fundamental operations in each LFK

designed to hide the impact of these latencies. Furthermore, the hardware is well matched to the workload presented by these LFKs. Tang and Davidson assume that the latencies of each function unit can be ignored, and instead focus on the function unit bandwidth. Patel [16] had proven that the controller for a pipelined floating-point unit can be designed to saturate at least one pipeline stage, assuming that the workload is known in advance and has an acyclic dependence graph. This theorem is roughly comparable to the requirement that an inner loop be vectorizable, and it was used as justification for focusing on bandwidth by assuming a saturated function unit. A lower bound on the number of processor clock is

$$C = \max(A, M, L + S).$$

Table 2 shows the value of C for each LFK. Memory contention due to IO or scalar operations, which could effectively reduce the available memory bandwidth, is ignored.

Tang and Davidson also developed an accurate timing model, based very closely on the processor microarchitecture and instruction issue constraints. The purpose of this timing model was to determine the performance of a compiled or hand coded LFK. Because of the complexity of this model, and considering

LFK	Time Bound (C)	Achieved Time	% of Bound
1	4	5.85	68
2	5	19.56	26
7	10	16.60	64
8	21	40.26	52
9	11	16.91	65
10	20	25.66	70
12	3	3.67	82

Table 2   Bounded vs. achieved performance on the Cray-1

that it is not fundamentally relevant to the issue of performance bounds, it will not be presented here. However, it is important to point out that the model proved to be very accurate, and was used to determine achieved performance for a given LFK.

Table 2 also shows the best achievable time, using the straight forward compilation techniques then provided by the Cray-1 Fortran compiler, for these kernels. Also shown is percentage of the performance bound achieved by these code schedules.

Table 2 clearly shows that each of the LFKs loses a significant fraction of the apparently available performance (when compared to the performance bound). The next step is to understand whether the performance bound really is achievable, and if so what factors account for this lost performance.

3.3   Sources of Lost Performance

The following factors were identified as important for explaining the difference between the performance bound and the achieved performance:

Misaligned Loads

LFK 1 (Figure 3) contains an example of a misaligned load. Each iteration of the inner loop contains a reference to ZX(K+10) and ZX(K+11). The bounds model assumes that after the K+11 term is used as an operand, it is kept in a processor register and used as the K+10 term for the successive iteration[2]. This sort of optimization can have an important impact on performance by reducing the required memory bandwidth, and is relatively easy to identify. Unfortunately, this optimization is poorly suited to register based vector machines. Taking advantage of this opportunity would imply a vector shift of each element in a given register, with final element being reloaded from memory or copied from a different vector register. The Cray-1 does not support this sort of operation, and thus the compiled code for LFK 1 contains an additional load over what the workload suggests is the minimum. The same phenomenon increases the memory traffic in kernels 2, 7, 8 and 12. Table 1 shows the increased memory traffic in parentheses for each LFK.

Effective Use Of Chaining

Although the Cray-1 directly supports chaining in hardware, experience indicates that careful instruction scheduling is required to enable chaining in practice. In particular, the Cray-1 provides an instruction called Vector to Scalar Transmission Instruction (VTSTI), which may be used to enable or disable operand chaining. The compiler or assembly programmer can insert these instructions in a stream of vector operations. Generally, the VTSTI refers to one of the vector elements in the result of the last vector instruction issued. The data must be read out of the vector register file, which effectively inhibits chaining on the function unit result bus and delays the execution of any succeeding vector instructions. However, VTSTI instructions can be necessary for enabling chaining in some situations, in effect lengthening some chains by breaking others.

By focusing on optimal performance, and the contrasting it to achievable performance, Tang and Davidson were able to identify the problem with VTSTI instruction use. They developed a set of four rules for when to insert these instructions into a code sequence in order to achieve increased performance.

Single Load Port

It is generally accepted that the single memory port on the Cray-1 is frequently the performance bottleneck. All succeeding Cray computers have increased memory bandwidth, relative to floating-point bandwidth. However, Tang and Davidson identified an additional problem with the single memory port design

---

[2] Without this assumption, an aggressive compiler could generate code that exceeded the performance bound.

on the first machine. Consider the case where the first operations in a kernel load a vector and multiply it by a constant (either vector or scalar). The multiplication can chain to the load operation, and concurrent execution is achieved. However, if the kernel begins by loading two vectors and multiplying them, chaining cannot be achieved and performance is lost. Because there is only a single load memory port, multiple loads can not be executed concurrently in an interleaved fashion. This will reduce performance, even in the case where the kernel is not fundamentally limited by memory bandwidth.

4 DATA DEPENDENCE AND SCALAR CPUS

Mangione-Smith, Abraham and Davidson began with the results of the Cray study just discussed, and extended it in two ways. First, they considered some kernels that are not strictly vectorizable, by including vector reduction and data dependent LFKs. Their workload consisted of the first twelve LFKs. Secondly, they extended and generalized the processor model to those machines without vector hardware. This included the Astronautics ZS-1 [19], the Mips R3000[6], and the IBM RS/6000 [15]. This section will focus on the ZS-1.

4.1 Astronautics ZS-1 Architecture

The Astronautics ZS-1 was a commercial decoupled access execute (DAE) computer. DAE computers attempt to separate the address generation section of a CPU from the function units that operate on data. Once this is done, operands can be read in from memory in advance of when they are actually needed. Several architectures exploit this parallelism in other ways: load/store machines and VLIW computers rely upon optimizing compilers to achieve early access, while memory-to-memory vector computers overlap long incremental sequences of memory requests with data operations. The IBM 360/91 was an early I-box/E-box machine where the two units have a clean interface and there is extensive hardware support for achieving early access.

The DAE architecture is an outgrowth of research carried on by J. E. Smith at the University of Wisconsin. At the same time, though independently, the Structured Memory Access (SMA) architecture was being developed at the university of Illinois. Both projects proposed using a network of queues to allow two processing units to execute semi-autonomously. However, the Wisconsin

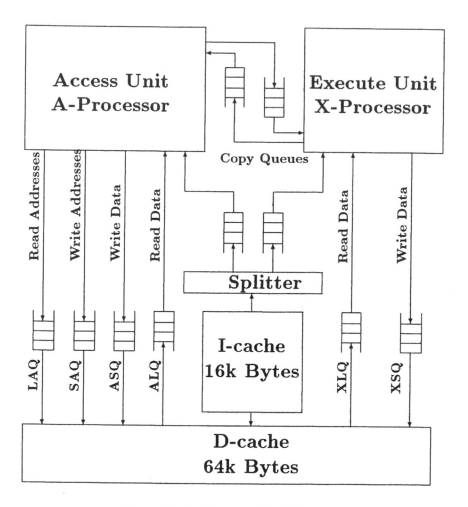

Figure 6   Architecture of the ZS-1 processor

project developed the characteristics of DAE as a modification of the Cray-1 scalar architecture, while the SMA project focused on memory access patters and support hardware. Smith started a company, later acquired by Astronautics, which developed the ZS-1 into a commercial product.

Figure 6 shows an overview of the ZS-1 CPU and cache memory. Even though the access processor (A-processor) and the execute processor (X-processor) execute one dynamic flow graph, they are not necessarily executing the same part of that graph concurrently.

The splitter maintains the program counter and fetches instructions from the instruction cache. Only instructions that will be execute are fetched, no branch prefetching is done. The splitter places each instruction in either the A-instruction queue or the X-instruction queue. However, because the splitter can fetch and split two instructions concurrently, the CPU has an instruction bandwidth of two instructions per clock cycle. Instruction splitting continues until one of the instruction queues is full or a conditional branch is encountered. For a conditional branch, the splitter stops execution until the branch flag is asserted, and the conditional branch is resolved. The splitter then resumes instruction fetching at the start of the next basic block.

The ZS-1 works best when executing iterative programs that make great use of the floating-point hardware. The X-processor uses the memory queues to read and write operands, without knowing the memory source or destination. The A-processor generates addresses and sets the branch flag to signal loop continuation or termination. Most fixed-point operations require only one clock cycle, and it is easy for the compiler to find efficient schedules for these instructions. The floating-point X-processor is more complex; its operations require more clock cycles and are pipelined. The latency of the floating-point units complicate the task of generating effective instruction schedules and increases the performance penalty of data dependencies. Because the A-processor tends to execute instructions at a higher average rate than the X-processor, it is often able to move ahead of the X-processor in the program flow path. This phenomenon, called *slip*, is responsible for hiding the effects of memory latency from the X-processor.

Whenever an operand for either processor is required from memory, the A-processor puts the operand's address into the load address queue (LAQ). Similarly, store addresses are placed in the store address queue (SAQ). The architecture specifies that all read requests will be fulfilled in order, as will all write requests. An address comparator is used to avoid potential read-after-write hazards. When a hazard is detected, the read request, and all later reads, are stalled until the pending write commits its result to memory.

The X-processor, which is responsible for floating-point operations, has pipelined function units for addition/subtraction, multiplication, and reciprocal approximation. The natural representation for floating-point numbers on the ZS-1 is 64-bit IEEE format, though 32-bit IEEE format is also supported.

4.2   Performance Bounds

Mangione-Smith, et al. modified the performance bound by splitting it into two components: one for modeling resource constraints, and a second for modeling dependence constraints. The aggregate performance bound is simply the larger of these two individual terms.

Resource Based Timing Model

The resource based model is a straight forward extension of the approach used by Tang and Davidson for the Cray-1. For scalar machines, such as the ZS-1, the instruction issue bandwidth is added to the model. The ZS-1 floating-point adder and multiplier have a bandwidth of one result every two clock cycles[3]. Thus, the resource based timing bound can be represented as:

$$C = \max(A + M, 2 * A, 2 * M, L + S).$$

In this case the first term models the instruction issue demands of the X-processor, the second is the floating-point additions, the third is the floating-point multiplication, and the last is memory operations (as well as A-processor instructions). Once again, this equation finds a bound on the minimum time per iteration of the inner-loop, not the execution time of the entire loop nest.

Dependence Based Timing Model

A *dependence* pseudo-unit is used to calculate a time bound for data dependent operations. The bandwidth of the dependence unit is a function of pipeline latencies and the workload characterization. The dependence unit has proved a convenient abstraction that lends consistency to the overall model.

The first step in finding the bandwidth of the dependence unit is to construct a dependence graph for the unrolled loop. Each node in this graph represents an operation on some X-processor resource, such as a read from the memory port or a floating-point multiplication. A-processor instructions, such as fixed-point calculations on induction variables or address calculations, are ignored under the assumption that the A-processor is rarely the system bottleneck and

---

[3]This chapter is modeling the original X-processor on the ZS-1, though Astronautics produced a later design which increased the throughput.

generally do not participate in dependence cycles[4]. Edges in the graph show data dependencies, and each edge has an associated cost which is equal to the time required for the pipeline latency. In particular, the floating-point pipelines have a latency of six clock cycles, so edges that begin at floating-point operation nodes cost six time units. A floating-point operation can refer to a data queue in the same way that registers are referred to, regardless of whether the queue is a data sink or source. In effect, each queue is a register that must be directly addressable by an instruction. The model assigns most memory operations a cost of zero when viewed through the X dependence graph, i.e. fully adequate slip is assumed.

The second step in finding the dependence unit time bound is to identify all simple cycles in the dependence graph. A simple cycle in the graph is any closed path where no edge occurs twice. Each cycle has an associated cost, i.e. the sum of the weights on its set of edges. Each cycle also has an associated iteration-span, i.e. the number of (unrolled) loop iterations contained in the cycle. Thus, each cycle impresses a time constraint on the iteration time, which is equal to the ratio of its cost over its iteration-span. The dependence time bound is then just the maximum of these values for all cycles in the dependence graph.

The dependence graph for loop 5, after it has been unrolled four times, is shown in Figure 7. This loop has a first order linear recurrence, which is manifested as a cycle in the dependence graph. Because of this dependence, the longest simple path through the graph is proportional to the degree of unrolling. The dependence unit provides a good time bound for loops with linear recurrence, as will be shown later in this section.

4.3 Achieved Performance and Bounds

Table 3 indicates the resource and dependence time bound for each of the loops. For the vector loops, dependence time for the *entire* loop execution is simply a constant that corresponds to the minimum time required to execute one iteration of the inner loop. For an arbitrarily long vector operation the dependence time *per iteration* is arbitrarily small. Thus, these LFKs are charged with zero dependence time (marked with a '-' in Table 3). For the reduction operations, a logarithmic term is added to account for the time required to evaluate a par-

---

[4] Actually, scalar induction variables do generally form dependence cycles, but most high performance compilers can remove these dependencies through loop unrolling and variable expansion.

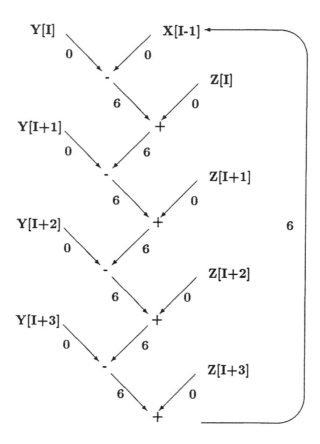

Figure 7   Dependence graph for LFK 5 after unrolling 4 times

LFK	Resource Time	Dependence Time	2 Clock Memory		64 Clock Memory	
			Achieved	% of Bound	Achieved	% of Bound
1	60	-	7.43	81%	7.52	80%
2	40	-	15.46	32%	19.06	26%
3	32	-	6.20	32%	6.24	32%
4	32	-	6.24	32%	6.29	32%
5	46	12	12.47	96%	16.66	72%
6	16	-	14.41	14%	28.50	7%
7	80	-	23.60	68%	23.84	67%
8	84	-	57.61	73%	59.77	70%
9	72	-	28.60	63%	28.94	62%
10	80	-	27.19	74%	27.80	72%
11	33	6	6.57	91%	10.52	57%
12	33	-	2.75	73%	2.78	72%

Table 3 Bounded vs. achieved performance on the ZS-1

allel summation tree, composed of the results of each iteration inside of a single unrolled iteration. Finally, for the linear recurrence LFKS this bound is equal to the time required for evaluation each iteration is series.

A detailed performance simulation study was conducted, using simulation tools available from Astronautics. These tools have been verified against the actual hardware, and will be used to determine the actual achievable performance for each LFK. A few modifications were made to the simulator before conducting these experiments. The lengths of the data queues were increased to 64 entries, so that queue full stalls would not impact performance. Also, the memory was changed to model a fully pipelined (i.e. no bank stall) design. The latency of memory accesses was allowed to vary, as an input parameter to the simulation.

Each run of the simulator executed 50,000 instructions. Table 3 contrasts the simulation results with those predicted by the performance model.

For pure vector loops, the data and control flow are almost completely data independent. The A-processor is able to slip far ahead of the X-processor, and the floating-point pipelines rarely need to wait for previous results to become available. Because of this slip, these loops have a higher achieved performance. With a memory latency of 2, these loops achieve a harmonic mean of 9.71

mflops. The harmonic mean of the performance bound is 15.83 mflops. The performance bound is reasonably close to the actual performance for these loops: the ratio of the harmonic mean of actual performance to the harmonic mean of the performance bound is 61%. This ratio increases to 72% when loop 2 is excluded from consideration.

It is difficult to speed up loops that contain linear recurrences because these loops have very strong data dependencies between iterations. The analytic model does a very good job of modeling this performance; the performance bound is tightest for this class of loops.

The bimodal operation of the vector reduction loops results in the combination of two performance bounds (resource and dependence), neither one of which does a good job of tightly bounding performance. These loops show the highest average disagreement between the performance bound and the actual performance.

4.4 Sources of the Performance Gap

Three primary sources of reduced performance were identified on the ZS-1, which serve to explain the gap between achieved and bounded performance.

Dataflow Analysis

It has been claimed that one of the chief advantages of the DAE architecture is that it can achieve vector like performance without requiring a vectorizing compiler. While this is true for some loops, there still remains a wide class of programs that would benefit from many of the techniques used by vector compilers.

Of all 12 LFKs, 2 and 6 achieve the smallest fraction of the performance bound. This is surprising, since both loops are generally vectorizable, and thus should achieve high performance.

This low performance occurs because the ZS-1 compiler relies upon hardware to avoid read-after-write hazards. For example, LFK 2 contains an array that is read from and written into, however there are no recurrences or hazards. Many vector compilers resolve this potential hazard at compile time and produce very effective vector code. Unfortunately, the ZS-1 Fortran compiler is not able to determine that there is no dependence. Because of this missed optimization, the compiler cannot reorder instructions to keep the floating-point pipelines full.

The dependence graph for this kernel can be constructed with this potential recurrence considered as an actual data dependence. When memory has a latency of 2 clocks this construction closes the gap between actual performance and the bound to 94%.

Misaligned Loads

As has already been discussed, misaligned loads occur in LFKs 1, 2, 7 and 12, and frequently occur in scientific algorithms. The ZS-1 code scheduler detects and eliminates misaligned loads in unrolled loops.

This optimization will not, however, always improve performance. None of the LFKs with misaligned loads are limited by the bandwidth of the memory port, and so the redundant reads could be left in the compiled code. This would require the A-processor to execute a few more read instructions but the A-processor is rarely a performance bottleneck.

The problem with removing these loads in the ZS-1 involves the X-processor. Each of the floating-point operations in the example loops execute in 6 clock cycles. All X instructions issue in the order in which they occur in the basic blocks, and most of the example loops encounter long sequences of instructions. However, the X register file has only one write port. A copy of the XLQ into the register requires one clock cycle. Because the register write port is often reserved by previously issued instructions (which require six clock cycles to complete), these copy instructions will often stall before being issued. This stall may reduce ZS-1 performance by blocking later instructions that could be otherwise issued.

Model Inaccuracies

Fortran requires that mathematical operations with equal precedence must be evaluated from left to right. The workload model, however, assumes that mathematical operations can execute concurrently, as long as dependence relations are not violated. Thus, ZS-1 performance for the reduction kernels (LFKs 3, 4 and 6) is much lower than the performance bound.

4.5   Followup Work

Mangione-Smith, Abraham and Davidson continued to refine their models, principly by developing a unified approach to representing data dependence with resource limits. They also used these techniques effectively to compare the ZS-1 to the Mips R3000 RISC and the IBM RS/6000 CPU.

5   MACS: A HIERARCHICAL PERFORMANCE MODEL

Boyd and Davidson [1] began with the work of Tang, Mangione-Smith, Abraham and Davidson as a starting point, and formalized a complete performance evaluation approach. The early work focused on machine/application performance and dealt with other issues (e.g. compiler optimizations and processor implementation details) in a somewhat ad hoc manner. This new model, called MACS, manages to clearly capture and isolate the impact on performance of several different factors: machine architecture, application program, high-level compiler optimizations, and low level compiler code scheduling. An M (machine) bound is associated with the peak performance of any application on a given architecture. This term is typically referred to as the machine's mflops rate, independent of application, and generally provides very little insight on performance issue. An MA bound (machine-application) factors in the actual work-load from a given application, and corresponds to the bounds presented so far. The MAC bound (machine-application-compiler) formally addresses the impact of high level compiler optimizations, such as misaligned load removal and loop unrolling. The final performance bound, $MACS$ (machine-application-compiler-schedule), further extends the bound to consider the impact of a specific code schedule. The MAC and MACS bounds specifically and formally address a number of issues that Mangione-Smith et al. and Tang and Davidson addressed through informal discussion.

As each factor is added to the performance bound (moving from M through to MACS), more issues are considered which could reduce performance. Thus, the performance bounds naturally form a hierarchy, with M the most idealized (and thus loosest), and MACS the closest to the actual achieved performance. In essence, moving up the hierarchy identifies a performance gap that can be associated with specific causes.

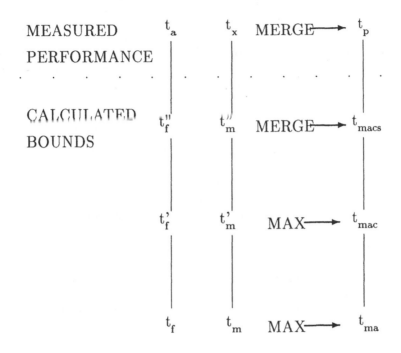

Figure 8 Hierarchy of MACS performance measures

Figure 8 gives a graphical view of this hierarchy. Each term will be discussed in detail in the following sections. The t_{ma} term is the MA time bound for each iteration, and is simply the maximum of the floating-point time bound (t_f) and the memory unit time bound (t_m). The MAC bound (t_{MAC}) takes into account the actual workload in the compiled code, and is the maximum of the real workload time bounds for the floating-point (t'_f) and memory (t'_m) units. The double primed time bounds correspond to actual code sequences, and interact in a complicated fashion to form the MACS bound t_{MACS}. t_a and t_x correspond to actual execution of just the memory or floating-point related instructions. These terms derive from a performance analysis approach developed by Windheiser and Jalby [23] which Boyd and Davidson applied to the C-240. However, this technique is orthogonal to the issue of performance bounds, and will not be discussed further here.

5.1 Convex C-240

Boyd and Davidson chose the Convex C-240 [2, 3] processor as the focus machine for their performance study. The C-240 is a four processor vector computer that is optimized for scientific computing. The system has a clock period of 40ns, yet still manages to achieve high performance on a number of scientific codes.

Only uniprocessor performance issues were considered. The C-240 provides a number of light-weight tasks in low level hardware, and can manage to quickly switch tasks with little or no operating system intervention[5]. Furthermore, multiprocessor memory traffic can cause unpredictable response time, even for processors executing the same application, as well as significantly degrade available bandwidth. These two factors combine to greatly complicate the task of modeling multiprogrammed or multiprocessor systems.

The vector processor (VP) on the C-240 employs a load-store model centered around eight vector registers with 128 elements each. The increased vector register length (relative to the Cray computers) helps to reduce the impact of pipeline latency (both in the function units and memory), though some recent research suggests that a more effective approach would have been to increase the number of available registers [7, 12]. Each VP has one memory port connected to its register file. There are 3 function units, providing memory port access, addition and multiplication. The memory port bypasses a data cache, which is reserved for scalar data. A number of computers have shown that transferring vector data through a cache can easily result in a flushed cache with little or no reuse of the streaming vector elements.

The VP function units support multiple concurrent independent instruction execution. Furthermore, a model of operand chaining is allowed which is more flexible than the Cray-1 or Cray-XMP. The vector registers are grouped into 4 pairs, {v0,v4}, {v1,v5}, {v2,v6} and {v3,v7}. Each pair of vector registers can support two read operations and one write operation simultaneously. The hardware necessary for sequencing access to each register has been moved out of the register itself, so that it is shared by both in the pair. There is no concept of chain slot time, as in the Cray-1, and thus the problem of instruction scheduling is greatly reduced.

---

[5]However, this mechanism is not nearly as fine grained as a multi-threaded (or barrel) processor, such as the Denelcor HEP [18].

The Address/Scalar Unit (ASU) is responsible for all scalar integer and logical operations. For example arithmetic, population count, and address operations occur within the ASU. The data cache only services ASU requests. The ASU is also responsible for all machine sequencing and control operations, such as operations on the VP.

A single multiported memory subsystem is shared by all four processors, as well as an I/O unit. There are 32 8-byte wide memory banks, with 8 clock access time. Thus, the memory can theoretically service one data operation (read or write) from each processor memory port per clock cycle, matching the bandwidth of the processor port. In practice non-unit stride accesses and multiprocessor contention tend to reduce this bandwidth to a significant degree.

5.2 MA Bound

The M bound is trivial to calculate based upon the VP function unit throughput and the processor clock speed. Since each arithmetic pipeline can produce a result each clock, and the processor has a clock frequency of 25 MHz, the M bound is 50 MFLOPS. This calculation reveals little information about real performance issues, and the M bound will not be discussed further.

The MA bound is essentially adapted from the same bound used for studying the ZS-1 earlier. It is assumed that each of the 3 function units will produce a single result each cycle, and all pipeline effects are ignored. However, because of the relatively long pipelines in the C-240, and the resulting poor performance on data dependent code, Boyd and Davidson choose to remove LFK 5 and 11 from their workload.

The MA model explicitly ignores the potential performance implication of:

☐ Fortran arithmetic rules

☐ The limited number of vector registers

☐ Instruction issue constraints

☐ Vector register length

☐ Operation chaining

☐ Sub-optimal memory performance secondary to memory contention, access patterns, or DRAM refresh

5.3 MAC Bound

The MAC bound improves on the MA bound by counting the actual operations present in the compiled workload. For example, the MAC bound uses a workload based on the actual memory references, rather than the required minimal number of references. These values are determined by inspecting the compiler output directly, and adjusting the workload accordingly to calculate $t_{MAC} = \max(t'_f, t'_m)$.

5.4 MACS Bound

The MACS bound further refines the MAC bound by adding information that is specific to a particular computer system and a given instruction schedule. In this case, Boyd and Davidson have developed a detailed timing model that reflects the processor and memory subsystem of the C-240. This timing model is similar to that developed for the Cray-1 by Tang and Davidson, and is used for similar purposes. A new implementation of the processor architecture would run the same compiled program binaries, but have a different timing model. By conservatively modeling only the phenomena that are certain to happen, the timing model can provide a lower bound on execution time tighter than the MAC bound.

Detailed Machine Model

The C-240 timing model is based primarily on 4 key features of the system: pipeline control, memory conflicts, dynamic memory and operation chaining. Each pipelined function unit can be modeled with a startup and shutdown constant. These terms capture the time required for exclusive access to that unit by each instruction, and will necessarily reduce the overall available bandwidth of the pipeline. Fortunately, these costs can be amortized over the instruction vector length, and these constants have values between 2 and 10 clock cycles.

Memory conflicts can come from references within the same program, other processors and IO in the system, as well as DRAM refreshing. While it is not possible to know a priori what references another processor will generate, it is sometimes possible to analyze the intra-processor reference stream. In particular, non-unit strides will reduce memory bandwidth and thus possibly performance. In addition, DRAM refresh operation will reduce available bandwidth for all processors by approximately 2%, based on specifications for the memory chips.

The most significant component of the timing model is a characterization of the chaining rules. Instructions that combine at runtime into chains and achieve concurrent execution do so by forming chimes. The term chime is used to refer to divide register based vector code schedules into non-overlapping time segments. All of the instructions in a given chime are effectively executed concurrently, either because they share no data or functional dependence, or because they can be chained together. By definition, chimes do not chain together, and so one chime ends by draining all vector elements (usually 128) into the data sink (either the register file or memory). If a code sequence accidentally breaks one chime into two, the runtime for the loop will increase by the vector length of the instruction. Clearly, an effective model for chaining rules can have a significant impact on the MACS performance bounds. These issues are similar to those related to the VTSTI instruction on the Çray-1.

Developing the MACS Bound

The MACS bound now corresponds to examining the compiled and scheduled assembly code, and applying it to the timing model. This results in the time bound for vector loops, and dividing by the instruction vector length determines the instruction MACS bound. This approach is different from the MAC and MA bounds, which had no dependence on the instruction vector length.

Consider the relationship between MA, MAC and MACS bounds. Each of these bounds assumes the same minimal set of operations for the base workload. Since MA models the best case execution of this minimal set, it follows that the MA bound will be looser than either MAC or MACS. Similarly, MAC considers the best possible execution of the actual workload, regardless of the actual code schedule. Clearly, the MA bound must be looser than the MACS bound, which corresponds to a specific schedule. However, if the exact same set of instructions could be reorganized in some manner without changing the computed result, as is often the case, the MACS bound would be invalidated while the MAC and MA bounds would still apply.

Unlike the previous bounds, MACS cannot be determined by simply taking the maximum of the separate memory and floating-point components after applying the timing model. These two code streams are intimately coupled through the chaining mechanism and chime rules, and are not useful in isolation as they are for the MA and MAC bounds.

5.5 Model Performance

LFK	f_m	f_a	f_a'	l_{fl}	s_{fl}	l_{fl}'
1	3	2	-	2	1	3
2	2	2	-	4	1	5
3	1	1	-	2	0	-
4	1	1	2	2	0	-
6	1	1	-	2	0	-
7	8	8	-	3	1	9
8	15	21	-	9	6	15
9	8	9	-	10	1	-
10	0	9	-	10	10	-
12	0	1	-	1	1	2

Table 4   LFK workload for MACS bound

Table 4 shows the workload for each of the performance models. The term t_a'
corresponds to the actual number of addition instructions, and l_{fl}' the actual
number of memory load instructions. The compiler did not insert unnecessary
multiplications. These counts are used for the MAC time bound.

LFK	t_{MA}	t_{MAC}	t_{MACS}	t_f	t_f'	t_f''	t_m	t_m'	t_m''
1	3	4	4.20	3	-	3.04	3	4	4.14
2	5	6	6.26	2	-	2.03	5	6	6.22
3	2	-	2.08	1	-	1.37	2	-	2.07
4	2	-	2.45	1	2	2.37	2	-	2.07
6	2	-	2.46	1	-	1.37	2	-	2.07
7	8	10	10.50	8	-	9.13	4	10	10.37
8	21	-	30.15	21	-	21.28	15	21	21.85
9	11	-	11.55	9	-	9.13	11	-	11.41
10	20	-	20.95	9	-	9.07	20	-	20.88
12	2	3	3.13	1	-	1.01	2	3	3.12

Table 5   Performance Bounds

Table 5 shows the result of applying the workload to the performance models.
A '-' in a column indicates that the value does not differ from either the baseline
workload or the baseline time bound respectively. Table 6 compares each of

the performance bounds to the actual achieved performance t_p, and indicates the performance gap for each type of bound.

LFK	t_{MA}	t_{MAC}	t_{MACS}	t_p	% of Bound		
					MA	MAC	MACS
1	0.60	0.80	0.84	0.85	70.4%	93.9%	98.6%
2	1.25	1.50	1.57	3.77	33.1%	39.8%	41.5%
3	1.00	1.00	1.04	1.13	88.7%	88.7%	92.6%
4	1.00	1.00	1.23	1.86	53.7%	53.7%	65.8%
6	1.00	1.00	1.22	2.63	38.0%	38.0%	46.4%
7	0.50	0.63	0.66	0.68	73.4%	91.8%	96.4%
8	0.58	0.58	0.82	0.86	67.9%	67.9%	97.7%
9	0.65	0.65	0.68	0.75	86.4%	86.4%	90.7%
10	2.22	2.22	2.33	2.44	91.0%	91.0%	95.3%
12	2.00	3.00	3.13	3.18	62.9%	94.3%	98.4%
AV	1.08	1.24	1.35	1.90	66.6%	74.6%	82.3%
MF	23.15	20.19	17.79	13.16			

Table 6   MACS bounds vs. achieved performance for the Convex C-240

The data shows very similar results to the Cray-1. The vector loops with misaligned loads execute unnecessary memory operations, and the result is a gap in performance. The vector reduction loops achieve poor performance which the performance bounds do not explain. This is due to a reduction operation on the C-240 which interacts with memory is an unexplained manner. Finally, vector codes that are difficult to analyze, such as LFK 2, result in a significant performance gap.

However, it is very revealing to compare the differences between the MA, MAC, and MACS performance gap for each LFK. Consider LFK 12, which has a MA gap of 37%. Mangione-Smith et al. would have studied this kernel in detail, searching for the source of the poor performance. Fortunately, the MACS bound indicates immediately that most of the performance (31%) is lost to unnecessary load operations (in the MAC model), while a bit more (4%) is lost in instruction scheduling. The MACS hierarchy identify and classify these performance losses automatically, without resulting to ad hoc analysis.

6   CONCLUSION

This chapter reviewed a performance evaluation methodology that focuses on bounded performance. This approach matches how scientific computer users think of performance, i.e. by considering peak potential rather than achieved metrics.

The performance bounds have been effective at identifying performance problems on a number of very different architectures, including the Cray-1, Astronautics ZS-1, and Convex C-240. Though the approach is currently limited to a small but important set of scientific codes, work continues to expand the applicable workload.

Exercises

8.1 Discuss how the techniques for bounding performance might be extended to handle library routines and function calls.

8.2 Present and discuss at least one approach to extending the techniques to conditional operations, such as *if* statements.

8.3 How would the performance models for the ZS-1 change if the splitter could only forward one instruction per clock cycle?

8.4 Develop the ZS-1 dependence bound for this inner loop: `X[I] = Z[I] * X[I-2]`, assuming that `I` increments by 1 for each loop trip.

8.5 What are the performance bounds on the ZS-1 if LFK 1 operated on integers rather than floating-point data?

8.6 What are the performance bounds on the ZS-1 if LFK 5 operated on integers rather than floating-point data?

8.7 The Mips R3010 floating-point unit can be modeled by two resources, which we will call A and B. A multiplication instruction uses the A unit exclusively for 5 clock cycles, and the B unit during clock 1 and 5. An addition uses the B unit for 2 consecutive clock cycles. Calculate the resource bounds for the vector loops.

8.8 Find the performance bound for LFK 8 on the R3010, and comment on the relevance of Patel's theorem [16].

8.9 Discuss the impact on the M, MA, MAC and MACS bounds if the C-240 had no chaining.

8.10 How could the performance bounding techniques be extended to effectively capture the impact of cache memories?

REFERENCES

[1] E. L. Boyd and E. S. Davidson. Hierarchical Performance Modeling with MACS: A Case Study of the Convex C-240. In *Proc. of the Int. Symp. on Computer Architecture*, pages pp. 203–212, 1993.

[2] CONVEX Architecture Reference (C200 Series). Technical Report 081-009330-000, Convex Computer Corporation, 1990.

[3] CONVEX Theory of Operation (C200 Series). Technical Report 081-005030-000, Convex Computer Corporation, 1990.

[4] An Introduction to the CRAY-1 Computer. Cray Research Inc., Chippewa Falls, WI, 1975.

[5] The Cray-2 Computer System Functional Description. Cray Research Inc., Chippewa Falls, WI, July 1987.

[6] Gerry Kane. *Mips RISC Architecture*. Prentice Hall, 1988.

[7] William Mangione-Smith, Santosh G. Abraham, and Edward S. Davidson. Register Requirements of Pipelined Processors. In *Proc. International Conference on Supercomputing*, 1992.

[8] William H. Mangione-Smith. *Performance Bounds and Buffer Space Requirements for Concurrent Processors*. PhD thesis, Univ. of Mich., EECS Dept., Univ. of Mich., Ann Arbor, MI, 1992.

[9] William H. Mangione-Smith, Santosh G. Abraham, and Edward S. Davidson. The Effects of Memory Latency and Fine-Grain Parallelism on Astronautics ZS-1 Performance. In *Proc. Twenty-Third Hawaii International Conference on System Sciences*, pages 288–296, 1990.

[10] William H. Mangione-Smith, Santosh G. Abraham, and Edward S. Davidson. A Performance Comparison of the IBM RS/6000 and the Astronautics ZS-1. *IEEE Computer*, 24(1), January 1991.

[11] William H. Mangione-Smith, Santosh G. Abraham, and Edward S. Davidson. Architectural vs. Delivered Performance of the IBM RS/6000 and the Astronautics ZS-1. In *Proc. Twenty-Fourth Hawaii International Conference on System Sciences*, January 1991.

[12] William H. Mangione-Smith, Santosh G. Abraham, and Edward S. Davidson. Vector Register Design for Polycyclic Vector Scheduling. In *Proc. Fourth Conference on Architectural Support for Programming Languages and Operating Systems*, April 1991.

[13] F. H. McMahon. The Livermore Fortran Kernels: A Computer Test of the Numerical Performance Range. Technical Report UCRL-53745, Lawrence Livermore National Laboratory, December 1986.

[14] J. O. Murphy and R. M. Wade. The IBM 360/195. *Datamation*, April 1970.

[15] R. R. Oehler and R. D. Groves. IBM RISC System/6000 Processor Architecture. *IBM Journal of Research and Development*, 34(1):23–36, January 1990.

[16] Janak H. Patel and Edward S. Davidson. Improving the Throughput of a Pipeline by Insertion of Delays. In *Proc. of the Int. Symp. on Computer Architecture*, pages 159–164, 1976.

[17] R. M. Russell. The CRAY-1 Computer System. *Communications of the ACM*, 21(1):214–248, 1978.

[18] B. J. Smith. A Pipelined Shared Resource MIMD Computer. In *Proc. of the International Conference on Parallel Processing*, 1978.

[19] James E. Smith et al. The ZS-1 Central Processor. In *Proc. of ASPLOS II*, pages 199–204, October 1987.

[20] Ju-Ho Tang. *Performance Evaluation of Vector Machine Architectures.* PhD thesis, CSRD, University of Illinois at Urbana-Champaign, 1989.

[21] Ju-ho Tang and Edward S. Davidson. An Evaluation of Cray-1 and Cray X-MP Performance on Vectorizable Livermore Fortran Kernels. In *Proc. of the 1988 International Conference on Supercomputing*, pages 510–518, July 1988.

[22] Ju-ho Tang, Edward S. Davidson, and Johau Tong. Polycyclic Vector Scheduling vs. Chaining on 1-Port Vector Supercomputers. In *Proc. of Supercomputing '88*, pages 122–129, 1988.

[23] Daniel Windheiser and William Jalby. Behavioral Characterization of Decoupled Access/Execute Architectures. In *1991 ACM International Conference on Supercomputing*, 1991.

INDEX

CPSIA information can be obtained at www.ICGtesting.com
Printed in the USA
LVOW011750210413

330169LV00003B/113/P

9 781461 360025